"At last an insightful book about martyrdom and suicide bombers. Too many so-called experts have dominated the stage without ever examining the life of a suicide bomber. Lankford, in a thorough and in-depth study, has identified the trauma, chronic depression, and suicidal behavior that characterize their lives. This is a fascinating book with profound implications."

—David Lester, former president of the
International Association for Suicide Prevention

"A coherent, must-read for all who would claim to be experts in terrorism—or just curious. Dr. Lankford's analytic rigor and willingness to examine assumptions make this a textbook example of how to do research and analysis. His conclusions? Suicidal martyrs are not heroes to be admired, but sick people to be pitied. Those who direct them are nothing more than evil. As Keynes once wrote: 'When someone persuades me I am wrong; I change my mind.' What will you do?"

—Jim Simon, former Asst. Director of Central Intelligence
for Administration, Central Intelligence Agency,
and Chair, Homeland Security Intelligence Council

"More than a decade after the 9/11 attack, scholars and commentators are still offering alternative explanations as to why the plotters were willing to commit suicide. Were they heroic martyrs so dedicated to cause of Islamic Jihad that they were willing to die? Or were they so mentally unbalanced that they wanted to die because their lives had become too depressing, too much filled with anxiety and failure? Adam Lankford explores these hypotheses, not only as they apply to the 9/11 plotters, but also to school shooters, airplane hijackers, lone wolf bombers, and the like. In a must-read book for those interested in these issues, he makes the case for the second hypothesis. He provides a benchmark that others will have to consider as they seek to reach their own conclusions."

—Donald Daniel, security studies professor,
Georgetown University, and former
Special Adviser to the Chairman,
National Intelligence Council

THE MYTH
OF
MARTYRDOM

THE MYTH
OF
MARTYRDOM

WHAT REALLY DRIVES SUICIDE BOMBERS,
RAMPAGE SHOOTERS, AND OTHER
SELF-DESTRUCTIVE KILLERS

ADAM LANKFORD

First published in 2013 by PALGRAVE MACMILLAN® in the U.S.—a
division of St. Martin's Press LLC, 175 Fifth Avenue, New York, NY
10010.

Where this book is distributed in the UK, Europe and the rest of the
world, this is by Palgrave Macmillan, a division of Macmillan Publishers
Limited, registered in England, company number 785998, of Houndmills,
Basingstoke, Hampshire RG21 6XS.

Palgrave Macmillan is the global academic imprint of the above
companies and has companies and representatives throughout the world.

Palgrave® and Macmillan® are registered trademarks in the United
States, the United Kingdom, Europe and other countries.

ISBN: 978-0-230-34213-2

Library of Congress Cataloging-in-Publication Data is available from the
Library of Congress.

A catalogue record of the book is available from the British Library.

Design by Letra Libre

First edition: January 2013

10 9 8 7 6 5 4 3 2 1

Printed in the United States of America.

CONTENTS

Acknowledgments   ix

1   The Myth of Martyrdom   1

2   Lies, Damn Lies, and Previous Research
    on Suicide Terrorism   21

3   Why Suicide Terrorists Are Suicidal   41

4   The Truth About 9/11   65

5   What Real Heroes Are Made Of   89

6   Murder-Suicide: The Natural Comparison   107

7   The Four Types of Suicide Terrorists   127

8   Mission Impossible? How to Stop Suicide Terrorism   151

Appendix A   177
Appendix B   191
Appendix C   195
Notes   199
Bibliography   233
Index   253

ACKNOWLEDGMENTS

Suicide terrorism can be a very dark and disturbing subject, and I spent more than three years investigating the intimate details of attackers' lives. For some, this might sound like a prison sentence, but I tried to maintain a sense of challenge and excitement as if working a puzzle, if only to preserve my *own* mental health.

At the beginning, when I realized that my findings directly contradicted the most well-known experts in the field, there was reason for concern. Sometimes there is resistance to an idea that challenges the conventional wisdom. Though I may have experienced this, fortunately there were anonymous peer reviewers who recognized the weight of the evidence and saw that it warranted publication in academic journals. Although I cannot thank them face-to-face, I am eternally grateful for their support. It is good to be reminded that there will always be open-minded people eager to embrace some new ideas.

A number of other scholars also assisted me along the way. They include Max Abrahms, who sent me his findings on the counterproductive nature of terrorist campaigns; Ken Ballen, who spoke with me about the results of his personal interviews with a number of terrorists; David Lester, who supported my early efforts to pursue research funding; Fielding McGehee, who spoke with me about what really happened at Jonestown in 1978; Ami Pedahzur and Arie Perliger, who sent me their database of past attacks; and Joseph Young, who sent me his findings on several terrorist profiles.

The superb work of many journalists who disseminated my early findings deserves recognition as well. Paul Kix's terrific piece for the

Boston Globe, "The Truth about Suicide Bombers," helped spark international interest in the topic. Articles by Anne-Catherine Simon for *Die Presse* in Austria, Poul Høi for *Berlingske Tidende* in Denmark, and Daniel Braw for *Helsingborgs Dagblad* in Sweden were also of great value, in addition to many other pieces that I have not listed here. I am hopeful that continued coverage of this research will help us to significantly reduce suicide attacks worldwide.

In addition, Andrew Nichols (Nick) Pratt, Colonel, USMC (Ret.), was kind enough to invite me to George C. Marshall European Center for Security Studies in Garmisch, Germany, where I was their suicide terrorism guest speaker for the Program on Terrorism and Security Studies. I greatly appreciated his support and directly benefited from the experience. As part of the program, I met with security officials from Afghanistan, Armenia, Australia, Bosnia and Herzegovina, Botswana, Bulgaria, Burkina Faso, Cameroon, Colombia, Congo, Czech Republic, Estonia, Georgia, Greece, India, Indonesia, Ireland, Jordan, Kazakhstan, Kosovo, Latvia, Lebanon, Macedonia, Mongolia, Montenegro, Morocco, the Palestinian territories, Poland, Romania, Saudi Arabia, Serbia, South Africa, Switzerland, Tunisia, Turkey, Uganda, Ukraine, the United States, and Uruguay. Their insights, observations, and questions directly inspired my research for the book's final two chapters.

Thanks also to my colleagues at The University of Alabama—Rebecca Howell, Ida Johnson, Mark Lanier, Bronwen Lichtenstein, Ariane Prohaska, Kathryn Seigfried-Spellar, and Jimmy Williams—who have been incredibly supportive throughout this process. They were always happy to offer advice or share a laugh, and my comfort in our department made it easy for me to focus on intellectual pursuits. Similarly, my students—whose insatiable desire for answers often mirrored my own—helped me to stay energized and motivated, with a healthy dose of curiosity.

Of course, it takes a certain degree of magic to create the finished product. Thanks to my agent Bob Mecoy, who played a vital role in getting this research into the right hands for publication. I particularly appreciate his enthusiasm and commitment, and I know that he went to bat for me on a number of occasions. And at Palgrave Macmillan, senior editor Emily Carleton, assistant editor Laura Lancaster, assistant production editor Victoria Wallis, and the rest of the team were instrumental in making this book possible. As we worked on the final drafts of the manuscript, Emily was like an angel on my shoulder—helping me to rein in my tendency to attack the critics, and instead focus on the more healthy excitement we can all enjoy from tackling new ideas.

Finally, thanks to my family and friends, who became regular participants in the creative process. I cannot begin to count how many times we sat at restaurants and spoke in hushed tones about the suicidal tendencies of violent attackers, all the while wary of disturbing those around us. Or how many conversations began with "I wonder why . . . ," only to be resolved by something thoughtful they said.

ONE

THE MYTH OF MARTYRDOM

Would you carry out a suicide attack?

After all, you want to kill Americans. Or maybe it's Europeans, or Jews, or some other "infidel" of the day. You want to make sure that your side wins and the other side loses. And you are willing to do whatever it takes.

It's really not that hard. Can you dress yourself? Okay, then pull on the bomb vest, one arm at a time, and then pull on another shirt to conceal the explosives. Can you walk? Okay, then stroll down the street to a crowded corner and wait for the perfect moment. Can you wiggle your thumb? Okay, then reach into your pocket and press that little button. It's really not that hard.[1]

In fact, it's so easy that donkeys have done it. In Afghanistan, Colombia, Iraq, Israel, and Lebanon, among other places, donkeys have carried out suicide bombings.[2] Of course, the donkeys weren't suicidal. I mean martyrs. The donkeys weren't martyrs. But you will be.

So let's get on with it. Wait, what? You're having second thoughts? You're thinking that maybe your life is worth more than a donkey's? And you've heard that in some countries, half of suicide bombers only manage to kill themselves. Yes—that's true.[3]

Now you're thinking that maybe you can contribute more some other way. Instead of blowing yourself up today, you could fight for twenty or thirty years, recruit new members, spy on the enemy, forge sensitive documents, build bombs, and strike from afar. And then at that future point, if *you're ready to "retire," you could blow yourself up in a suicide attack, satisfied with the knowledge that you did everything you could.*

I guess you're right—carrying out that suicide attack doesn't make much sense. Even if you're not afraid to die, in the vast majority of cases it's still not worth it. As they say, give a man a bomb vest, and he kills for a day. Teach a man to make bombs, and he kills for a lifetime. That's one of the reasons the U.S. military had so much trouble in Iraq. It wasn't until they started hunting down the bomb makers, instead of the bombs, that they really made any progress.[4]

But it all comes down to a very personal question.

Would you rather live or die?

A FAILURE OF IMAGINATION

Most people do not know the truth about 9/11. But it is not because of a conspiracy. And not because they have been lied to.

It is because, when it comes to the motives and psychology of the nineteen terrorist hijackers who set the world on fire that fateful September day, the experts got it wrong. Why were these suicide terrorists willing to kill themselves, along with nearly three thousand innocent civilians who they had never even met? In the aftermath of the deadliest attack on perhaps the most powerful nation in human history, our experts made the same types of mistakes they have made many times before.

As the bipartisan National Commission on Terrorist Attacks Upon the United States concluded, the strikes on the World Trade Center and the Pentagon were successful because of our "failure of imagination." After a nearly three-year investigation, including interviews with more than one thousand individuals in ten countries, at a total cost of nearly $15 million, the 9/11 Commission determined that "Across the government, there were failures of imagination, policy, capabilities, and management."[5] But by far, "the most important failure was one of imagination."[6] It was our inability to think.

This book won't make that mistake. At the beginning of this chapter, we were playing pretend, inside the head of a potential suicide bomber. Is that science? No. But it's a useful exercise because it stretches our brains and can bring us a step closer to the truth. In many cases, human be-havior is far too complex to be rigidly sorted into predetermined boxes. That's why we refer to the "art" of homicide investigation and the "art" of interrogation. These complex challenges often defy any strict order of operations or previously determined formulas. Ask any skilled terrorist interrogator or homicide detective if they could successfully be replaced by someone with a "how-to" cheat sheet. Maybe on the simplest of as-signments. But not on the tough cases, because a search for hidden truths requires instinct, improvisation, and imagination.

The irony is that the average man or woman on the street is some-times better at this than the scholars and government experts we count on. Professional success in these fields is often based on conformity: how well you follow a prescribed set of rules, and whether you can play the game without upsetting anyone. But research suggests that when it comes to skills like "divergent thinking," which is associated with cre-ativity and imagination and is critical for advanced problem solving, the less formal education you have received, the better off you may be.

As revolutionary education specialist Sir Ken Robinson recounts, a few years back there was a study of divergent thinking that required subjects to generate new possibilities from scratch. A sample question would be "How many different uses can you think of for a paper clip?" In the counterterrorism realm, we might ask about different uses for bombs or hijacked airplanes instead of paper clips—but more on that to come. Anyway, the study's results were fascinating:

> They gave a series of tests to 1,600 three-to-five year olds. . . . Of the 1,600 children, 98% scored at the genius level or higher for divergent thinking. They gave the same tests to the same children five years later at the ages of 8 to 10. Then 32% scored at the genius level in divergent thinking. They gave the same test to the same children at the ages of 14-to–15 and the result was 10%. Interestingly, they gave the same test to over 200,000 adults and the figure was 2%.[7]

Why do most people become less imaginative and less capable of generating new ideas as they grow older? There are many potential explanations. To some degree, it may be hardwired and almost inevitable: part of the cognitive maturation process required for survival.[8] But Robinson suggests that it's also the fault of our education system, because much of "what we teach in education is about not being wrong, about not taking risks."[9]

But if you're too scared of being wrong, it's awfully hard to get it right.

THE CONVENTIONAL WISDOM

So what glaring error did the so-called experts on suicide terrorism make in their diagnoses of the 9/11 hijackers?

They normalized them. They made the logical leap that in terms of their psychology, suicide terrorists were essentially just like ordinary people. "Sure, the 9/11 hijackers had extreme political and religious beliefs," the experts admitted. But were they unstable? No. Were they suicidal? No. Were they struggling with serious personal problems? Of course not. They just really, really believed that they were serving the greater good.

Believe it or not, this was actually the least risky perspective at the time. It fit squarely with past psychological experiments, studies of genocide and mass killing, and studies of institutional violence that had helped identify why large groups of people do such very bad things.[10] In addition, it seemed to reinforce previous findings that the vast majority of terrorists do not have personal pathologies or psychological disorders—they were relatively ordinary individuals before they were recruited and indoctrinated by terrorist organizations.[11] The truth is, this is an accurate characterization of most terrorist leaders and operatives— but not of those who carry out suicide attacks.

The assumption that suicide terrorists were psychologically normal may have also been appealing because it contradicted the public outrage. Everyone knows you can't trust the judgment of angry mobs recently traumatized by a terrorist attack, right? After 9/11, most people figured that anyone who would intentionally crash an airplane into a building must have something deeply wrong with him. The experts laughed and said no.

Consider the following statements, made by leading authorities around the world:

- Jerrold Post, founder of the CIA's Center for the Analysis of Personality and Political Behavior, chair of the American Psychiatric Association's Task Force for National and International Terrorism and Violence, and director of the political psychology program at George Washington University: "We'd like to believe these are crazed fanatics, and some sort of madmen in the grip of a psychosis. Not true . . . as individuals, this is normal behavior."[12]

- Robert Pape, former adviser for two presidential campaigns and professor at the University of Chicago: "The uncomfortable fact is that suicide terrorists are far more normal than many of us would like to believe."[13]

- Scott Atran, professor at the University of Michigan who has made presentations to the U.S. State Department, the U.K. House of Lords, and the U.S. National Security Council at the White House: "No instances of religious or political suicide terrorism stem from lone actions of cowering or unstable bombers."[14]

- Riaz Hassan, Australian Research Council fellow, former visiting professor at Yale University, and professor emeritus at Flinders University: "Most suicide bombers are psychologically normal."[15]

- Robert Brym, Royal Society of Canada fellow and professor at the University of Toronto: "Virtually all suicide bombers are psychologically stable."[16]

- Ellen Townsend, professor at the University of Nottingham: "Suicide terrorists are not truly suicidal."[17]

- Adel Sadeq, head of psychiatry at Ain Shams University: "The psychological make-up [of a suicide bomber] is that of a person who loves life."[18]

There is far more where that came from. Experts have also claimed that suicide terrorists are:

- "qualitatively similar to countless people throughout history who have given their lives for a higher cause"[19] (Larry Pastor, George Washington University Medical Center);
- "much like ordinary soldiers with a strong sense of duty and a willingness to sacrifice all for the common good"[20] (Robert Pape, the University of Chicago);
- "not significantly different from other rebels or soldiers around the world who are willing to engage in high-risk activism out of a sense of duty and obligation"[21] (Mohammed Hafez, Naval Postgraduate School).

Among those who share these views: a U.S. presidential candidate, scores of high-ranking government officials, and a number of world-renowned social scientists.[22]

However, this is one of those cases where laypeople were right to trust their instincts. One of those times when six-year-old kids intuitively understood more than sixty-year-old "experts." One of those opportunities for us to use our imaginations—while we still can.

THE FEAR FACTOR

I'm afraid to die. And I bet you are, too.

When I was fifteen, I got hit in the head with a baseball, no helmet. Internal bleeding produced a three-ounce blood clot. Think of a soda can filled to the one-quarter mark with blood, and then imagine that much blood lodged between the inside of the skull and the outer covering of the brain. The technical phrase was "extradural hemorrhage," but it doesn't take a neurologist to realize that internal bleeding causes a lot of pressure to build up and that pressure causes pain.

I was rushed to the emergency room with violent nausea, a debilitating headache, and numbness across half my body. After several tests,

I was told that the doctors were going to have to cut open my skull to drain the clot.

My immediate response: "Let's do it."

Now, an onlooker may have mistaken my statement for bravery. After all, I had just been informed that a doctor was going to perform some life-threatening procedure that I didn't fully understand, within inches of my brain. You only get equipped with one of those brains, and you only get one life. But I didn't flinch.

The truth is, there was not an ounce of courage in my response. I was so overwhelmed by the agony of the moment that I would have jumped at any potential solution—anything that would get me out of the present crisis. I was not courageously marching into surgery—I was desperately seeking to escape unbearable pain.

A similar misconception often surrounds suicide. Famed English writer Charles Caleb Colton once remarked, "Suicide sometimes proceeds from cowardice, but not always, for cowardice sometimes prevents it; since as many live because they are afraid to die, as die because they are afraid to live."[23]

To some degree, he's right. One reason why many people *do not* commit suicide when "the going gets tough" is because they are afraid of death. And the same fear also prevents many acts of suicide terrorism. Regardless of their beliefs, most ordinary people would be far too afraid of dying to strap explosives to their bodies and intentionally blow themselves up, much less hijack an airplane and deliberately crash it into a skyscraper.

But far too many commentators have taken this a step too far, concluding that because suicide terrorists do what we are afraid to do, this makes them brave. Worse yet, in some social contexts, these individuals are not only considered brave, but also glorified as heroic sacrificers—"martyrs."

However, as this book will show, suicide terrorists have a dirty little secret. They're afraid too—but of life. Much like my response when waiting in the emergency room, suicide terrorists are often desperate to escape unbearable pain—be it real or imagined, physical or psychological.

In fact, many suicide terrorists appear to be overwhelmed by far more fears than the average individual. They don't jettison our fears of death and boldly embrace their fate—they just stack their own fears on top. As the moment of their final act draws near, a natural survival instinct often sets in, and many have second thoughts. For instance, as a preemptively arrested suicide bomber known as Ali explained, "Even in the morning of the operation, I was very brave in my mind . . . . [But] from the minute I put on the explosive belt . . . I thought how frightening the belt was, that I was going to explode into pieces."[24] Many suicide terrorists get caught between a rock and a hard place: afraid to live and afraid to die. Blowing themselves up offers a permanent solution to this temporary problem.

But make no mistake, this is not a sacrifice. "Sacrifice" is defined as "the forfeiture of something highly valued for the sake of one considered to have a greater value or claim."[25] But as we will see, most suicide terrorists are so consumed by pain, fear, crisis, and other personal problems that the opportunity cost of their suicide becomes quite affordable. By definition, this also means that their attacks cannot be considered a true "sacrifice," because the suicide terrorists are not forfeiting "something highly valued." Even according to their own statements, they are trading something they put a low value on (their lives in this transient, unhappy, and corrupt world) for something they value highly (heaven and paradise). There is nothing noble or brave about that kind of bargain.

It is not only inaccurate to label these suicide terrorists "normal," "stable," "sacrificial," or "martyrs," but it is also dangerous. It plays directly into the hands of terrorist leaders, increasing the power of their propaganda. It allows them to glorify yesterday's suicide bombers as they recruit new ones for tomorrow. It also helps terrorist organizations conceal that they are exploiting desperate people for their own purposes: capitalizing on the psychological pain of individuals who could live in peace, if only they got the help they needed.

ARE SUICIDE TERRORISTS SUICIDAL?

In December 2010, esteemed journalist Paul Kix wrote an article for the *Boston Globe* titled "The Truth about Suicide Bombers." In the piece, which made headlines worldwide, he cited findings from recent studies and suggested that at their core, suicide terrorists "just want to commit suicide."[26]

Kix's powerful opening speaks for itself. He starts us off with the case of a suicide bomber from Afghanistan:

Qari Sami did something strange the day he killed himself. The university student from Kabul had long since grown a bushy, Taliban-style beard and favored the baggy tunics and trousers of the terrorists he idolized. He had even talked of waging jihad. But on the day in 2005 that he strapped the bomb to his chest and walked into the crowded Kabul Internet cafe, Sami kept walking—between the rows of tables, beyond the crowd, along the back wall, until he was in the bathroom, with the door closed.

The blast killed a customer and a United Nations worker, and injured five more. But the carnage could have been far worse. . . . One day after the attack, [Professor Brian Williams] stood before the cafe's hollowed-out wreckage and wondered why any suicide bomber would do what Sami had done: deliberately walk away from the target before setting off the explosives. . . .

Eventually a fuller portrait emerged. Sami was a young man who kept to himself, a brooder. He was upset by the U.S. forces' ouster of the Taliban in the months following 9/11—but mostly Sami was just upset. He took antidepressants daily. One of Sami's few friends told the media he was "depressed."

Today Williams thinks that Sami never really cared for martyrdom; more likely, he was suicidal. "That's why he went to the bathroom [before blowing himself up]," Williams said.[27]

This is just one example, but it's the first chink in the armor for those experts who insist that suicide terrorists are psychologically normal, that they "love life," and that they behave like ordinary soldiers.

Sami was clearly struggling with mental health problems, which is why he took antidepressants. He had also indicated to a friend that the drugs were not working—which could explain his desperation for a permanent way out. If Sami had truly been a committed ideologue, set on maximizing the destructive effects of his death, he would have blown himself up in the middle of the café. Instead, like many suicidal people, he needed to be alone—so he walked away from the enemy before ending his life.

As the starting point for a more sophisticated theory, this book takes the view that, by definition, all suicide terrorists are suicidal. Every act of suicide terrorism fits the definition of suicide: (1) death of the actor, (2) intention of dying, and (3) self-orchestration of that death.[28] And every suicide terrorist demonstrates at least a few behaviors on the continuum of suicidality:

- Suicide ideation [i.e., suicidal thoughts] (fleeting)
- Suicide ideation [i.e., suicidal thoughts] (chronic)
- Suicide-like gestures
- Diffuse, risky lifestyle
- Suicide plan (vague, nonlethal)
- Suicide plan (specific, lethal)
- Non-serious (low-lethality) suicide attempt
- Serious (high-lethality) suicide attempt
- Completed suicide.[29]

This may seem simplistic at first, but as our journey into the minds of suicide terrorists will reveal, there is tremendous variation in the way suicidal urges develop and take shape. Different suicide terrorists carry out similar attacks for a range of different reasons. In addition, it can be very difficult to determine if someone is suicidal, because these individuals are often so ashamed of their innermost pain that they deliberately hide the truth from those around them. We will tackle these challenges, and many more, in the pages to come.

A MOMENT OF SELF-REFLECTION

In that same *Boston Globe* article, Kix cites my research at length and points out that I am "at the forefront" of this subject.[30]

That may be good for the ego, but I wish he were wrong. A young professor should not be able to uncover the secret motives of suicide terrorists in just a few years, while the rest of the world essentially failed to do so in the decade that followed 9/11. Not if that young professor began with no grant funding, no research assistants, no government connections, no security clearance, and no privileged access, while the leading academic experts and government authorities are backed by tens of millions of dollars and access to any data they desire.

The fact that it's played out this way seems like a frightening condemnation of the systems we depend upon for knowledge. After all, these are the leaders we count on to keep us safe so we can sleep at night. I never anticipated that they could be so wrong, or worse yet, so closed-minded to the seemingly obvious possibility that suicide terrorists are suicidal.

When I began studying suicide terrorists, I had no agenda, just curiosity. Are these people selflessly sacrificing their lives so they can help others, or do they actually want to die? My hunch was that they were closer to the former, but I kept an open mind. And then, as I began watching the martyrdom videos and reading the suicide notes these attackers left behind, the evidence began piling up so high that I could no longer ignore it.

So I began looking for scholars who were saying what I was seeing. I began searching for leaders who had taken the next step: using research on suicidal behavior to catch these offenders and prevent their attacks. I expected to find hundreds of experts who could tell me more, who could help me understand the intricacies of this terrible threat. There were a few who had asked the right questions, but none who provided many answers.

To be fair, this book benefits from a lot of legwork conducted by others who studied suicide terrorism. They traveled extensively, conducted many valuable interviews, and gathered a great deal of information upon which I have relied. My work would not be possible without their work. But with a few exceptions,[31] they came to the wrong conclusions.

In addition, there are almost certainly other government experts and psychologists, sociologists, criminologists, and political scientists who were capable of doing this work, but their time was dedicated to other projects instead. Much like myself, until the last few years, they were content to let others study suicide terrorism in depth and simply trust their conclusions.

The fact remains that the basic premise of this book was apparent to the average man and woman on the street immediately after 9/11, if not earlier. Suicide terrorists are suicidal. It did not take a genius to follow up on these instincts. It just took an open mind and the ability to connect the dots, as others should have done long ago.

OUR MISSION

Today, there are more than ninety million people around the world who believe that suicide bombings are "often" or "sometimes" justified.[32] Within the United States, more than two hundred thousand people share this exact same view.[33] And that's the low estimate. It may be more like five hundred million people around the world, and more than a million people in the United States.[34] However, most of these individuals are entirely peaceful. We may disagree with them, but they are no more likely to carry out a suicide attack than you or I.

So how can we figure out who really is a threat and who isn't—before it's too late? In the years since 9/11, billions of dollars have been invested in counterterrorism efforts, but no one has successfully answered this question. Experts have talked about "radicalization" and "brainwashing," suggesting that ordinary people can be transformed into deadly terrorists by sophisticated social psychological techniques. However, they have yet to produce a reliable profile of who becomes a terrorist, much less a suicide bomber. Even among the tens of thousands of terrorists around the globe, very few are willing to blow themselves up for the cause. That's why in recent years, fewer than 3 percent of terrorists attacks have been suicidal in nature.[35] Most terrorists want to live.

Knowing someone's religion, political preference, or personal opinions about suicide bombings is simply not enough. Even with this information, we can only narrow our sights to many millions of "potential" killers. We must be more precise, because the decision to become a suicide terrorist is about much more than just ideology.

A useful comparison can be made with those who attempt political assassinations. On the surface, there is no one more clearly motivated by radical ideology than those who want to eliminate government leaders. And much like suicide terrorists, individuals who attempt political assassinations are often educated, with no prior record of violent offenses, and appear to have rational, strategic objectives.[36] However, a U.S. Secret Service study of all eighty-three individuals who mounted assassination attempts between 1949 and 1998 revealed that the true cause of their actions was much deeper. Sixty-one percent of perpetrators had received previous treatment for mental health problems, 44 percent had struggled with serious depression, 43 percent had a history of delusional ideas, and 41 percent had made suicidal threats in the past. Many of these attackers had also struggled with a range of other personal problems, including social isolation, substance abuse, and perceived victimization.[37]

New research provides a similar window into the motives of suicide terrorists. What makes them unique is their individual psychology. To truly understand them, we must try to know everything about them— who they were, what they wanted, what they feared, and what finally pushed them over the edge. Previous attempts to explain suicide bombers have focused solely on social and situational factors, glossing over the details of each individual's life. And that's why the truth about suicide terrorism has remained a mystery. Until now.

JOE STACK

Joe Stack is smiling. He sits in the living room with his young grandson, who is dressed in green pajamas, cuddling on his lap. Alongside them are Stack's daughter and granddaughter, wearing equally sunny expressions, as if the photographer didn't even need to say "Cheese!" The quintessential picture of a happy, healthy family.

And yet, in February 2010, the same man would pen an angry manifesto against the U.S. government, take off in a single-engine airplane, and deliberately crash it into the IRS building in Austin, Texas. Two people were killed, including Stack, and thirteen others were injured.

For those who insist that suicide terrorists are psychologically normal, it would be easy to label Stack a "martyr" and reject the possibility that he was suicidal. After all, to those who do not really understand suicide, the portrait of Stack's happy relationship with his daughter and grandkids would suggest a lack of mental health problems.

And based on Stack's manifesto, it would be easy to assume that he was so committed to his political beliefs that he was willing to sacrifice his life. Since his writing is relatively clear and he does not sound like a crazy person, it is tempting to think that he was just a normal guy fighting for a cause. As Stack wrote:

> Why is it that a handful of thugs and plunderers can commit unthinkable atrocities (and in the case of the GM executives, for scores of years) and when it's time for their gravy train to crash under the weight of their gluttony and overwhelming stupidity, the force of the full federal government has no difficulty coming to their aid within days, if not hours? Yet at the same time, the joke we call the American medical system, including the drug and insurance companies, are murdering tens of thousands of people a year and stealing from the corpses and victims they cripple, and this country's leaders don't see this as important as bailing out a few of their vile, rich cronies. Yet, the political "representatives" (thieves, liars, and self-serving scumbags is far more accurate) have endless time to sit around for year after year and debate the state of the "terrible health care problem." It's clear they see no crisis as long as the dead people don't get in the way of their corporate profits rolling in.
>
> And justice? You've got to be kidding! . . .
>
> I know I'm hardly the first one to decide I have had all I can stand. . . . But I also know that by not adding my body to the count, I ensure nothing will change. I choose to not keep looking over my shoulder at "big brother" while he strips my carcass, I choose not to ignore what is going on all around me, I choose not to pretend that business as usual won't continue; I have just had enough. . . .

I can only hope that the numbers quickly get too big to be white-
washed and ignored, that the American zombies wake up and revolt; it
will take nothing less. I would only hope that by striking a nerve that
stimulates the inevitable double standard, knee-jerk government reaction that results in more stupid draconian restrictions, people wake up
and begin to see the pompous political thugs and their mindless min-
ions for what they are. . . .

I am finally ready to stop this insanity. Well, Mr. Big Brother IRS
man, let's try something different; take my pound of flesh and sleep
well.[38]

This part of Stack's manifesto appears to directly support the view that
he was motivated purely by politics.

And not surprisingly, after Stack's suicide attack, his daughter essentially tried to make him the American version of a martyr. She insisted
that he was a "hero" who gave his life for the greater good: "I think too
many people lay around and wait for things to happen. But if nobody
comes out and speaks up on behalf of injustice, then nothing will ever be
accomplished . . . now maybe people will listen."[39]

We could stop here. That's exactly what most people who study suicide terrorists do. They look quickly for a political or religious motive,
circle it, and move on. Offender motive = political. Case closed. Now,
who's up for coffee?

However, simple logic dictates that Stack's suicide attack was not
really the product of his antigovernment ideology. Sure, his rage was
real. But there are millions of Americans who share Stack's anger about
political corruption—and the IRS is probably the most hated institu-
tion in the entire United States. Despite these beliefs, even radical political activists who attack the government generally do not end up
dead. They lash out, for better or worse, but live to tell the tale. So
why didn't Stack? Beyond ideology, there must be something different
about him.

When we dig a little deeper, we see that in the same manifesto, Stack
actually admitted to his mental health problems and alluded to his suicidal intentions:

If you're reading this, you're no doubt asking yourself, "Why did this have to happen?" The simple truth is that it is complicated and has been coming for a long time. The writing process, started many months ago, was intended to be therapy in the face of the looming realization that there isn't enough therapy in the world that can fix what is really broken.

Needless to say, this rant could fill volumes with example after example if I would let it. I find the process of writing it frustrating, tedious, and probably pointless . . . especially given my gross inability to gracefully articulate my thoughts in light of the storm raging in my head. Exactly what is therapeutic about that I'm not sure, but desperate times call for desperate measures. . . .

So now we come to the present. After my experience with the CPA world, following the business crash, I swore that I'd never enter another accountant's office again. But here I am with a new marriage and a boatload of undocumented income, not to mention an expensive new business asset, a piano, which I had no idea how to handle. . . .

This left me stuck in the middle of this disaster trying to defend transactions that have no relationship to anything tax-related (at least the tax-related transactions were poorly documented). Things I never knew anything about and things my wife had no clue would ever matter to anyone. The end result is . . . well, just look around.

I remember reading about the stock market crash before the "great" depression and how there were wealthy bankers and businessmen jumping out of windows when they realized they screwed up and lost everything. . . . Now when the wealthy fuck up, the poor get to die for the mistakes. . . . isn't that a clever, tidy solution.[40]

In just these few paragraphs, Stack reveals his belief that "there isn't enough therapy in the world that can fix what is really broken [with me]." He describes himself as a "frustrated" man "with a storm raging in my head." He also admits feeling trapped (a classic suicidal risk factor)—or as he puts it, "stuck in the middle of this disaster." While looking for a way out, Stack suggests that "desperate times call for desperate measures"—and then compares himself to the 1929 Wall Street

Crash window jumpers who committed suicide "when they realized they screwed up and lost everything." It isn't hard to understand why Stack made this parallel: he was in the midst of being audited by the IRS and had lost most of his retirement savings.

Ultimately, no matter what others try to claim, we know that Stack's primary motive was not political heroism, it was suicide. As he admitted, he felt helpless and hopeless in the midst of a deep psychological crisis. And he knew exactly how to escape those feelings, because of a powerful lesson his mother had taught him a long time ago. When Stack was just a seven-year-old boy, his single mother killed herself, leaving young Joe and his siblings to fend for themselves as orphans.[41]

We are very lucky that Stack was so honest about his mental condition and so open about his pain and despair. If he had written only the political portion of his manifesto, it would have been even easier for people to claim that he was psychologically normal and just fighting for a cause. And in a different social or religious context, he might have simply spouted extremist rhetoric. The fact that Stack gave us a glimpse into his innermost thoughts is of great value.[42]

But it's also unusual. Completely honest suicide terrorists are hard to find. This is no shock, given what we know about suicidal people. As suicidologist Edwin Shneidman has explained, "some desperately suicidal people . . . can dissemble and hide their true feelings from the world. If it is true that all the world's a stage, then some players on occasion may wear their masks."[43] Some bury their deepest and darkest secrets, then put on smiles for all the world to see.

However, that doesn't mean we have to fall for it and therefore misunderstand these perpetrators. We can do better, dig deeper, and learn more.

OVERVIEW

This book takes you on a journey through the minds of suicide bombers, airplane hijackers, lone-wolf terrorists, cult members, school shooters, kamikaze pilots, and more. The result is an astonishing account of fear, failure, guilt, shame, and rage, told through case studies, suicide notes, love letters, diary entries, and martyrdom videos. The psychopathology of these killers is contrasted with the courage and bravery of heroic soldiers, true martyrs, and average citizens who sacrifice their lives for what they believe in. It is only by exploring the deepest, darkest secrets of suicide terrorists—and discovering exactly how they differ from true heroes—that we will ever be able to stop them.

Here is a general road map to our investigation of suicide terrorism.

Chapter 2 examines previous explanations of suicide terrorism and why they have been so very wrong. For years, terrorist leaders and spokesmen have insisted that their "martyrs" are ordinary people who selflessly sacrifice their lives for the cause. Unfortunately, in the Middle East, Asia, and the Western world, most government experts and scholars have taken them at their word. This chapter will expose the common misconceptions that have allowed terrorist leaders to essentially trick the world's smartest men and women into spreading this dangerous propaganda for them.

Chapter 3 explores the initial evidence that more than 130 suicide terrorists have exhibited classic suicidal traits. By drawing connections between a hundred years of research on conventional suicide and the details from suicide notes, martyrdom videos, and interviews with terrorists, we can begin to recognize the critical patterns. Specific case studies include a suicide terrorist who shot himself in the head on the top floor of the Empire State Building, another who had previously overdosed on pills after being dumped by a girlfriend, and a third who admitted that he agreed to become a suicide bomber "not because I belonged to the organization, but to realize my wish to die."[44]

Chapter 4 presents a psychological autopsy of 9/11 ringleader Mohamed Atta, arguably the most infamous and influential suicide terrorist in human history. Stunningly, Atta has been fundamentally misunderstood for nearly a decade by presumed experts who have claimed that he was just following Osama bin Laden's orders, and that he was "not readily characterized as depressed, not unable to enjoy life, not detached from friends and society."[45] The reality is quite different: Atta struggled with social isolation, depression, guilt, shame, and hopelessness for many years, and he repeatedly doubted and disobeyed bin Laden before finally killing himself on September 11, 2001.

Chapter 5 explores what real heroes are made of. Those who subscribe to the "myth of martyrdom" suggest that suicide terrorists are essentially the psychological equivalent of the firefighters who died on 9/11 while pulling people from burning buildings. By this distorted logic, both types can be considered legitimate heroes by their supporters because they were sacrificing their lives in an attempt to save others. But there are critical differences, and this chapter exposes the fakers. The power of real heroism is illustrated by stories of Secret Service agents willing to take a bullet for the president and soldiers who jumped on grenades to protect their comrades.

Chapter 6 challenges us to expand our thinking. If suicide terrorists are indeed suicidal, who else should we study to understand this behavior more accurately? The natural comparison is to other perpetrators of murder-suicide, including workplace killers and rampage shooters. For instance, is it a mere coincidence that a week before he opened fire at a Pennsylvania gym and then shot himself in the head, George Sodini considered blowing himself up on a bus, like a Palestinian suicide bomber? Is it a mere coincidence that the Columbine school shooters discussed a plan to "hijack a hell of a lot of bombs and crash a plane into NYC with us inside," nearly three years before Al Qaeda did almost that exact same thing? Perhaps these various types of killers have far more in common than we ever realized.

Chapter 7 argues that there are four primary types of terrorists who become suicidal: conventional, coerced, escapist, and indirect. We'll draw comparisons to the famous bunker suicides of Adolf Hitler and his followers during the collapse of Nazi Germany; the Jonestown tragedy, where hundreds of cult members drank Kool-Aid laced with poison; the kamikaze pilots of Japan, who have long been misunderstood; and the deadly game of Russian roulette, where players point revolvers at their heads and leave their future "up to fate." In addition, we'll look at firsthand accounts from teenagers who were kidnapped for suicide missions, others who were threatened with decapitation for disobedience, and

Osama bin Laden's own bodyguard, who details the terrorist leader's initial plans for suicide when he feared capture after 9/11.

Finally, Chapter 8 presents some solutions. Now that we understand the psychology of suicide terrorists, we should be able to predict where their attacks are most likely to occur—and then take decisive steps to stop them. For instance, the wild story of the Underwear Bomber, whose own father contacted the CIA in an attempt to prevent his son's suicide attack, suggests that the families of suicide terrorists are an untapped resource that should be mobilized. And recent discoveries of a five-minute computer test that identifies suicidal people could potentially revolutionize airport security. But major progress is only possible if we push the limits of our collective imagination. This chapter offers powerful short-term and long-term recommendations for counterterrorism officials around the world.

Past experts have gotten it wrong. The proof is in the pudding. From 2001 to 2010, global suicide attacks increased by more than 300 percent.[46] And with the exception of the fence Israel built to keep Palestinian suicide terrorists out of their cities, most attempts to combat this deadliest of threats have been an utter failure.[47] Of course, Israel's strategy is clearly not applicable everywhere. In most societies, our enemies walk among us.

That's why we need to be able to find them and stop them. Before it's too late.

TWO

LIES, DAMN LIES, AND PREVIOUS RESEARCH ON SUICIDE TERRORISM

The simplest way to try to understand people's motives is just to ask them. Short of hiring a psychic, breaking out the tarot cards, or tracing the lines across someone's palm, the easiest way to know what's going on inside people's brains is to listen to what comes out of their mouths.

This is how social scientists often get their information: by administering surveys and conducting interviews, then tallying the results. They love this approach, because it gives them new, exclusive, and empirical data, seemingly untainted by their own opinions. When these scholars see strong patterns among the data—when essentially "everyone" is telling them the same thing—they usually assume that their subjects' statements can be trusted. So they run with them.

But you can't believe everything you hear.

Respondents may give consistently unreliable answers for many reasons. They may be influenced by social and cultural biases. They may be lying, with ulterior motives. They may be in psychological denial because admitting the truth, even to themselves, would be far too painful. Or they may simply lack the knowledge or information to provide accurate answers. If you asked "everyone" in the 1400s whether the Earth orbited the Sun, or the Sun orbited the Earth, you would get a very consistent answer. And much like the answer researchers often receive when they simply ask about the motives of suicide terrorists, it would be consistently wrong.

Sometimes the truth does not simply jump from the tips of respondents' tongues to the pages of our articles and books. Sometimes we have to dig for it.

Take the case of failed Palestinian suicide bomber Wafa al-Biss. Ask her why she attempted to blow up an Israeli hospital. Then ask her mother. Ask her father. Ask the two terrorists from the Al-Aqsa Martyrs Brigades who oversaw her operation. All five people will tell you the same thing: that she acted purely for political and religious reasons, self-lessly attempting to sacrifice her life for a noble cause.[1]

The two terrorists explained that Wafa was motivated by "a great determination and perseverance to undertake a sacred mission for God."[2] Her mother remarked that "it was the love of her country and her dedication to her country that led her to do this."[3] These sentiments were echoed by Wafa and her father. Five for five.

There's just one tiny problem. It's not true. With a little detective work, we can see that in the same interviews in which they insisted that Wafa was purely motivated by ideology, all five sources revealed that their own statements cannot be trusted.

THE TERRORIST LEADERS

During an interview, the terrorist militants who ran Wafa's operation repeatedly contradicted themselves and spouted propaganda, attempt-ing to infuse the attempted suicide attack with far more legitimacy and significance than it actually held. One of the men's crossed legs shook incessantly as he spoke—maybe he had to use the bathroom, or maybe at some deeper level he was uncomfortable with the lies he told.[4]

At one moment, the terrorists were insisting that "nobody opposes" women being used as suicide bombers: "We have never heard of anyone objecting to women. There has been no disagreement on this topic."[5] But in fact there are widespread cultural debates about this practice, and Wafa's father had specifically expressed the opinion that only men should be suicide bombers.[6]

A minute later, the terrorists were claiming that Wafa's parents had been happy about their daughter's decision to blow herself up, "like any Palestinian" would be.[7] Of course, even in Palestine, where suicide attacks are widely celebrated, most families do not want their children used for such purposes. In fact, some parents have literally threatened to kill terrorist recruiters for using their children as suicide bombers.[8] And in Wafa's case, both of her parents had specifically forbidden her from carrying out an attack.

Lies and more lies, but we shouldn't be surprised. Terrorist leaders and other rank-and-file terrorists commonly insist that those who carry out "martyrdom" attacks are not suicidal. For instance, Hamas cofounder Mahmoud al-Zahar has stated, "These are not suicide operations. This is a despicable term used by the Israelis in order to say that these are suicide operations, knowing that suicide is forbidden in Islam. . . . These are martyrdom-seeking operations, approved by all the authorities of the Islamic nation, who consider them to be the highest level of martyrdom."[9]

These claims belie the true agenda of terrorist leaders and their supporters: to slander their enemies, mobilize hatred against them, and preserve and protect the reputation of the suicide bombers upon which their organizations depend.[10] Al-Zahar's assertion that *all* Islamic leaders support suicide attacks is clearly untrue, so why should he—or other leaders making similar claims—be trusted to provide accurate psychological assessments of their suicide bombers?

THE FAMILY

During interviews with Wafa's parents, her mother cried and her father sat stone-faced, trying to choke back emotion. Like many traumatized parents, they deeply wanted to believe that their child was motivated by heroic impulses, rather than weakness, and that there was nothing they could have done to prevent her tragic fate. However, in the course of the interview, they also revealed that Wafa had wanted to kill herself for much of her tortured existence, and that her father had locked her in the house for more than a month and had often beaten and abused the crying girl. As former CIA officer Robert Baer later observed, if anything, it seems that the father's brutal treatment of his own daughter increased her desire to die.[11]

It's not surprising that family accounts of the intentions of suicide terrorists are unreliable. Whatever the facts, it is much easier for family members to tell themselves that their loved one was attempting to be heroic than to admit that their death may have been preventable. This pretense not only implies that the deceased is in paradise instead of hell, but also negates the family's own responsibility for not intervening.

The comments of the father of Palestinian suicide bomber Tariq Hamid on this subject are typical. "Some people claim that all these young mujahideen who blow themselves up are desperate people with no money and no homes. These claims are wrong. These are lies and clear Zionist propaganda. . . . They lack nothing. The only thing they need is to reach Paradise, by means of defense and martyrdom for the sake of Allah."[12] Tariq's father and other parents of suicide terrorists may wish to believe that their children lacked nothing on earth, simply because they were well provided for and not starving or homeless. But mental health is rarely that simple: suicidal people may still lack things they desperately need, such as meaningful social connections, purpose, or hope.

Even family members who are not in denial still cannot be trusted to give an accurate evaluation of their loved one's motives. This fact often arises in cases of conventional suicide in the Islamic world, where families have been to known to lie and cover up the true reasons for their child's death, in order to avoid disgrace and shame.[13] When it comes to suicide terrorism, if a few small lies help preserve the reputation of their son or daughter, it is a small price to pay.

Furthermore, much like terrorist leaders, most family members of suicide terrorists are not qualified to recognize the warning signs of suicide. For example, many parents speak glowingly of how energetic and happy their loved ones seemed in the hours before their attacks, because they think this shows that their child was motivated by selfless heroism, not suicide.[14] However, what they fail to realize is that this spike in energy before killing oneself is actually a classic suicidal symptom.[15] Outside the terrorism context, suicidal individuals often appear noticeably more energetic and at peace in the days or hours before they kill themselves, because they have been looking forward to escaping their lives and are genuinely excited that the end is near.

THE SUICIDE TERRORISTS THEMSELVES

Wafa's own statements were similarly unreliable. At first, she sounds like any other indoctrinated terrorist, claiming that the Israelis "have killed many Palestinian children," so she "wanted to kill 20, 50 Jews. Yes! . . . even babies. You kill our babies."[16] But she later admitted that she had never been particularly interested in politics and had not even cared which terrorist organization sponsored her attack. She had actually gone from group to group, looking for anyone who would provide the twenty-two pounds of explosive she could strap to her body to escape her problems.

Furthermore, after her arrest at an Israeli checkpoint, Wafa insisted that she was never serious about her attack and that "when I got to the gate, I wanted to live, like you!"[17] But video evidence directly contradicts these statements. Locked in an enclosure at the gate by suspicious security officials, Wafa repeatedly reached into her pocket to press the detonation button, jerking the cord out with frustration and pounding the button with her thumb when she failed to explode.

Wafa's desire to blow herself up at the gate, even when her death would accomplish nothing for the cause, is another indication that her motives were not political or religious. Even at that desperate point, if she were a true ideologue, she should have allowed herself to be arrested, because she would eventually be released and could live to fight another day.[18] In fact, some preemptively arrested suicide bombers have received prison sentences as short as four years. However, Wafa didn't care about any of that. More than anything, she wanted to die. So she tried and failed to detonate her explosives while standing *all alone* in the gated enclosure, and then was forcibly arrested after it became clear that her bomb did not function properly.

Further investigations reveal that the real reason behind Wafa's suicide attack was her mental health problems. Throughout her teens, she had talked about wanting to "martyr" herself. Then at age eighteen, she had tried to throw herself out a window but lost her nerve. Two years later, she attempted suicide by setting the kitchen stove on fire and blowing herself up. The flames consumed her body, and she suffered third-degree burns across her chest, neck, and arms. But she was rushed to an Israeli hospital and survived.[19]

When the time came for her release from the hospital, she cried, pleaded to remain, and had to be removed on a stretcher. The doctors strongly recommended counseling for Wafa, but her family refused because of the social shame it would bring upon them.[20] In another context, where the stigma against mental health treatment is less widespread, she might have received the help she needed. In Palestine, she found a different way out. She decided to become a suicide bomber, and then plotted to blow up the very same hospital that had done her the disservice of keeping her alive.

Much like the statements of terrorist leaders and family members, the words of the suicide terrorists themselves cannot be automatically trusted. Suicide terrorists commonly try to portray themselves as being as far from suicidal as possible: as confident, secure, and heroic.[21] They're most likely in denial, because the reality is often quite different. For instance, in Al Qaeda suicide terrorist Abu Muhammad Al-San'ani's final video before he blew himself up in Afghanistan, he claimed that "I feel a great calm. . . . I've never felt so calm in my life."[22] However, as he spoke, his voice was audibly shaking.

It is common for suicidal people to deny their death wish, but suicide terrorists are particularly likely to engage in self-deception, given the social expectation that they act like brave heroes. And even if they recognize their true intentions, there is no incentive for them to admit it.[23] If they are going to die either way, why would they choose shame and disgrace, instead of being praised and honored as sacrificial "martyrs" for years after their deaths?

COMPOUNDING THE PROBLEM

As the case of Wafa al-Biss shows, when it comes to the motives of suicide terrorists, we cannot automatically trust the words of the individual attackers, their family members, terrorist leaders, or anyone else. Not if they have strong incentives to be deceitful. Not if we care about getting it right.

Unfortunately, many scholars have made this exact mistake. For instance, in 2007, psychology professor Ellen Townsend published an article titled "Suicide Terrorists: Are They Suicidal?" in one of the most widely read journals on suicidal behavior. Her answer was a resounding no. As she explained, "The results of [her] review strongly suggest that suicide terrorists are not truly suicidal, and that attempting to find commonalities between suicide terrorists and others who die by suicide is likely to be an unhelpful path for any discipline wishing to further understanding of suicidal behavior."[24]

How did Townsend come to this conclusion? By reviewing five "empirical reports": three that depended largely upon interviews of the deceased suicide terrorist's friends and family members and two that were based on interviews of regular terrorists, not suicide terrorists.[25] She simply took what they had to say at face value, published her article, and then reasserted her conclusions in December 2010.[26]

But she's not the only one. The conventional wisdom among experts that "most suicide bombers are psychologically normal," that they are "much like ordinary soldiers," and that they "are not truly suicidal"[27] is like a house of cards. It's built on six extremely shaky misconceptions. And it's about to come crashing down.

Misconception #1: Consistent sources are automatically reliable.

As we've seen, the assumption that consistent sources are automatically reliable—and that you can simply trust what they say—is remarkably flawed. But it's just the first of many common misconceptions among the presumed experts. There are also fundamental misunderstandings of suicide, mental illness, who becomes a suicide terrorist, and why.

Misconception #2: Suicidal people are easily identifiable.

Tony Dungy won a Super Bowl as the football coach of the Indianapolis Colts. But he's no Bill Parcells or Rex Ryan. His success was not based on how mean he could look or how loud he could yell. In fact, as a board member of the Positive Coaching Alliance and the author of two books on leadership, Dungy has been a pioneer for a different type of coaching. As a *New York Times* feature put it, "Dungy does not belittle his players or scream at them. He guides instead of goads . . . [and prioritizes] being a teacher instead of screaming and yelling."[28]

As professional sports have become a sophisticated multibillion-dollar industry, teams have increasingly recognized that they need leaders who understand people. And Dungy was the perfect fit: someone blessed with the ability to quickly connect with fifty-three individual millionaire athletes from a wide variety of backgrounds, discover what motivates them, and inspire them to make the most of their short time on this earth.

And yet, at 1:45 A.M. on December 22, 2005, Tony Dungy awoke to the worst shock a parent can get. His eighteen-year-old son, James, had committed suicide.

Family and friends were stunned. At the time, virtually all indications were that James was a happy, healthy kid. His parents had seen no signs that James was struggling with mental health issues. And as one friend explained, James "didn't seem like he was depressed. . . . He was an easygoing person. He joked around all the time, and it didn't seem like he had any problems. He was a nice guy to be around."[29] Another friend said that James had just called her very recently and they made plans to get together the next week.[30] And a third friend who had gone to the movies with James just hours before he took his own life described his behavior as normal. "He was cracking jokes, just being himself," she said. "This morning, it was so surreal."[31]

Sometimes, suicidal people openly discuss their suicidal thoughts, or display such abnormal behavior that our suspicions are immediately aroused. But as all too many parents, siblings, friends, and loved ones have learned the hard way, we are often unaware of the suicidal people among us, blind to their secret pain.

Of course, the same holds true for suicide terrorists. And yet, unless they specifically admit that they are suicidal, or unless they conform to the most simplistic stereotype of what a suicidal person "looks like," most scholars are quick to dismiss the possibility.

Renowned suicidologist David Lester and his colleagues expose this type of claim in the work of Riaz Hassan, a presumed suicide terrorism expert who has taught at institutions such as Yale University:

> Hassan (2001) asserts that none of the suicide bombers in the Middle East have a "typical" suicide profile, which Hassan says is uneducated, desperately poor, simpleminded, or depressed! This profile would come as a great surprise to suicidologists, let alone Ernest Hemmingway, Judas Iscariot, Yukio Mishima, Cleopatra, or Adolf Hitler, all of whom committed suicide.[32]

Lester further explains that Hassan's "suicide profile" is essentially made up. It's what someone might guess about suicide if they had never studied the behavior. And other scholars have made this same error and even more egregious ones, based on their fundamental misunderstandings of suicide and mental illness.

For instance, in his 2005 book *Dying to Win,* University of Chicago professor Robert Pape presents the results from what he called "the most comprehensive and reliable survey now available." It was a study of "the universe of suicide terrorist attackers from 1980 to the end of 2003, a total of 462 suicide attackers in all."[33] As he explains, his study

> found *no documented mental illness, such as depression,* psychosis, or past suicide attempts . . . no evidence of major criminal behavior . . . [and] not a single report that a suicide attacker was gay, an adulterer, or otherwise living in a way that would bring shame in a traditional society. . . . Rather, the uncomfortable fact is that suicide terrorists are far more normal than many of us would like to believe.[34]

At first glance, it might sound like Pape is presenting very impressive evidence that suicide terrorists are psychologically normal. His book was widely praised by the mainstream media, including the *Washington Post* and CNN, and was widely cited by other scholars. Many people have been quick to embrace Pape's findings and then repeat them, disseminating this information as good science.[35] In fact, Pape's research is taken so seriously that he has served as an adviser for two presidential campaigns.[36]

But let's stop and think for a moment. We can start with Pape's claim that not a single one of the 462 suicide bombers from 1980 to 2003 was depressed.

How likely is it that you could walk into a room with 462 people anywhere on the globe and not a single depressed person would be present? This is actually something we can calculate. The U.S. Centers for Disease Control and Prevention reports that approximately 5 percent of the population is depressed.[37] (We might expect a higher percentage to struggle with depression in Palestine, Iraq, and Afghanistan, given the strains and trauma affecting those who live there. But more on that to come.) So if about 5 percent of the population is depressed, in a room of 462 people, we would expect approximately 23 depressed individuals.

What is the probability that zero of 462 are depressed? It is calculated as $(1-0.05)^{462}$, which equals 1 in 19,574,665,823. For comparison's sake, you'd be about one hundred times more likely to hit the Powerball jackpot, after walking into an Exxon station and buying a one-dollar lottery ticket.[38]

Either Pape has unintentionally discovered that suicide bombing is the most remarkable cure for depression, mental illness, major crime, and adultery in human history, or there is something seriously wrong with his so-called "comprehensive and reliable" approach.

The key here is that *not finding* signs of depression, other mental health problems, or suicidal tendencies is easy. It's like not finding the clues needed to solve a murder. Anyone can do it. And it becomes even easier to not find signs of suicidality among suicide terrorists when you subscribe to the misconception that suicidal people are easily identifiable. If you expect them to wave their hands in your face or jump up onto your desk and blurt out their innermost feelings, you will miss most of the critical clues. By contrast, digging deeper, finding the evidence, and connecting the dots requires much more knowledge, effort, and skill.

Misconception #3: Suicidal people are crazy and irrational.

In the wake of the September 11, 2001, attacks, there was a popular rush to condemn Al Qaeda's suicide terrorists as "crazy," as "lunatics," and as "monsters."[39] Fortunately, many scholars quickly fought back against this hasty characterization. As they rightly argued, although terrorists' crimes may be unforgivable and it may be comforting to label our enemies in dismissive terms, we should not distort the truth simply to make ourselves feel better.

However, many of these same scholars made a major mistake by conflating concepts like "crazy" and "irrational"—on the one hand—with "suicidal" or "mentally ill"—on the other. There is a broad spectrum of people who struggle with suicidal urges and mental health problems. Some of them may suffer from delusions and have no grasp of rationality, but many do not. This faulty view that suicidal people are crazy and irrational is related to misconception #2: the belief that suicidal people are easily identifiable. When commentators essentially assume that suicidal people walk around crying, drooling, or hallucinating, anyone who does not act that way gets a prematurely clean bill of health.

For instance, in an anonymous review, one presumed expert wrote the following comment when insisting that 9/11 ringleader Mohamed Atta could not have been depressed or suicidal. (An in-depth study of Atta is presented in Chapter 4). "A true depressive would not have had the ability to achieve a college [degree], let alone a graduate degree, or have any type of passion or interest in religion or any cause whatsoever."[40]

This shows a fundamental misunderstanding of mental illness. Major depression and suicidal desires can rise and fall, and profoundly afflicted individuals can graduate from school, publish novels, plan sophisticated attacks, and carry out many other complex activities requiring prolonged concentration, careful calculation, and lasting effort.

Some scholars have become further wedded to this misconception because of previous research on regular, non-suicide terrorists. It has been well established that the vast majority of terrorists are not crazy or insane, and they do not appear to suffer from serious pathologies, early childhood traumas, or severe personality disorders.[41] This is probably true. However, when it comes to suicide terrorists, these findings appear to have led to a common syllogistic leap:

1. Terrorists are not crazy or irrational.
2. Suicide is crazy and irrational.
3. Therefore, terrorists do not commit suicide.

The first point is generally accurate, and has been documented by terrorism expert Bruce Hoffman, among many others.[42] Indeed, it was the rationality of terrorist leaders like Osama bin Laden or Ayman al-Zawahiri, who sounded like CEOs rattling off the complex elements of their strategies, that made them such formidable adversaries.[43] In addition, rational choice models have been used, with some success, to explain terrorist organizations' behavior.[44]

However, the second and third points are a major oversimplification. Suicidal people often appear to be rational actors who behave in calculated and premeditated ways.[45] Even in their final moments, they may carefully plan and stage their deaths for symbolic effect.

Furthermore, rational and psychologically healthy people can suddenly become suicidal, depending on a range of social and situational factors.[46] People change. A relatively normal Chechen or Al Qaeda terrorist could become suicidal, just like a relatively normal high school student, businessman, or soldier. This does not necessarily mean that most suicide terrorists were ever insane, or that they were born with some inherent mental flaw.

Misconception #4: Suicide terrorists are a representative sample of regular terrorists.

Imagine that you are the leader of a terrorist organization. You need someone to carry out a suicide attack. How do you select this person?

Do you walk into a room with one hundred of your followers, cover your eyes, spin around, and then blindly point at one unlucky soul? Do you ask everyone to write their names on pieces of paper, fold them in half, and drop them in a hat, which you shake and then pick from at random? Do you tell your fellow terrorists that they should stand in a circle and draw lots to see who will blow themselves up?

Of course not. Why would you? No successful leader makes important decisions this way. Sure, many terrorist spokesmen like to claim that every member of their organization is willing to sacrifice his or her life for the cause. But again, this is simply propaganda. There is no evidence that suicide terrorists are selected in this manner.

And yet, a remarkable number of scholars and government officials take it for granted that suicide terrorists are a random or representative sample of regular terrorists. When making broad pronouncements about the motives of suicide terrorists, they simply cite previous research on regular terrorists and assume it automatically applies. For instance, a 2009 journal article titled "The Psychology of Suicide Terrorism" asserts, "Understanding the psychology of suicide terrorism must necessarily be rooted in an understanding of the psychology of terrorism."[47] It then goes on to make a number of claims about why people become suicide terrorists by recapitulating why people become terrorists.

At first, this might seem reasonable. However, upon closer examination, the problem becomes clear.

Many suicide attackers are people from local communities with *no previous terrorism experience*.[48] Others come from within the terrorist organizations themselves. But in both cases, these individuals are often self-selected.[49] As the 9/11 Commission's multimillion-dollar investigation revealed, "operatives volunteered for suicide operations and, for the most part, were not pressured to martyr themselves."[50] And whether it's carrying out suicide attacks, answering an online opinion poll, or having a second helping of ice cream, people who volunteer for any activity are different from those who do not. Their volunteerism sets them apart.

The misconception that suicide terrorists are a representative sample of regular terrorists has been further exposed by Israeli psychologist Ariel Merari and his colleagues. They recently interviewed fifteen preemptively arrested suicide bombers, twelve terrorists arrested in non-suicide missions, and fourteen arrested organizers of suicide attacks.[51]

Unlike the suicide bombers, when the regular terrorists were asked if they had ever considered carrying out a "martyrdom operation," eleven of twelve insisted that they had not.[52] They bluntly rejected the possibility, making statements such as "I am incapable of doing it," "I simply am not interested," "I cannot see myself dead," and "This is no way to die."[53]

Similarly, when the organizers of suicide attacks were asked if they considered intentionally martyring themselves, nine of fourteen said they had not.[54] Most put far too much value on their own lives to simply die for one attack. They offered a range of dismissals, such as "I didn't want to do it myself," "I wasn't ready to do it myself," "I wouldn't be willing to carry out a martyrdom operation," and "I didn't want to go on a martyrdom operation . . . the thought of being a martyr didn't cross my mind."[55] As an organizer from Palestine Islamic Jihad further explained, "No. It's very difficult. Every man has different character and traits. I was destined to organize and others were destined to perform martyrdom operations. I am willing to fight but not to die in a suicide attack. For me life is something basic."[56] Indeed, it is.

Since we don't want to repeat the mistakes of previous scholars, we should be skeptical about what terrorists tell us. However, it is hard to imagine why these committed ideologues—who openly admitted their hatred for infidels and their desire to fight and kill—would lie about this. What would be their ulterior motive? These admissions directly contradict terrorist propaganda, which purports that all members are willing to intentionally die for the cause. And in their social context, admitting that they would not volunteer for "martyrdom operations" is almost like saying that they don't have what it takes to be heroes. It is very unusual for people to consistently lie to make themselves look worse. In fact, the U.S. legal system has a special classification for admissions people make against their own self-interest. The rationale is that when a speaker "reveals something incriminating, embarrassing, or otherwise damaging . . . the lack of incentive to make a damaging statement is an indication of the statement's reliability."[57]

So they were probably telling the truth. Unlike suicide terrorists, the vast majority of regular terrorists are not willing to intentionally kill themselves—for any reason.[58] There are fundamental differences between those who will and those who won't.

Misconception #5: Terrorist organizations would not use unstable or mentally ill people.

Many terrorist leaders insist that they would never use unstable or mentally ill people for suicide terrorism attacks.[59] However, despite how absurd these statements might seem on their face, many scholars disseminate these ideas with reckless abandon.

For instance, sociologist Robert Brym draws parallels between suicide bombers in Lebanon and the September 11 hijackers, in order to dismiss the views of the masses and claim that suicide terrorists are "psychologically stable":

> Several psychologists characterized the Beirut bombers as "unstable individuals with a death wish." Government and media sources made similar assertions in the immediate aftermath of the suicide attacks on the United States on September 11, 2001. Yet these claims were purely speculative. . . . On reflection, it is not difficult to understand why virtually all suicide bombers are psychologically stable. The organizers of suicide attacks do not want to jeopardize their missions by recruiting unreliable people.[60]

These same sentiments are echoed by Jerrold Post, one of the key figures the U.S. government relies upon to develop its homeland security strategies. Currently a political psychology professor, Post had a twenty-one-year career in the CIA, founded the agency's Center for the Analysis of Personality and Political Behavior, is chair of the Task Force for National and International Terrorism and Violence for the American Psychiatric Association, and has consulted for the U.S. Department of Justice, House Armed Services Committee, House Foreign Affairs Committee, Senate Armed Services Committee, and United Nations International Atomic Energy Agency.[61] As he explains:

We'd like to believe these are crazed fanatics, and some sort of madmen in the grip of a psychosis. Not true. . . . One of the most striking aspects about the psychology of terrorists is that as individuals, this is normal behavior. . . . In fact, terrorist groups make it a point to expel, or not to admit, emotionally unstable people. After all, they'd be a security risk. You wouldn't want an emotionally unstable person in the Green Berets; you wouldn't want an emotionally unstable person in a terrorist operation or cell. So, the issue is not individual psychology.[62]

These statements are remarkably similar, reflecting groupthink. All around the world, the same claims about terrorist organizations not wanting to use unstable people have been repeated in briefings, conferences, lectures, and boardrooms.[63]

Unfortunately, these opinions are convincing enough to be dangerous. After all, the points about the potential security risk *seem* to make sense, which encourages people to repeat them ad nauseam until you hear them so often that they *must be true.*

But the reality is that recruiters of suicide terrorists have often *deliberately targeted unstable individuals* because they are consistently easier to exploit.[64] Like anyone handling a potentially dangerous substance or weapon, terrorist organizations naturally take precautions to minimize risks. They don't take a suicidal recruit, give him directions to their leaders' houses, give him a map of all hidden weapons caches, and then give him that month's schedule of upcoming attacks.

However, just because someone is unstable, that does not necessarily mean that he or she cannot be strategically used. Along with the aforementioned cases of donkey bombs (and how reliable is a donkey walking alone, without its master?), suicide terrorists have struggled with depression, hopelessness, guilt, shame, rage, personal crises, and even severe mental health problems such as Down's syndrome.[65]

Terrorist leaders will use any asset—reliable, unreliable, stable, or unstable—that can potentially help their cause. As even a chess novice will tell you, there's no reason to sacrifice your dependable rooks, bishops, and knights if you have otherwise worthless pawns that will do the job just as well.

Misconception #6: The political function of an act = the individual's primary motive.

The final misconception in the suicide-versus-martyrdom debate involves the actor's intent. True martyrdom is primarily motivated by the desire to serve other people, while suicide is primarily motivated by the desire to serve oneself.[66] Unfortunately, since human motives can be so hard to gauge, the political function of a suicide terrorist's attack is commonly assumed to be his or her primary goal. But this is an egregious oversimplification.

When we see a news headline about a suicide bombing in Iraq or Afghanistan, we tend to interpret it in the broader political context, precisely because it is this context—and not the personal psychological problems of the individuals involved—that has the biggest effect on our lives. We are far more scared of Al Qaeda and Islamic fundamentalism than we are of some random suicidal person in the Middle East. And we probably care more about large-scale military deployments and international oil prices than we do about a few strangers' mental health problems thousands of miles away. Clearly, terrorist organizations sponsor suicide attacks for political purposes. But that doesn't mean the individuals carrying them out are pursuing the same thing.

Assuming that all suicide terrorists are motivated by politics is like assuming that all people who attend charity fund-raisers are motivated by their passionate commitment to the charity's cause. In reality, some people attend charity events for their *own* benefit first, and the cause second (if at all). They want to network for professional purposes. They want to meet the love, or lust, of their life. They want to gorge on fancy food and drinks. And so on. Of course, these people probably don't hate the charity whose event they attend. You wouldn't go to a Ku Klux Klan rally just for the food. But the political cause is not necessarily their top priority—and it may not rank highly at all.

Similarly, suicide terrorists appear to carry out suicide attacks to kill themselves first, and to serve the organization second (if at all).[67] Do they have the same basic ideology and belief in God as the terrorist organizations that arm them? Sure. Do they share the same underlying anger and desires for revenge? Sure, some do. In fact, like many suicidal people, they may be especially disposed to see themselves as helpless victims, and thus to blame others for their own problems. But again, millions of terrorist sympathizers and tens of thousands of regular terrorists share these same opinions. What makes suicide terrorists behaviorally different is that their primary intent is to die.

It should come as no surprise that with both charity-event attendees and suicide terrorists, those who are primarily motivated by personal goals instead of collective ones still wish to appear selfless and altruistic. After all, what's the alternative?

HELPING THE ENEMY

You're a terrorist leader. You sit on a creaky wooden chair in a small room with no windows. In front of you, a small color television rests on a desk, along with stacks of recent newspapers from around the world.

You can't believe your good fortune. Your attacks were strategically designed to attract attention, but you didn't expect the media coverage to be this good. Sure, the commentators call you killers. Sure, they whine about "innocent" victims. Hypocrites. They've been terrorizing your people for decades. But you couldn't have hired a better publicist if you tried.

Praise God, the world's leading academic scholars and government experts have been doing your bidding for years, and they don't even realize it. Yale University?[68] Check. The University of Chicago?[69] Check. The University of Nottingham, the University of Toronto, and Ain Shams University in Cairo?[70] Check, check, check. And that's just the beginning.

They interview you about suicide terrorists, and then simply believe what you tell them.[71] They trot out ridiculous studies claiming that for twenty-year spans, not a single suicide bomber was depressed.[72] They insist that you would never use mentally unstable people for suicide attacks.[73] They say that suicide terrorists are psychologically normal, and that their attacks are caused by the West's military occupation of your lands.[74] They claim that your "martyrs" are the equivalent of ordinary soldiers and Green Berets.[75] And then they support the illusion that all terrorists are the same, and that every one of them would be willing to kill themselves for the cause.

The best part is that none of it is true. You specifically recruit "sad guys" and girls, people who are depressed, hopeless, bitter, and suicidal.[76] In fact, there's one scheduled for tomorrow. You heard that she was raped, and would rather kill herself than suffer the shame of living as a victim. But you don't want to know the details. She's trying to be brave—she'll do. And if she fails and gets arrested, so be it. There's always another desperate soul out there.

You glance at the screen, where an "expert" is testifying before the United States Congress, spreading your propaganda for you. Then you lean back in your chair.

And you laugh.

THREE

WHY SUICIDE TERRORISTS ARE SUICIDAL

We don't know much about Ali Hassan Abu Kamal.

Did he ever consider slitting his wrists, jumping out of a window, or hanging himself? Did he cry at night, have terrible nightmares, or wake up afraid of each new day? Did some final, traumatic crisis push him over the edge? We don't know.

Investigations into the lives of suicide terrorists sometimes leave us with more questions than answers. And the case of Abu Kamal is no exception. However, based on his *actions*, we do know that the sixty-nine-year-old Palestinian English teacher was, in the end, suicidal.

On December 24, 1996, Abu Kamal took a plane from Egypt to the United States. After a brief stop in New York, he flew to Florida and checked into a cheap motel, where he stayed for approximately three weeks. While there, he displayed strange behavior for a Muslim man, including standing nude in an open doorway, propositioning a maid, and bringing prostitutes to his room.[1]

In late January, he received his temporary-resident identification card and quickly proceeded to a local gun shop. Abu Kamal's weapon of choice was a .380 caliber Beretta semiautomatic handgun, which costs about five hundred dollars and can hold fourteen bullets at a time.[2] He paid in cash and picked up the firearm five days later, after the required waiting period.

At that point, Abu Kamal returned to New York City, and on Saturday, February 22, 1997, he visited the Empire State Building. As if he was just another tourist, Abu Kamal rode up to the eighty-sixth-floor observation deck and took in the sights. Why was he there? Perhaps he was unarmed and conducting surveillance—checking for security guards, metal detectors, and any other potential obstacles to his mission at the national landmark. Or as a federal law enforcement officer later speculated, "He may have gone up there with his gun and he simply chickened out."[3] Again, we don't know for sure.

The next day Abu Kamal returned, rode back up to the eighty-sixth floor, stepped out onto the observation deck, and opened fire. He shot seven people: several locals, along with tourists from Argentina, Switzerland, and France. His attack was hasty and unfocused: of the seven victims, all but one survived.[4] Then Abu Kamal, who had tucked a two-and-a-half-page suicide note into a pouch around his neck, did something suicide terrorists almost never do, at least by this method. He turned the gun around and shot himself in the head.

Abu Kamal's suicide note provides evidence that his underlying motives were personal more than political. However, at first, his justification for striking the Empire State Building sounds like a classic terrorist creed:

Charter of Honour

Out of revenge for prestige, patriotism and retarding tyranny and suppression, I consider those mentioned below as my bitter enemies and they must be annihilated & exterminated –

1. The First Enemy: Americans–Britons–French (though the French now seem friendly after Chirac's visit to Palestine) and the Zionists. These 3 Big Powers are the first enemy to the Palestinians ever since their three-partite Declaration in the early fifties, and they are responsible for turning our people, the Palestinians, homeless. The Zionists are the paw that carried out their savage aggression. My restless aspiration is to murder as many of them as possible, and I have decided to strike at their own den in New York, and at the very Empire State Building in particular. The Zionists have usurped my father's land at

Abbassiya near Lydda Airport and which is now worth ten million U.S. dollars at least.[5]

So far, spot-on for a brainwashed political activist who was supposedly willing to sacrifice anything for his ideological beliefs.

However, as the note goes on, the former English teacher reveals the true sources of his anger and pain, which are deeply personal:

2. The Second Enemy: a gang of rogues who attacked me on Saturday 26/6/1993 at my office in Gaza (Daraj), because I didn't agree to their command asking me to help them cheat in the final examination (Tawjihi). They were seven, and I have so far identified two of them, viz: Amar Khaleed Darweesh and Mohamed Awadh (the latter has a shop for selling water-pipes in Gaza [Zeitoun]). If I could identify the others, ready to pay a reward for knowing them, I will kill all of them in revenge for this brutal attack, if I had the chance after the first strike.

3. The third one: A ranking officer in the Egyptian Police Force, who had insulted and beaten me savagely for some passport formalities when I was in Cairo in the early Eighties and without any justification. I didn't know his name, but I located his residence at Sebki Street at Dekki in Cairo, near Egypt Farm Company, and he must be killed with his brother who helped him.

4. The Fourth Target: Three students in Cherkassy town in Ukraine: Mohammad Al-Hadeedy, Sami Abu Amra and Mahmoud Al-Mohtasseb (the latter's residence telephone in Gaza is 561168), all of Gaza, because they had beaten and blackmailed my son Al-Ameer. Sami Abu Amra usurped $250 from my son and brutally beat him when he was sick. The first two: Hadeedy and Abu Amra must be killed.[6]

The many similarities between suicide terrorists and others who commit murder-suicide will be explored in Chapter 6. But for now, it suffices to say that Abu Kamal's deep sense of victimization, his desire to blame others for his problems, and his inability to let go of past grudges make him remarkably similar to other suicidal killers.[7]

Like them, he plotted his revenge ahead of time. Like them, he ended up killing many innocent people who had nothing to do with his problems, while letting those who had actually wronged him go unharmed. And like them, he became so consumed by his pain and rage that he ultimately took his own life. Not because it would help others, but because after his murderous actions, he genuinely wanted to die.

There are additional clues about Abu Kamal's suicidal motives. For instance, he was apparently a very proud man who had accumulated nearly $500,000 in savings over the course of a fifty-year career. He had told his family that he was going to the United States to establish a business with friends as part of an "investment scheme," and that he would eventually bring his wife and children to join him and start a better life. However, a friend in New York reported that shortly after arriving in the United States, Abu Kamal had been defrauded out of his life savings and was now essentially broke. There were also some indications that he was ashamed about no longer being able to afford his son's college tuition.[8]

WHY DIE?

Ultimately, the reasons why Abu Kamal committed suicide may be less compelling than the nature of his death. His case is important because his acts of terrorism and suicide were actually separate, not combined. Instead of blowing himself up at the exact same instant as his enemies, he killed people first, and then shot himself in the head. Because his terrorist attack was separate from his suicidal action—even by just a few seconds—this makes his suicidal intent undeniable.

Abu Kamal's decision to launch a terrorist attack against a symbol of American power could make sense, from a certain twisted, radical perspective. After all, some Islamic fundamentalists may genuinely believe that his attack would serve the greater good. However, his decision to shoot himself in the head after the attack only makes sense as a form of suicide. No one benefited from Abu Kamal's suicide *except Abu Kamal,* who escaped the consequences of his crime. There was nothing selfless or sacrificial about it. He acted just like many other people who commit murder-suicide. They kill others first, out of rage or revenge. And then they kill themselves.

Many people get hung up on the fact that suicide terrorism attacks seem to *require* the death of the perpetrator. For instance, it's impossible for suicide bombers with explosive belts strapped around their waists to kill their enemies without also killing themselves. After all, the explosives are not equipped with a time delay, so they can't be planted and left to explode on their own, and they are not designed to be thrown from afar, like grenades. Therefore, one could argue that suicide bombers do not want to die—*they must die*—if they wish to successfully harm the enemy. Because in suicide terrorism the act of killing and the act of suicide are usually combined, many commentators become convinced that the perpetrator must be selflessly sacrificing his or her life to ensure the mission's success.

And sometimes the attacker's death really does have a strategic purpose. For instance, it would have been nearly impossible for the 9/11 terrorists to successfully bring down the Twin Towers if they had insisted on their own survival. Imagine if they had wanted to jump out of the hijacked airplanes at the last minute, parachute to safety, and somehow still ensure that their specific targets were destroyed. A convoluted plan like that would have almost certainly failed. So being willing to die significantly increased their ability to kill—although their motives still may have been suicidal, as we'll see in Chapter 4.

However, in many cases the suicide terrorist's death adds nothing of tactical value. Dying does not increase the likelihood of success nor the expected magnitude of destruction. In fact, the terrorists' broader cause is potentially *harmed* by the death of these attackers, because they cannot return to fight another day.

So why do they kill themselves? For their own reasons. A classic example is the infamous July 7, 2005, London transportation-system attack, which left fifty-six people dead, including the four suicide terrorists. As former CIA official Robert Baer explained afterward, there was no tactical, logistical, or strategic reason for the attackers to commit suicide: they could have simply dropped off their bombs and walked away.[9] The reason they stayed is clear: they preferred to die.

When we assess the motives and psychology of suicide terrorists, we should consider whether their deaths add significant value to their attacks. Human beings aren't always rational, but rational choice theory suggests that they are more likely to weigh the pros and cons when it comes to the most significant decisions of their lives.[10] If you're buying a magazine, you might do it on impulse, without any cost-benefit analysis. But if you're buying a house, you generally try to do your homework, run the numbers, and make sure you'll get what you pay for.

Now imagine that you were considering doing something that would cost you *your life*. If there was another way to accomplish the exact same goal without dying, wouldn't you take that path? Of course you would. Just like the tens of thousands of regular terrorists who do so every year as they shoot, bomb, kill—and live to fight another day.

Unless, of course, dying is actually your goal. As it was when, for no other discernible reason, Abu Kamal put the gun to his temple and pulled the trigger.

AN IMPRESSIVE STUDY

As discussed briefly in Chapter 2, Merari's Israeli research group recently conducted psychological tests of three groups of Palestinian terrorists: fifteen preemptively arrested suicide bombers, twelve regular terrorists, and fourteen organizers of suicide attacks. These individuals were associated with some of the most active Palestinian organizations running suicide operations: Hamas, Palestinian Islamic Jihad, and the Al-Aqsa Martyrs Brigades.

The results were fascinating: there were very clear differences between the groups.

The would-be suicide bombers had a lot of mental health problems. Sixty percent were diagnosed as dependent-avoidant: a disorder characterized by lack of self-confidence, lack of independence, and fear of shame, rejection, and ridicule. In addition, 53.3 percent displayed depressive tendencies, 40 percent displayed suicidal tendencies, 20 percent showed signs of post-traumatic stress disorder, and 13.3 percent had previously attempted suicide, unrelated to terrorism.[11]

By contrast, the regular terrorists and organizers of suicide attacks were far more psychologically normal. Only 16.7 percent of the regular terrorists were diagnosed as dependent-avoidant types, only 8.3 percent displayed depressive tendencies, and none exhibited suicidal tendencies, signs of PTSD, or had ever attempted suicide. In turn, the organizers of suicide attacks displayed consistently higher ego strength than the suicide terrorists, and none exhibited suicidal tendencies, signs of PTSD, or had ever attempted suicide, while only 21.4 percent had depressive tendencies. These results are summarized in Table 3.1.[12]

Overall, Merari's findings provide extremely compelling evidence that at least some suicide terrorists are suicidal.

One example from the study is a suicide bomber named Rafik.[13] During the prison interviews, Rafik shed some light on his troubled past:

> As a child, I was a recluse. . . . I had no friends in school. I had very
> few relationships—if I was with one or two, that was enough. And it
> has been like this until now. I don't like to talk much with people. I'm
> not afraid, but embarrassed. . . . Since I liked to be alone, I had a room
> of my own. Most of the time I locked myself in my room and watched
> television. . . . Sometimes, when I am nervous and no one can talk to
> me, then if somebody says "hi" to me I can beat him up. On the other

Table 3.1   *A Psychological Assessment of Suicide Terrorists, Regular Terrorists, and Organizers of Suicide Attacks*[a]

Diagnosis	Suicide Terrorists (n = 15)	Regular Terrorists (n = 12)	Organizers (n = 14)
Suicidal tendencies	40.0%	0%	0%
Depressive tendencies	53.3%	8.3%	21.4%
Dependent/avoidant personality	60.0%	16.7%	n/a
Post-traumatic stress disorder	20.0%	0%	0%
Previous (non-terrorist) suicide attempts	13.3%	0%	0%

a. Merari, *Driven to Death.*

hand, when I see a small child crying, I may cry with him. I have these kinds of extremes.[14]

Rafik recounts similarly unstable behavior throughout his life, including one episode when he was ten years old and threw a tray of hot tea on his father, burning him. Despite these types of incidents, his father eventually became his closest friend—his one true confidant.

And then crisis struck. When Rafik was just twenty years old, his father suffered a sudden heart attack. Rafik rushed him to the hospital, but they were too late. Furious and distraught, Rafik actually threatened to kill the doctor before departing. Then reality began to set in. As Rafik explained, "After his death, I did not want to go out. I thought, 'who would I be with—with whom would I talk without him?' I thought of committing suicide by cutting my veins, and had my mother not come into my room at that time, I might have done it."[15]

Instead, less than a year later, Rafik volunteered to become a suicide bomber. Although he was ultimately arrested and imprisoned before he could blow himself up, he later admitted that even in prison, he had been stockpiling painkillers and had considered another suicide attempt just days before his interview.[16]

More powerful evidence that suicide terrorists are suicidal comes from a teenage suicide bomber named Zuheir.[17] As he confessed, his life was characterized by pain and suffering:

> The truth is that my relationship with my parents was very bad. Both my father and my mother hurt me. They used to beat me hard, with the broomstick too, and insulted me with harsh words. . . . My parents forced me to wear clothes I didn't like and didn't let me leave the house except for school. All in all, my life was very, very miserable. My parents hit me almost daily, every time they thought I misbehaved. They claimed that people told them I behaved badly outside home. I didn't know who told them such things. . . . My pleadings didn't change their humiliating attitude. This was my life and I reached such a state of despair that I wanted to kill myself.[18]

As Zuheir explains further, given his need to escape his terrible situation, he began to look for a permanent way out.

> I used to stand in front of Israeli tanks, hoping they would shoot me. I tried more than once, but it didn't work. . . . I developed a mental complex from thinking a lot whether to commit suicide or not. Then I met people who offered me a chance to carry out an act of *istishhad* [martyrdom]. I had been thinking for a long time about an opportunity to die, and when these men showed up, I said to myself this was a good opportunity to enjoy a few days with the money they gave me, buy nice clothes, and have a short haircut as I liked, before I die and rest from my life. . . . I thought hard and decided to accept their offer to carry out an act of *istishhad,* not because I belonged to the organization, but to realize my wish to die.[19]

Like Rafik, Zuheir was ultimately arrested before he could carry out his suicide attack.

WHAT ABOUT THE OTHERS?

These findings clearly show that at least some suicide terrorists are suicidal. In addition, they demonstrate that many of these attackers are motivated by their desire to escape their lives, more than by any political or religious beliefs. In fact, this is why some suicide bombers have even been atheists who did not believe in God or heaven: as long as they wanted to die, blowing themselves up could appeal as their way out.[20]

Overall, it's not surprising that terrorist leaders continue to claim that their suicide attackers are psychologically stable, ideologically committed, selfless "martyrs." Like certain politicians, they'll say anything to win.

What's more shocking is that despite the evidence, academic scholars and government experts continue to spread this terrorist propaganda. Some insist that Rafik and Zuheir are the rare exceptions, and that somehow Merari's findings are a fluke. For instance, sociologists

Robert Brym and Bader Araj have claimed that Merari's sample may not be representative of the larger population of suicide bombers.[21] However, this is a wholly unsubstantiated critique, and Brym and Araj admit that if Merari's sample is somehow not representative, it is likely in ways that are still "unknown."[22] Others point out that Merari's results show that 53 percent of the suicide bombers had depressive tendencies and 40 percent had suicidal tendencies, but this still leaves a large percentage who may have been "normal." This is a more legitimate objection.

However, there are several important reasons why Merari's study, if anything, may have significantly *underdiagnosed* suicidality among its subjects. In other words, every suicide bomber the researchers assessed may have been suicidal, but some could have easily slipped through the cracks.

First, it should be emphasized that despite more than one hundred years of research on suicidal behavior, mental health professionals sometimes fail to identify suicidal desires among their own clients until it's too late. Even trained psychologists can be fooled by a mentally ill person who wears the mask of someone with less serious problems. Frankly, when people are diagnosed as suicidal, it's usually because they either admit to having suicidal thoughts or because they already attempted suicide.[23] In the absence of this evidence, it can be hard to know for sure. And in Palestine, where suicidal thoughts and mental health problems are severely stigmatized, we would expect a large percentage of afflicted individuals to deliberately conceal the signs.

Second, Merari's team of psychologists intentionally ignored the most obvious indicator that their subjects were suicidal: the fact that they had planned to blow themselves up. This is understandable, because the assessments were intended to determine whether the subjects showed any *additional* signs of mental illness or suicidality. However, far fewer therapy patients in any practice would be diagnosed as suicidal if we specifically ignored their most blatant self-destructive behaviors.

Third, suicidal urges commonly ebb and flow. Just because the suicide terrorists may have been suicidal in the days, hours, or minutes before their suicide attacks does not necessarily mean they would still be suicidal when assessed during Merari's study. For instance, although Zuheir was admittedly suicidal outside prison, once he was arrested, that temporarily resolved his crisis. Behind bars, he explained, "The truth is I like my life in prison much better than my life with my parents."[24] Given the prestige and status bestowed upon even failed suicide bombers, some may genuinely be healthier and happier after incarceration than they were before their arrest.[25]

Finally, Merari's research team was assessing individuals for conventional suicidal tendencies, which has its limitations. For example, they did not classify a suicide bomber named Hamed as suicidal, despite the fact that he had very low self-esteem and had struggled for years with social marginalization, parental disapproval, and difficulties in school.[26] Similarly, Sabri, a depressed teenage suicide bomber who broke into tears when recalling several traumatic crises from his past, was not diagnosed as suicidal in the conventional sense.[27] However, some percentage of suicide terrorists appear to have been suicidal in *unconventional* ways—for instance, because they were coerced, felt threatened by security forces, or were indirectly self-destructive. These variations of suicidality will be explored in Chapter 7.

OPRAH TAKES THE STAGE

Oprah Winfrey is not a suicide bomber. She's a famous television host, a billionaire, and arguably the most powerful woman in the world.[28]

But if a teenage Oprah had been in the wrong place at the wrong time, she may have snuck out of her house, filmed a martyrdom video, cursed the infidels, strapped explosives to her chest, and blown herself up.

As the media mogul recently admitted, she seriously contemplated suicide as a teenager. When she was sent to live with her father in Tennessee, the strict man laid out the rules in no uncertain terms, explaining that "I would rather see a daughter of mine floating down the Cumberland River than to bring shame on this family [with] the indecency of an illegitimate child."[29]

Little did he know, it was already too late: the teenage Oprah had been pregnant when she arrived. Her immediate thought was "Before the baby is born, I'm going to have to kill myself."[30] Eventually, she made at least one attempt, which included "stupid things like drinking detergent and all that kind of crazy stuff that you do when you're trying to get attention, when you're really just trying to cry for help."[31] As it turned out, the baby—to whom Oprah said she felt "no connection to whatsoever"—died in the hospital.[32] And Oprah gradually grew into the strong woman she is today.

Unfortunately, not everyone is so resilient—or so fortunate. There are at least two Palestinian girls who similarly experienced unwanted pregnancies and similarly contemplated suicide: Ayat al-Akhras and Andalib Takatka Suleiman.[33] However, in their social and religious context, the easiest way out was not to drink detergent and hope for the best. No, because they were Muslim, a conventional suicide would have been "one of the greatest wrong-doings" they could commit: "Allah says: 'Do not kill yourselves . . . he that does that through wickedness and injustice shall be burnt in fire.'"[34] Although most cultures and religions discourage suicide, Islamic prohibitions function as a particularly strong form of deterrence because many Muslims believe—in the literal sense—that they would suffer punishments for all of eternity after killing themselves.[35] This is one of the reasons why suicide rates in the Muslim world are so low.[36]

However, there is one loophole—and the two pregnant girls quickly grasped for it. By carrying out suicide bombings and pretending to be "martyrs," they could simultaneously kill themselves, escape their problems, and avoid breaking religious law. Or at least, this was the myth that they desperately wanted to believe and that they eventually bought into.

So instead of attempting conventional suicide like teenage Oprah, Ayat rushed to film a martyrdom video, where she claimed "that she chose this path in order to protect the Palestinian people and to show the Arab leaders who neglected the Palestinian cause what one woman was capable of doing."[37] And then she blew herself up at the entrance to a supermarket, killing two bystanders. Shortly after her death, word of Ayat's premarital sex and impending pregnancy began spreading through the community. Just two weeks later, Andalib carried out her own suicide attack. Like Ayat, she claimed to be ideologically motivated—although her statement that "We are suffering; we are dying while we are still alive" sounds like she was describing her own pain and desperation more than that of the community.[38] As with Ayat, shortly after Andalib's death rumors of her unwanted pregnancy began circulating. But ultimately, in both of these cases, the girls' escape plans had been successful. They were dead and had avoided public humiliation, which is really what they wanted—whether they helped the terrorist cause or not.

The idea that we would call the teenage Oprah "suicidal," while labeling Ayat and Andalib "psychologically normal," is an absurd and inaccurate double standard. Ultimately, all three were desperate girls who became pregnant by mistake. Like thousands of girls in similar situations around the world, all three feared the shame, dishonor, and other consequences that would result from their secrets being exposed. And all three tried suicide as a way out.

Of course, just because Oprah, Ayat, and Andalib shared the same underlying motive, that does not mean their situations were identical. The most obvious difference between them was context, which is why we can only guess at what would have happened if Oprah had been born in Palestine, where she would have been shaped and prodded by terrorist organizations and their suicide-justifying propaganda.

CONVERTED "KILLERS"

At the same time, not all suicide terrorists are simply a product of their context. For instance, in Europe, there have been some attackers who seemingly did everything they could to defy the social norms around them.

Consider the separate examples of suicide bombers Nicky Reilly and Muriel Degauque. Both were white and European, so they do not fit the popular stereotype of such attackers. But both made a conscious decision to convert to Islam several years before their attacks. Reilly changed his name to Mohamad Abdulaziz Rashid Saeed, began worshipping at an Islamic center close to his home, and grew a traditional beard.[39] Degauque married a Muslim man, began wearing traditional Islamic dress, and started reading the Quran.[40] The easy explanation for their actions is that they were primarily motivated by religion. And in both cases, their families blamed their suicide attacks on their religious conversions.

In addition, Reilly wrote a religious-based justification for his attack:

> In the name of God most gracious, most merciful: why I did it.
>
> Everywhere Muslims are suffering at the hands of Britain, Israel and America. We are sick of taking all the brutality from you. You have imprisoned over 1,000 Muslims in Britain alone in your war on Islam. You torture and destroy Muslim lives by taking a father or a son or a brother, even you torture Muslim women. In Britain it's OK for a girl to have sex without marriage and if she gets pregnant she can get an abortion so easily. When you are getting drunk on Friday and Saturday night your behavior is worse than animals. You have sex in nightclub toilets. You urinate in shop doorways. You shout your foul and disgusting mouth off in the street. It is unacceptable to Allah and the true religion Islam. . . .
>
> Sheikh Usama [bin Laden] has told you the solution on how to end this war between us, and many others have as well, but you ignore us. Our words are dead until we give them life with our blood. Leave our lands and stop your support for Israel. . . . I have simply seen for myself the brutality and corruption of America, Britain and Israel for myself and my common sense told me it is unacceptable and wrong. The word is the word of the sword until the wrongs have been righted.[41]

Reilly's suicide note is intriguing: it starts off religious and political, and then seems to devolve into the personal—describing a series of offensive behaviors that the twenty-two-year-old likely witnessed or heard about firsthand. And then it returns to religious justifications, referring to Allah, Islam, and "Sheik Usama" bin Laden. Elsewhere, the note contains a preemptive strike against any accusations of manipulation or mental illness: Reilly insists that "I have not been brainwashed or indoctrinated. I am not insane. I am not doing it to escape a life of problems or hardships. I am doing what God wants from his mujahideen. We love death as you love life."[42]

As you might guess by now, the true cause of Reilly's radical behavior lay far deeper than his religion or politics. In fact, even the local Muslims with whom he prayed were surprised by his violent actions. As one recounted, "He always struck me as being not quite well in the head, but he seemed like a nice guy."[43] Further investigations by psychiatrists revealed that Reilly had an IQ of 83, was thought to have the mental age of a ten-year-old, and suffered from Asperger's syndrome and obsessive-compulsive disorder, among other psychological problems.[44] His family was also a disaster: his parents separated before he was born, his stepfather was a convicted heroin dealer, and his younger brother was sent to prison for six years after robbing a man and beating him unconscious.[45]

Notably, Reilly also made several suicide attempts before getting involved with terrorism. The first time was apparently when he was sixteen. After a girlfriend broke up with him, he intentionally overdosed on drugs. The second time, he went to a local park and stabbed himself in the stomach, but he ultimately survived to try again. He apparently attempted slitting his wrists several times as well.[46]

Acquaintances recall that after 9/11, Reilly became "fascinated by the attack on the Twin Towers," that he used an image of the towers burning for his computer's screensaver, and that he would often "watch beheadings on the internet."[47] All of that is entirely possible—and yet in this case, it seems more symptomatic of his limited mental capacity than of a true ideological commitment to the cause.

Based on his prior suicidal actions, Reilly was a ticking time bomb. Islamic fundamentalism became the vehicle for his anger and his suicidal impulses, but even if he had never stumbled across that path, it was only a matter of time before he killed himself or harmed others. If the September 11 attacks had not caught his attention, something else, such as the neo-Nazi movement, may have instead. Counterterrorism investigators believe that despite his claims, Reilly was manipulated by extremists he met in online chat rooms, who encouraged him to carry out a suicide attack and instructed him on how to build a homemade bomb.[48]

Reilly's self-destructive tendencies eventually got the best of him. When he mounted his attack at the Giraffe restaurant in Exeter, the nail bombs he had constructed literally blew up in his face. He was seriously wounded, but no one else was harmed. Instead of finally committing suicide, it was yet another failed attempt for Reilly, who will hopefully get the treatment he needs behind bars.[49]

By contrast, Degauque appeared to be in much better control of her mental facilities, but was only marginally more effective than Reilly as a suicide bomber. When she finally blew herself up in the Iraqi town of Baquba, she was the only fatality, and just a single enemy soldier was wounded.[50] Of course, if her primary objective was suicide—as was likely—then she was quite successful.

Degauque's problems did not begin until her teenage years. As a friend recalls, early on "she was an adorable little girl, smiling all the time. But then, later, everything became . . . different. She was really weak and very easily influenced."[51] Around sixteen, she began using drugs and dropped out of school. Not surprisingly, her parents found her hard to control, and that caused turmoil—as did her illicit activities with a seemingly endless stream of boys. At least once, she ran away from home and was found nearly one hundred miles away.[52]

However, the major blow to her psyche came in her early twenties, when her older brother was killed in a motorcycle accident. Degauque had been extremely close to him—he was apparently adored by every-one—and she was left with the horrible task of having to break the news to her family. Acquaintances recall that she and her parents were never the same. At the funeral, Degauque broke down, "consumed with grief and guilt."[53] As one of her closest friends remembers, "When Jean-Paul died, she completely changed. She was always sad and she told me that it was unfair that her brother had died, and that *she should have died in his place.*"[54]

In the time that followed, Degauque seemed like a lost soul. She had trouble holding a job, and when she got one, she was frequently late or missing. She began living off unemployment checks, increasingly used drugs, and drifted away from her childhood friends. She married a Belgian man, but divorced him after just a few years. Her relationship with her parents grew worse and worse. And then she married a much younger man—a radical Islamist known to police as Issam Goris. As part of this new relationship, Degauque began observing strict religious customs.[55]

At some point, the couple disappeared, and then resurfaced in Iraq. In what appears to have been a suicide pact, Degauque and her husband launched their attacks at separate locations on the same day. Goris was shot and killed by soldiers before his bomb exploded. But Degauque was not so lucky: she detonated her explosives, but was only seriously wounded and did not immediately die. Eventually, however, the pain overcame her and her suicide was complete.[56]

As we look back, it becomes clear that Reilly and Degauque were both desperate people searching for answers. Their religious conversions were not the solution—they were just failed attempts to fix something deep inside them that was severely damaged. Ultimately, the same personal issues and psychological pain that led to their religious transformations also led to their suicide attacks. Despite converting to Islam, Reilly was still plagued by severe mental disorders and suicidal urges. And nothing could bring Degauque's brother back or heal the deep pain within her.

THE EVIDENCE GROWS

One of the first post-9/11 articles to suggest a connection between conventional suicide and suicide terrorism was written by David Lester, former president of the International Association for Suicide Prevention, president-elect of the American Association of Suicidology, and distinguished professor of psychology at Richard Stockton College. As he and his colleagues pointed out in 2004, the few cases they studied indicated that "many suicide bombers may indeed have the risk factors for conventional suicide and that previous commentators have not sought out the required information."[57] In their recommendations for future research, they suggested that "if detailed biographies of terrorists and suicide bombers were to be collected, evidence might well be found of a high frequency of risk factors for suicide."[58]

This made sense, but it was easier said than done. The biggest obstacle was our general lack of information about suicide terrorists' lives.

Often we know next to nothing about the individual perpetrators. Even in the best of cases, the data are woefully incomplete.

However, even incomplete data are useful. After all, the conventional wisdom about suicide terrorists' psychological normalcy has been so rigid and closed-minded that it should be easy to disprove. For years, terrorist leaders and presumed experts alike have essentially claimed that suicidal suicide terrorists *don't exist*. Recall, for instance, Atran's assertion that "*no instances* of religious or political suicide terrorism stem from lone actions of cowering or unstable bombers."[59] Or Pape's claim that not a single one of the 462 suicide terrorists from 1980 to 2003 exhibited "mental illness, such as depression, psychosis, or past suicide attempts . . . major criminal behavior . . . [or] was gay, an adulterer, or otherwise living in a way that would bring shame in a traditional society."[60]

This rigidity works in our favor, because when you're searching for something assumed to be nonexistent, even a few solid cases will do. Ride just one unicorn around your neighborhood and watch what happens. People will start to question their assumptions.

In any case, Lester's call has now been answered. Based on my in-depth review of electronic news and video archives, existing data sets, legal documents, government reports, previous scholarly research, and other relevant sources, new evidence suggests that more than 130 suicide terrorists appear to have had classic risk factors for suicide (see Table 3.2). This list is summarized here and presented in full as Appendix A.[61]

For starters, Qari Sami, Joe Stack, Wafa al-Biss, Ali Hassan Abu Kamal, Rafik, Zuheir, Hamed, Sabri, Ayat al-Akhras, Andalib Takatka Suleiman, Nicky Reilly, and Muriel Degauque are not exceptions. They are not twelve individual flukes. They're closer to the norm. They were all struggling with serious personal problems, and these problems appear to have made them suicidal.

Many other suicide terrorists kill themselves for the same reasons people commit conventional suicide. For instance, intelligence officials in Afghanistan and security analysts in Pakistan have independently reported that heroin addicts have been carrying out suicide attacks in that region.[62] Given the well-established link between substance abuse and conventional suicide, this makes a lot of sense. Other precursors to suicide terrorism include mental illness, divorce, adultery scandals, financial problems, job problems, poor health, and the death of a loved one.[63]

Of course, this is not an exhaustive list. Life is complicated, and it seems that people commit suicide for an infinite number of different reasons. The same is true of suicide terrorists. If Murphy's law is "Anything that can go wrong will go wrong," a useful extension might be "Anything that can go wrong will go wrong—and that may push someone over the edge."

But let's look at a few representative cases:

- Wafa Idris, the first Palestinian female suicide bomber, suffered a miscarriage that left her unable to get pregnant again, and was subsequently divorced by her husband. Intensely shamed, she returned home to live with her mother, and then eventually blew herself up.[64]

- Bilal Fahs had been abandoned by his father as a child, but when he was seventeen, he fell deeply in love with a terrific girl and they got engaged. However, to his dismay, he was legally prohibited from marrying his fiancée due to his invalid civil status. Overcome by this news, he ultimately crashed a car loaded with explosives into an Israeli military convoy.[65]

- Reem Raiyshi committed the crime of adultery and apparently feared the social repercussions within her highly religious community. For her, carrying out a suicide attack was akin to a self-inflicted honor killing: it was the only way to escape the impending shame and try to make amends.[66]

- Shadi Nassar suffered a permanent disability as a child, and for the rest of his life he struggled with chronic epileptic episodes. He was constantly rejected, humiliated, and mocked by his peers, and he became lonely and depressed. Then one day, he was insulted and abused by enemy soldiers. This was apparently the last straw: shortly thereafter, he carried out a suicide attack.[67]

- Murad suffered from a degenerative eye condition. Ultimately, he expressed the desire to die rather than live as a handicapped person. He prepared to carry out a suicide bombing, but was arrested before he could successfully blow himself up.[68]

- Arien Ahmed had a troubled past: her father died when she was a child, and her mother abandoned her to the care of relatives. When her lover was killed by enemy soldiers, she could no longer cope and decided to become a suicide bomber. As she explained, upon his death, "I lost all my future."[69]

- Hanadi Jaradat was traumatized by the death of her brother, cousin, and fiancé. As her mother recounted, she "was full of pain. She saw them taking the body [of her brother] from the hospital to the morgue, and she was different after that. Some nights she woke up screaming, saying she had nightmares about Fadi."[70] A few months later, Jaradat blew herself up at an Israeli restaurant.

- Thenmozhi Rajaratnam, also known as Dhanu, was reportedly gang-raped by Indian soldiers during their involvement in the Sri Lankan civil war. In addition, her four brothers were all killed. Deeply scarred by these traumatic events, the Tamil woman eventually blew herself up at the foot of Indian president Rajiv Gandhi.[71]

Again, this is just a brief sample. The personal problems that drive suicide terrorists are seemingly endless. A teenage boy contracted the HIV virus and could not handle the stigma of the "homosexual" disease.[72] A man received serious threats against his debt-ridden father and family, but believed the terrorist organization would settle his affairs if he carried out a suicide attack.[73] A woman missed what she thought was her last chance for marriage, and explained that at that point, "my life wasn't worth anything and my father wouldn't let me marry the boy I wanted to, so I . . . volunteered, to get back at my father."[74] And so on. In each of these cases, you could easily match the suicide terrorist with someone who committed conventional suicide for almost exactly the same reason.

These findings are just the beginning: there may be thousands of suicide terrorists with classic risk factors for suicide, but at least for now,

Table 3.2   Initial Evidence of Suicide Terrorists with Risk Factors for Suicide

Risk Factors for Suicide	Number of Suicide Terrorists[b]
Serious physical injury or disability	12
Depression, PTSD, or other mental health problems	44
Unexpected death of a loved one or close friend	66
Precipitating crisis event	104
Raped or sexually assaulted	Multiple
Heroin addiction	Multiple
Other physical disabilities	Multiple
Other mental health problems	Multiple
Threatened with punishment of self or family	Multiple
Other	8

See Appendix A for a full list of cases.

"Afghan Officer Kills Nine at Base," *MSN News,* April 28, 2011, accessed June 11, 2011, http://news.uk.msn.com/world/articles.aspx?cp-documentid=157196750; Rogelio Alonso and Fernando Reinares, "Maghreb Immigrants Becoming Suicide Terrorists: A Case Study on Religious Radicalization Processes in Spain," in *Root Causes of Suicide Terrorism: The Globalization of Martyrdom,* ed. Ami Pedahzur, 179–98 (New York: Routledge, 2006); Robert Baer, *The Cult of the Suicide Bomber 2* [DVD] (London: Many Rivers Films, 2008); Robert Baer, *The Cult of the Suicide Bomber* [DVD] (London: Many Rivers Films, 2005); Anat Berko, *The Path to Paradise: The Inner World of Suicide Bombers and Their Dispatchers* (London: Praeger, 2007); Anat Berko and Edna Erez, "'Ordinary People' and 'Death Work': Palestinian Suicide Bombers as Victimizers and Victims," *Violence and Victims* 20 (2005): 603–23; Anat Berko and Edna Erez, "Martyrs or Murderers? Victims or Victimizers? The Voices of Would-Be Palestinian Female Suicide Bombers," in *Female Terrorism and Militancy: Agency, Utility and Organization,* ed. Cindy D. Ness, 146–66 (London: Routledge, 2008); Eli Berman and David Laitin, "Hard Targets: Evidence on the Tactical Use of Suicide Attacks," *National Bureau of Economic Research Working Papers,* 2005, accessed July 26, 2011, http://www.nber.org/papers/w11740; "Blackmailing Young Women into Suicide Terrorism," *Israeli Ministry of Foreign Affairs,* February 12, 2002, accessed May 27, 2012, http://www.mfa.gov.il/MFA/Government/Communiques/2003/Blackmailing+Young+Women+into+Suicide+Terrorism+-.htm; Mia Bloom, *Bombshell: The Many Faces of Women Terrorists* (Toronto: Penguin, 2011); Mia Bloom, *Dying to Kill: The Allure of Suicide Terror* (New York: Columbia University Press, 2005); Robert Brym and Bader Araj, "Are Suicide Bombers Suicidal?" *Studies in Conflict & Terrorism* 35 (2012): 432-43; Dave Cullen, *Columbine* (New York: Twelve, 2009); Christine Fair, *Suicide Attacks in Afghanistan: 2001–2007* (United Nations Assistance Mission in Afghanistan, 2007); Christine Fair and Frederic Grare, "Suicide Attacks in Afghanistan," *Carnegie Endowment for International Peace,* October 19, 2007, accessed July 27, 2011, http://www.carnegieendowment.org/events/?fa=eventDetail&id=1067; Stephen Farrell, "Murky Trail for 'Loner' in Attack on C.I.A." *New York Times,* January 7, 2010, accessed May 26, 2012, http://www.nytimes.com/2010/01/08/world/middleeast/08jordan.html; Sonya Fatah, "Why the Disabled Do Taliban's Deadly Work: With So Few Rehabilitation Services Available, Suicide Attacks Can Offer Easy Escape," *Globe and Mail,* May 7, 2001, accessed September 27, 2010, http://www.theglobeandmail.com/servlet/story/LAC.20070507.SUICIDE07/TPStory/Front; Peter Finn and Joby Warrick, "In Afghanistan Attack, CIA Fell Victim to Series of Miscalculations About Informant," *Washington Post,* January 16, 2010, accessed May 25, 2012, http://www

.washingtonpost.com/wp-dyn/content/article/2010/01/15/AR2010011504068_pf.html; Leonard Greene, "Sex Torment Drove Him Nuts," *New York Post,* December 31, 2009, accessed October 25, 2011, http://www.nypost.com/p/news/national/sex_torment _jiHq0SZCZ0zevbRKdpjEKM; Helle Lho Hansen and Andreas Karker, "Lors' Mor: Han Ville Dø I København," *B.T.,* September 28, 2010, accessed June 16, 2011, http:// www.bt.dk/krimi/lors-mor-han-ville-doe-i-koebenhavn; "'I'm Off to Kill Someone': Knifeman Planned to Kill Train Passenger to Commit 'Suicide by Cop,'" *Daily Mail,* March 1, 2011, accessed July 1, 2011, http://www.dailymail.co.uk/news/article-1361836 /Im-kill-Knifeman-planned-kill-train-passenger-commit-suicide-cop.html; "Iraq's 'Female Bomber Recruiter,'" *BBC News,* February 4, 2009, accessed July 27, 2011, http://news.bbc.co.uk/2/hi/7869570.stm; "Jurors Sequestered in CIA Shooting Case," *CNN,* November 12, 1997, accessed July 27, 2011, http://cgi.cnn.com/US/9711/12/cia .shooting.trial/index.html; Lankford, "Do Suicide Terrorists Exhibit Clinically Suicidal Risk Factors? A Review of Initial Evidence and Call for Future Research," *Aggression and Violent Behavior* 15 (2010): 334–40; David Leppard and Abul Taher, "MI5 Fears Jihadis Will Use Mentally Ill as Suicide Bombers," *Times Online,* May 25, 2008, accessed June 4, 2011, http://www.timesonline.co.uk/tol/news/uk/article3999058.ece; David Lester, Bijou Yang, and Mark Lindsay, "Suicide Bombers: Are Psychological Profiles Possible?" *Studies in Conflict & Terrorism* 27 (2004): 283-95; Damien McElroy, "Baghdad Market Bombers 'Mentally Impaired,'" *Telegraph,* February 2, 2008, accessed June 8, 2011, http://www.telegraph.co.uk/news/worldnews/1577373/Baghdad-market -bombers-mentally-impaired.html; Ariel Merari, *Driven to Death: Psychological and Social Aspects of Suicide Terrorism* (Oxford: Oxford University Press, 2010); "Militant Held Over Iraq Suicide Bombings," *CNN,* February 20, 2010, accessed July 27, 2011, http://www.cnn.com/2010/WORLD/meast/02/20/iraq.bomber.arrest/index.html; Soraya Nelson, "Disabled Often Carry Out Afghan Suicide Missions," *National Public Radio,* October 15, 2007, accessed July 27, 2011, http://www.npr.org/templates/story/story .php?storyId=15276485; Larry Neumeister and Tom Hays, "2 NY Collaborators Give Firsthand Look at Al-Qaida," *Yahoo News,* May 6, 2012, accessed May 7, 2012, http://news.yahoo.com/2-ny-cooperators-firsthand-look-al-qaida-211626418.html; Robert A. Pape, *Dying to Win: The Strategic Logic of Suicide Terrorism* (New York: Random House, 2005); Ami Pedahzur, *Suicide Terrorism* (Cambridge: Polity, 2005); "Police: Tampa Flyer Voiced Support For Bin Laden," *CNN,* January 6, 2002, accessed July 27, 2011, http://articles.cnn.com/2002-01-06/us/tampa.crash_1_plane-charles-j -bishop-crash?_s=PM:US; "Qian Mingqi Blew Himself Up to Demand Justice and Call Attention to His Plight," *Asia News,* May 28, 2011, accessed December 27, 2011, http:// www.asianews.it/news-en/Qian-Mingqi-blew-himself-up-to-demand-justice-and-call -attention-to-his-plight-21688.html; Ravi Somaiya, "Swedish Bombing Suspect's Drift to Extremism," *New York Times,* December 13, 2010, accessed July 27, 2011, http://www .nytimes.com/2010/12/14/world/europe/14suspect.html?hp=& ; Anne Speckhard and Khapta Ahkmedova, "The Making of a Martyr: Chechen Suicide Terrorism," *Studies in Conflict and Terrorism* 29 (2006): 429–92; Kevin Toolis, "Face to Face With The Women Suicide Bombers," *Daily Mail,* February 7, 2009, accessed February 8, 2009, http:// www.dailymail.co.uk/femail/article-1138298/Face-face-women-suicide-bombers.html; Nick Walsh, "Man Opens Fire on Americans in Kabul; 9 Dead," *CNN,* April 28, 2011, accessed June 11, 2011, http://www.cnn.com/2011/WORLD/asiapcf/04/27/afghanistan .violence/index.html; Carrie Weimar, "Teen Pilot's Family Drops Drug Lawsuit: The 15-Year-Old Killed Himself by Crashing a Plane into a High-Rise," *St. Petersburg Times,* June 28, 2007, accessed July 18, 2011, http://www.sptimes.com/2007/06/28/news_pf /Hillsborough/Teen_pilot_s_family_d.shtml; Michael Wilson, "From Smiling Coffee Vendor to Terror Suspect," *New York Times,* September 25, 2009, accessed May 26, 2012, http://www.nytimes.com/2009/09/26/nyregion/26profile.htm. Additional evidence for this table is discussed in more depth throughout the text and cited accordingly.

their secrets remain hidden. Naturally, it was far easier to uncover evidence that past suicide terrorists had event-based risk factors for suicide, which were more likely to be documented, than it was to identify their psychological problems, which do not necessarily show up in observable ways.

Considering how much evidence could be compiled despite such limited information, we can only imagine how many cases of suicidal tendencies, mental health problems, and personal crises may have gone undocumented. Of course, that does not mean these factors didn't exist, or that these secretive attackers were some mysterious strain of purely ideologically motivated, sacrificial "martyrs."

The truth is out there, and every shred of evidence helps. So let's keep digging.

FOUR
THE TRUTH ABOUT 9/11

Mohamed Atta is the most infamous and influential suicide terrorist in human history.

As the ringleader of the nineteen hijackers who struck on September 11, 2001, and the first pilot to crash into the World Trade Center towers, Atta directly brought about the death of nearly three thousand Americans. In addition, he indirectly triggered the United States' "Global War On Terror," along with its costly invasions of Afghanistan and Iraq. Recent estimates have put the toll of those wars at nearly $4 trillion and approximately 225,000 civilians and soldiers dead.[1]

It's conceivable that, if not for Atta, most of those funds could have been dedicated to more humane purposes, and most of those victims would still walk among us.

Stunningly, considering his importance, Atta has been fundamentally misunderstood for more than a decade. For instance, presidential campaign adviser and political scientist Robert Pape has claimed that Atta was relatively normal, and that he was "not readily characterized as depressed, not unable to enjoy life, not detached from friends and society."[2] He further asserts that Atta's "psychological history, motivations, and behavior do not appear terribly different from those of . . . many soldiers from many cultures who saw their societies in desperate struggles for survival."[3]

Others have similarly suggested that Atta's actions were solely the product of his ideological commitment to the cause, "not individual psychology."[4] According to this view, Atta was just following orders. As former CIA expert and renowned government consultant Jerrold Post has explained, "as we've come to understand, the terrorists involved in 9/11 had subordinated their individuality to the group. And whatever their destructive, charismatic leader, Osama bin Laden said was the right thing to do for the sake of the cause was what they would do."[5] For them, he insists, "Osama bin Laden [was] an almost God-like figure."[6]

The facts say otherwise. When Atta was in Germany, some other Islamic fundamentalists would praise bin Laden to the heavens. But Atta remained skeptical and unconvinced. Unlike the others, he said that maybe bin Laden was a great man—or maybe not.[7]

Then, after meeting the Al Qaeda leader in Afghanistan and agreeing to lead the "planes operation," Atta repeatedly disobeyed him.[8] Their first disagreement was about the targets for terror. Osama bin Laden wanted one of the planes to strike the White House, but Atta preferred the U.S. Capitol Building. Twice, bin Laden had a middleman instruct Atta that the White House was their priority. Twice, Atta deflected those orders. At one point, Atta even considered striking a nuclear facility, although it had never been approved as a target by Al Qaeda leadership.[9]

Their second disagreement was about the strike date. Bin Laden was concerned about having so many terrorists in the United States at one time, with an ever-increasing risk of exposure. So he wanted the attacks to occur as soon as possible: as early as July 2001. As it turned out, this concern was well founded. That same summer, potential 9/11 hijacker Zacarias Moussaoui raised the suspicions of his flight instructor, was arrested by government agents, and jeopardized the entire plot.[10] But Atta stubbornly insisted that he wasn't ready and refused to strike until September. This reportedly made bin Ladin so frustrated that he exclaimed, "I will make it happen even if I do it by myself!"[11] As this clearly shows, Atta was not just following orders. He was not so blindly committed to the cause, so in awe of bin Laden, or so brainwashed by terrorist teachings that he simply did what he was told.

No—the truth is that Atta had his own agenda. Like many suicidal people, he was not willing to take his own life until *he* was ready: he wouldn't be rushed into it, and it needed to be on his terms. In fact, unlike a professional soldier or ideologically committed Green Beret, he was willing to jeopardize the mission's success in order to meet his own objectives.

PUTTING THE PUZZLE PIECES TOGETHER

There is much more to this story. But we're going to have to work for it. Atta is dead and he's not coming back, so it's too late to assess his psychology face-to-face. However, we can still perform a psychological autopsy, which is designed "to produce as full and accurate a picture of the deceased as possible with a view to understanding why they killed themselves."[12] This is a valuable method that expert suicidologists believe "offers the most direct technique currently available for examining the relationship between particular antecedents and suicide."[13]

Of course, we can't expect Atta to have made it easy for us. Given strict Islamic prohibitions against suicide, we should assume that even if Atta recognized that he was suicidal, he would have tried to disguise the truth. In some sense, there may have been multiple Mohamed Attas: the person he claimed to be, the person people thought he was, and the person he really was underneath it all.[14]

It is quite clear that the people who knew Atta did not know him nearly as well as they thought they did, because apart from his fellow hijackers, almost everyone was shocked by his violent suicide attack.[15] Of course, these people were not experts on depression or suicide, and even mental health professionals can miss the warning signs. But with the exception of a flight instructor who described Atta as having the personality of "a walking dead man,"[16] there does not appear to be a single associate or family member who labeled Atta "suicidal" when they were interviewed after 9/11.

This actually makes their accounts of Atta more trustworthy, not less. These sources did not have ulterior motives or agendas to portray Atta as suicidal. They were just a bunch of witnesses who recalled statements Atta made or things he did. Their observations are still valuable evidence, even though they did not understand the significance of what they saw.[17]

Each one provided a few pieces of the puzzle. Now it's up to us to put them together.

SOCIAL ISOLATION

Ever since his childhood, Atta was socially isolated, and social isolation is a major risk factor for both depression and suicide.[18]

In large part, Atta's childhood isolation was promoted by his strict and overbearing father, who proudly proclaimed, "We are people who keep to themselves. We don't mix a lot with people, and we are all successful."[19] This characterization of Atta's upbringing is corroborated by those who knew him as a child. Neighbor Mohammed Gamel Khamees remembers that "There was no hanging around, no friends, very strict rules. . . . [The family was] like a set of rings interlocked with one another. They didn't visit and weren't visited."[20] Similarly, classmate Mohammed Hassan Attiya recalls that "I never saw him playing. . . . We did not like him very much, and I think he wanted to play with the rest of the boys, but his father wanted him to always perform in school in an excellent way."[21] Atta did have some friends at school, or at least acquaintances, but he was much more isolated than his peers.

However, despite his lack of social connections, there does not appear to be much evidence that Atta was depressed or suicidal as a youth. It may thus be more accurate to understand his restricted social life during childhood as a precursor to his social isolation as an adult.

After finishing college and essentially being forced by his father to move to Germany to pursue a graduate degree, Atta faced his new life alone. This was something he was clearly unprepared for. As Atta's father explained, "My son is a very sensitive man; he is soft and was extremely attached to his mother. I almost tricked him to go to Germany to continue his education. Otherwise, he never wanted to leave Egypt."[22] In general, as psychologist Ronald W. Maris and his colleagues summarize, "suicides tend either to be socially isolated or to have negative social interactions. Indicators of social isolation . . . include being single . . . living alone; having no or minimal family relations or social support; having few, if any close friends."[23] And at least for several years, Atta's life in Germany fit every single one of these criteria.[24]

When Atta arrived in Germany, the only people he knew in the entire country were a few family connections who gave him a place to live. He made very few friends, and when he moved into a small apartment with some other college kids, Atta's social life went from nonexistent to downright hostile.[25]

In this unhealthy living situation that lasted more than three years, Atta's two male roommates grew to avoid him, and then to hate him. This was largely due to Atta's resistance to doing chores, his rigid puritanism, his refusal to let his guard down and relax, and his general unsociability.[26] Eventually, an extremely aggressive undercurrent took hold in the small apartment—and this should not be underestimated, in terms of its psychological impact on Atta. Apart from depression and social isolation, another risk factor for suicide is the loss of security,[27] and it would be hard to imagine that Atta felt very secure living among those who mocked and despised him. One of his roommates' girlfriends became so upset at Atta's rudeness that she pushed her boyfriend to taunt him for his puritan behavior. So the roommate posted sexual images in the apartment's only bathroom, where Atta would be forced to see them every day.[28]

When the roommates went out to socialize, they would often make fun of Atta behind his back. In a remarkably prescient moment, perhaps inspired by his sense of Atta's rage and depression, one roommate joked with friends that "he hoped Atta wasn't back at the apartment making a bomb to blow himself up with."[29]

Eventually Atta moved out, and in 1995, he went on the hajj: a pilgrimage to Mecca in Saudi Arabia. As Volker Hauth, one of his few friends, remembers, when Atta returned to Germany he was "even more quiet, more introverted, and more fervent in his religious practice."[30] Hauth further recalls that "Over the years, [Atta] became more and more isolated and bitter, developed a tunnel vision. . . . He didn't feel at home in Hamburg."[31] Atta began teaching Islamic classes to younger Muslims, but his antisocial style alienated most of them as well. They would attend his class a few times but then never return.[32]

A fellow Egyptian student in Germany tried to reach out to Atta, but as he remembers, it was as though Atta was keeping a "wall" between himself and others.[33] Notably, this was also how Atta's original hosts in Germany described his self-imposed isolation. As his landlady recalls, there was "always a wall between him and the family."[34]

Ultimately, Atta did join a group of devout Muslims in Hamburg. It included Marwan al-Shehhi and Ziad Jarrah, who eventually became two of the 9/11 pilots. However, the social bonds that this group offered did not reduce Atta's risk for suicide. As Maris et al. explain, "not all social relations protect against suicide. Obviously, if you were a member of the Hemlock Society, were in the Jonestown cult, were a Japanese kamikaze pilot in World War II, or a Muslim terrorist, then social support would *increase* the suicide rate in your group. In general, when the group norms are pro-suicide . . . or social relations or interactions are negative . . . they tend to *raise* suicide rates."[35] Based on these principles, it is relatively easy to imagine that instead of healing him, Atta's new social group may have exacerbated his suicidal intentions by glorifying the myth of martyrdom.

Also, Atta's experiences in this group were actually much more negative than commonly assumed. Well after joining the group, Atta still complained to a former classmate about his continued social isolation, lamenting that he had made very few friends in Germany.[36] And as esteemed investigatory journalist Terry McDermott explains, even within the Hamburg group, "When [Atta] was not around, the other men mocked his sternness and complained about all his rules."[37] Atta "had also begun to use a sort of rouge makeup; no one knew why. People made fun of him for that too."[38]

He was not just ridiculed behind his back—he was also confronted directly. And at times, his social vulnerability surfaced. After arguing with a fellow group member named Ahmed Maglad, Atta seems to have been plagued by a sense of personal rejection. As Maglad recalls, "One evening he suddenly stopped me in a parking lot and asked me:

'Ahmed, why don't you love me?'"[39] Later, in the months before their attacks, fellow 9/11 pilot Jarrah became so upset at Atta's pushiness that he threatened to withdraw from the plot completely.[40] Yet again, Atta's social failings were causing him problems, and others had to intervene. Overall, this may have been the closest thing to a group of "friends" Atta had his entire life, yet he still seemed incapable of truly fitting in.

DEPRESSION

One of the most common risk factors for suicide is depression.[41] There is growing evidence that a significant percentage of suicide terrorists were depressed before carrying out their attacks, and Atta is no exception.[42]

According to the U.S. National Institute of Mental Health, there are eleven primary signs and symptoms of depression among men. Many men who suffer from depression display only a few of these symptoms; others exhibit more. The symptoms are as follows:

1. Persistent sad, anxious, or "empty" mood
2. Feelings of hopelessness, pessimism
3. Feelings of guilt, worthlessness, helplessness
4. Loss of interest or pleasure in hobbies and activities
5. Decreased energy, fatigue, being "slowed down"
6. Difficulty concentrating, remembering, making decisions
7. Difficulty sleeping, early-morning awakening, or oversleeping
8. Appetite and/or weight changes
9. Thoughts of death or suicide; suicide attempts
10. Restlessness, irritability
11. Persistent physical symptoms [such as aches or pains that do not ease with treatment].[43]

Atta exhibited at least eight of these symptoms. At least for now, there is no clear evidence that Atta had "difficulty concentrating, remembering, making decisions," "difficulty sleeping, early-morning awakening, or oversleeping," or "persistent physical symptoms" such as aches or pains. However, he seems to have displayed each one of the other symptoms of depression prior to his suicide attack.

Persistent sad, anxious, or "empty" mood

Atta's mood could often be described as "empty." As a Muslim convert named Philip Kay recalled, Atta showed "no emotional excesses or peaks."[44] He often seemed devoid of passion, a sign that he may have been struggling with depression. Because of this emptiness, Kay and others "eventually came to wonder whether Atta might be missing some essential human part."[45]

Atta's emptiness, and perhaps his inner sadness, was most noticeable in his virtual unwillingness or inability to express positive emotions. For instance, those who knew Atta as an adult have very few memories of him ever laughing. Doris Michaels, in whose home Atta stayed when he arrived in Germany, could recall Atta laughing only when he played with her grandchild.[46] Similarly, Kay could think of only a single example of Atta laughing: when he played briefly with another child whom he met on the street.[47] And Chrilla Wendt, an instructor who helped Atta finish his graduate thesis, could not even recall him ever smiling.[48]

This was not simply a product of Atta's religious devotion. In fact, among the devout Muslims with whom Atta studied, prayed, and plotted, his constant, somber mood stood out as very unusual. As Maglad recalls, "He thought that the heart would die through fun. . . . He was convinced that there was not enough time in one's life to have fun."[49] When Atta was asked by a fellow Muslim why he never laughed, he responded, "How can you laugh when people are dying in Palestine?"[50] Another time, he told someone that "Joy kills the heart."[51]

Even in the widely seen video of Atta and Ziad Jarrah reading Islamic scripts approximately a year before 9/11, it is actually Jarrah who breaks into uncontrollable laughter. Atta cracks an awkward smile once at Jarrah's outburst, and then quickly stifles it. Like all of us, Atta must have experienced emotional peaks and valleys. But his inability to express them is a key indicator that he may have been clinically depressed.

Feelings of hopelessness, pessimism and feelings
of guilt, worthlessness, helplessness

Because these traits are not only symptoms of depression, but also direct risk factors for suicide,[52] they will be discussed in depth later in this chapter.

Loss of interest or pleasure in hobbies and activities

There is so little evidence of Atta ever playing that it becomes hard to document the disappearance of this behavior. Certainly Atta must have had fun as a youth, but interviews of those who knew the family contain no mention of toys inside the house or games outside it. As mentioned earlier, Atta's father was extremely strict, prioritizing education and studying above all else.[53] Perhaps the only story of Atta "playing" as a child is a recollection of him holding secret, back-alley conversations with other boys, perched at adjacent windows from the upper levels of their homes.[54]

In Germany, Atta almost never socialized, went to dance clubs or bars, or attended sporting events.[55] He went to a movie once—*The Jungle Book*—and was so upset about the excited crowd that he never went to the movies again.[56] Furthermore, as journalist John Crewdson summarizes, based on interviews of the terrorist's associates, "Atta thought that no music of any kind had a place in the life of a devout Muslim, and that the same went for good food and fun."[57] When group member Maglad would bring home delicious food, Atta would not partake, complaining, "You are living your life like in paradise, and people are dying elsewhere."[58] As another roommate summarized, Atta "was reluctant to any pleasure."[59]

By contrast, most Islamic fundamentalists find a way to balance their ideology and their natural desire to enjoy life. However, because Atta was so deeply depressed—and because he refused to admit it—he tried to frame his refusal to have fun as an act of religious devotion.

Decreased energy, fatigue, being "slowed down"

Depressed people often feel burned out and fatigued, even when there is no clear reason for them to be tired.[60] In Atta's case, this particular symptom could also signify "life weariness," which is associated both with having a death wish and committing suicide.[61]

In 1999, shortly before he set off with other members of his group to find a path to "martyrdom," Atta returned home to Egypt. He lied to his father, telling him that he was about to enter a Ph.D. program in the United States. But he confided in his mother, the only person with whom he appears to have shared true emotional intimacy his entire life. Unfortunately, his mother was suffering from diabetes and was in declining health. As McDermott recounts, Atta told his mother that "he was unsure about continuing his education. What he really wanted to do was stay; *he said he was tired*. He wanted to remain in Cairo and take care of her."[62] In this case, it appears that Atta was expressing life weariness: he did not feel tired because of a long day's work, but because of a long seven years away from home in what apparently felt like a long and painful life.

Suicidal people are commonly motivated by a desire to escape,[63] and it seems clear that the weary Atta had decided he needed a way out. He had struggled for seven years to complete his master's degree, and spent seven years socially isolated, far away from the home he never wanted to leave in the first place. It had been seven years of anger, hostility, depression, and a strict religious purity that he had defined as almost completely devoid of pleasure. And now he was tired of it all. Two paths lay in front of Atta: a violent suicide attack that would end his pain forever, or a return to the only place he had ever felt safe, and to the only person he could really trust.

He pleaded with his mother, asking her to persuade his father to allow him to stay in Egypt. She said no. She insisted that he must do what his father wanted, and travel to America to pursue his doctorate.[64] Like a good son, Atta promised to obey, but a few months later he was in Afghanistan, pledging to bin Laden that he was ready to die.

Appetite and/or weight changes

As mentioned earlier, Atta would complain when other members of his group would bring home delicious food, which seems odd considering the lack of a true religious justification for this stance.

At one point, Atta even expressed displeasure at having to eat to stay alive. As one of his prior roommates recalls, "I remember sitting down at the table and Mohamed sighing, 'This is boring. Eating is boring.' He said it wasn't just that he wanted different food, it was just the *act* of eating."[65]

This statement stands as additional evidence that Atta was suffering from depression. It also supports the indications that he was plagued by a growing sense of life weariness. Even simple pleasures had begun to feel like loathsome chores.

Thoughts of death or suicide; suicide attempts

Did Atta ever consider hanging himself, slitting his wrists, or putting a bullet through his brain? Not that we know of. But this is not surprising, given Islam's strict prohibition of suicide. In Atta's mind, killing himself through conventional means would have been a one-way ticket to hell.[66]

However, there was that one loophole which Atta spent a great deal of time thinking about. "Martyrdom" had essentially become the only socially approved form of suicide in the Islamic world: a method of escape for suicidal individuals who still wanted to go to paradise.[67] It is not clear precisely when Atta became fixated on this idea, but it seems likely that it was during his earliest, most socially isolated, and most depressed years in Germany. Eventually, he would spend a great deal of time debating the morality of "martyrdom" with the other devout Muslims in his group. In fact, there were periods when they spent many hours every day discussing the issue.[68]

On April 11, 1996, Atta wrote and signed his last will and testament.[69] He was just twenty-seven years old. There are several notable things about Atta's will, which he divided into eighteen points. First, he had not imagined the September 11, 2001, attacks at that point.[70] He was planning his premature death, but he had not decided on the specific manner of his exit. In addition, although the purpose of a will is primarily to govern the disposition of personal property, Atta said almost nothing about whom he wanted to receive his possessions. He did not mention a single friend or family member by name.[71]

The document actually reads more like a suicide note than a will: it has a strong undercurrent of anger and pain, and it was filled with specific instructions for what should be done with Atta's body after he died.[72] Of the eighteen points, a third of them begin with the phrase "I don't want," and then follow with some specific restriction. "I don't want anyone to weep and cry." "I don't want anyone to visit me who didn't get along with me while I was alive." And so on.[73]

You can almost feel Atta's personal grudges and social bitterness oozing through his words. These are not the statements of a psychologically healthy person who was getting ready to sacrifice his life for a sacred cause. This is someone who was angry, depressed, and suicidal.

Overall, the document is a powerful example of Atta's state of mind: he had clearly spent a significant amount of time imagining his lifeless body, how it would be treated, and who would pay their respects after his death.[74]

Restlessness, irritability

Whenever Atta's control was threatened, or whenever he momentarily lost power over a situation, he became extremely irritable.

For example, when some of his teachers in Germany tried to do Atta a favor by helping him with a visa application, he became inexplicably hostile. "I am grown up now; I can take care of that myself," Atta snapped at them.[75] This was well before he had developed an alias or considered carrying out a terrorist attack, so his reaction probably cannot be attributed to a legitimate fear of exposure.

Similarly, during his one experience at a movie theater in Germany, Atta was extremely upset by the crowd chatting before the film began. "Chaos, chaos," he muttered in disgust, and when he returned home, he stomped into his bedroom and slammed his door in anger.[76] The entire outing had been ruined.

Along these same lines, when Atta began leading Islamic prayer groups, he was very rigid and stern with the other students, and he would critique them quite frequently: for their hair, their jewelry, their music, even the way they prayed.[77] Their sessions were also strictly structured.

If, during the group's discussion of religious texts, "anyone attempted to deviate from the established routine, Atta would grow visibly upset, chewing on his lower lip in agitation."[78] This irritability was likely the product of his broader struggles with depression. And again, depression is a major risk factor for suicide.[79]

GUILT AND SHAME

Guilt and shame are not only symptoms of depression, but they are also direct risk factors for suicide.[80] Atta appears to have struggled with these feelings, but like many people in pain, he tried to keep it a secret.

For instance, Atta seemed preoccupied with seeking forgiveness, but he almost always framed his desire for forgiveness in general terms, never specifying the sources of his guilt. Some signs of this appear in Atta's last will and testament, which contains the following pleas:

> The people who will prepare my body should be good Muslims because this will remind me of God and his forgiveness . . . pray that I will go to heaven . . . pray for me to be with the angels. . . . You must speed my funeral procession and I would like many people there to pray for me. . . . Everyone who attends my funeral should ask that I will be forgiven for what I have done in the past (not this action).[81]

Although it is possible that Atta was simply asking for forgiveness in a general way, it seems more likely that he was prompted by specific guilt from his own life. His last statement, asking that he "be forgiven for what I have done in the past," is particularly suggestive of personal guilt.

Similarly, his "suicide note," which was found in his suitcase after 9/11 and which he had apparently distributed to the other hijackers, includes the following statements: "Purify your soul from all unclean things . . . erase your sins. . . . The angels will ask for your forgiveness . . . and will pray for you. . . . Lord, forgive our sins and excesses."[82] Here, Atta's reference to "unclean things" seems particularly indicative of guilt and shame.

When it comes to the specific reasons for Atta's guilt and shame, we can only speculate. Most proximate to the September 11 attacks was Atta's mysterious August 2001 trip to Las Vegas, the so-called City of Sin. Atta and his fellow terrorists occasionally flew cross-country trips for reconnaissance purposes, but this trip did not appear to serve that function. As the authors of the *9/11 Commission Report* conclude, "Beyond Las Vegas's reputation for welcoming tourists, we have seen no credible evidence explaining why, on this occasion and others, the operatives flew to or met in Las Vegas."[83] Journalist Evan Thomas takes the next logical step: "They stayed in cheap hotels on a dreary stretch of the Strip frequented by dope dealers and $10 street hookers. Perhaps they wished to be fortified for their mission by visiting a shrine to American decadence."[84]

On the one hand, the notion of Atta having sex with prostitutes is completely at odds with everything we know about his personality. Other members of Atta's group acknowledged their sexual desires, flirted with women on the street, and even boasted of sexual conquests.[85] But Atta appears to have been the polar opposite. His German friend Hauth believed that Atta must have died a virgin, and Atta's father described his son as being so nonsexual that he was "like a virgin girl in his politeness and shyness."[86]

On the other hand, sometimes it is those who appear to be the most repressed or inhibited who are actually the most likely to engage in risky sexual behaviors, given the opportunity.[87] As renowned expert on sexual psychology Michael Bader explains, "Sexual fantasies always find a way of turning the 'no' of guilt into the 'yes' of pleasure."[88] If, despite his fundamentalism, Atta had sexual contact with prostitutes, this could certainly explain his guilt over "unclean things" and his growing desire to commit suicide.

However, even if this never occurred, it seems quite clear that for some deeply personal reason, Atta experienced overwhelming guilt and shame about his sexual desires. Cousin Essam Omar Rashad recalls that during their adolescence in Cairo, Atta would leave the room whenever belly-dancing programs came on television.[89] This behavior was particularly odd because these programs were quite normal in that culture. In turn, Atta's schoolmates remember him as "extremely shy about girls."[90] And when he came to Germany, Atta's guilt and shame about his sexual desires were seemingly amplified. Doris Michaels, his first landlord, similarly remembers Atta "putting his hands over his eyes and leaving the room when anything remotely explicit appeared on television."[91] And as McDermott explains, "Even sleeveless blouses caused him to grimace."[92] At times, Atta would even take detours on his way home, in order to avoid streets with scantily clad women.[93] Again, Atta's personal discomfort about sex was not solely the product of his religion. The other devout Muslims in his group acted more like normal young men.

It is unknown why the subject of sex provoked such shame in Atta, so we can only speculate. Sexual shame and guilt are often rooted in childhood experiences.[94] Perhaps Atta's father, who desperately wanted for his young son to "toughen up,"[95] unintentionally triggered his son's sexual insecurity. After all, his father admitted that "I used to tell [Atta's mother] that she is raising him like a girl, and that I have three girls, but she never stopped pampering him."[96] To make things worse, Atta's father mockingly called him "Bolbol," which is Arabic for "nightingale."[97] Given this type of tough love, it may have been inevitable that Atta would lack the confidence to approach attractive girls as a youth or women as an adult. Hauth recalls that Atta "had no experience with women," and that he was so awkward and uncomfortable when talking with them that they often thought him quite rude.[98]

Unfortunately, this type of shame and insecurity can breed still more sexual frustration—which Atta admitted to his landlord in his early twenties[99]—along with outright anger. By the time Atta wrote his last will and testament in 1996, his hostility toward women was overt. He first insisted that "I don't want a pregnant woman or a person who is not clean to come and say good-bye to me because I don't approve [of] it," then added that "I don't want women to come to my house to apologize for my death," and ultimately determined that "I don't want any women to go to my grave at all during my funeral or on any occasion thereafter."[100]

Of course, Atta may have experienced guilt and shame for other reasons as well. It is certainly possible that he was ashamed of his professional struggles and failure to live up to his father's expectations. In addition, Atta may have experienced "separation guilt" for abandoning his mother and moving to Germany. In his absence, his mother was diagnosed with diabetes and became estranged from his father.[101] At some level, Atta may have blamed himself for these developments, believing that things would have been different if he'd never left her. Separation guilt is surprisingly common, often unconscious, and frequently linked to sexual repression.[102]

In any case, it is clear that Atta's guilt, shame, and insecurities were not normal, even for an Islamic fundamentalist. And this seems like part of the explanation for both why he was so depressed and why he ultimately wanted to die.

HOPELESSNESS

Hopelessness is both a symptom of depression and a direct risk factor for suicide itself.[103] Hopelessness is particularly relevant to suicide because it is a distinctly future-oriented feeling, and suicidal individuals are almost uniformly pessimistic about their future. Depression can be based on the past or present, yet still allow for future improvement. But people who struggle with hopelessness generally feel that their life is not likely to get much better—it's only going to get worse.[104]

Atta's hopelessness appears to have derived from the mounting pressures on him to acquire his doctorate, get married, and establish a family.[105] These expectations had been etched in stone ever since Atta's childhood, when his father insisted that his offspring settle for nothing less than elite levels of professional success. Atta's two older sisters had obediently flourished: one became a cardiologist and the other became a professor of zoology. However, as Atta's father explains, he expected even more from his only son: "I told him I needed to hear the word 'doctor' in front of his name. We told him 'Your sisters are doctors and their husbands are doctors and you are the man of the family.'"[106]

At least initially, Atta seemed to share his father's goals, and despite struggling much more than his sisters did in college, he was determined to be successful. During his early years in Germany, Atta told Hauth that his dream was to return to Egypt "as an Arab to Arabia" to work as an urban planner and help people build better lives. However, as the years passed, Atta became increasingly afraid that he would never be able to establish a home in his native country because of Egypt's intolerance for Islamic fundamentalism.[107] As Hauth explains, "He lived in fear of being criminalized for his religious beliefs."[108] In addition, Hauth recalls that "increasingly, I felt a sense of despair in him, on a personal level."[109]

By 1999, after seven dark years in Germany, Atta was barely any closer to meeting his goals—or those of his father. In fact, they increasingly seemed out of reach. During one of Atta's brief trips home in 1999, his former classmate Ahmed Khalifa ran into him on the street. He described Atta as being depressed about not having a career, many friends, or his own family back in Germany.[110] As Khalifa recalls, "I think he felt that he had just been studying all those years."[111] Khalifa further remembers Atta's own hopelessness as almost being contagious: "When I said goodbye, I was sad."[112] This was during the same trip when Atta's mother rejected his plea to stay with her and insisted that he go to America to pursue his doctorate.

Ultimately, Atta did travel to the United States, but not with education on his mind. He apparently believed that his original life plan was no longer possible. And Atta alludes to his failure in his 2001 suicide note: "How much time have we wasted in our lives?" he asked.[113] In some sense, Atta's personal clock was ticking: ever since he had left Egypt in 1999, he had been lying to his parents about being in an American Ph.D. program.[114] But that lie had an expiration date—he could not pretend to be a successful doctoral student forever.

Atta was also facing growing pressures to get married and start a family, and that, too, seemed impossible. As former landlord Doris Michaels recalls, Atta once admitted "that for him, being a practicing Muslim, it was not easy to be 24 years old and unmarried."[115] If the social pressures for Atta to get married were stressful for him at age twenty-four, we can only imagine how hopeless—and perhaps ashamed—he must have felt due to his lack of progress by age thirty-three. McDermott provides useful context for these pressures, which highlights the extent of Atta's abnormality:

In general, remaining single is frowned upon within Islam. Yusuf al-Qaradawi, a Qatari cleric popular among [Atta's] Hamburg group, has written . . . that Muslims are compelled to marry: "As long as he possesses the means to marry, the Muslim is not permitted to refrain from marriage on the grounds that he has dedicated himself to the service or the worship of Allah or to a life of monasticism and renunciation of the world."[116]

These pressures, coupled with Islamic prohibitions against sex before marriage and the normal urges of most young men, mean that the majority of devout Muslims marry at an early age.[117] Osama bin Laden married his first wife when he was seventeen or eighteen, ended up marrying several additional wives, and fathered as many as twenty-four children.[118] And fellow 9/11 pilots and Hamburg group members Jarrah and al-Shehhi had girlfriends to whom they were at least unofficially married, despite being seven and ten years younger than Atta.[119] But at age thirty-three, Atta had never been in a single romantic relationship.

Curiously, several acquaintances report that Atta "seemed uninterested in women."[120] Fellow Muslim group member Shahid Nickels explained that when Atta talked about marriage, he seemed to do so only "symbolically."[121] Furthermore, when Muslim convert Heidi Jane Finke told Atta that she knew of a young Islamic woman who "would suit him well," Atta told her that he was not interested.[122] In fact, there are only a few accounts of Atta ever expressing interest in a woman, and even then, it was always in a secret conversation behind her back.[123]

Perhaps the most likely explanation for Atta's avoidance of women and marriage is his sexual guilt, shame, and insecurities. Given Atta's insistence on always being in control, it is easy to imagine that his sexual discomfort would have prompted him to avoid the apparent "threat" of female companionship. As everyone who has ever started a relationship knows, dating requires some willingness to show vulnerability and take risks. Ironically, this may have been one risk that the man who crashed a plane into the World Trade Center was simply unwilling to face.

However, there was a potential light at the end of the tunnel, although it may have felt more like an oncoming train. When Atta returned home to Egypt in 1999, his overbearing father took matters into his own hands. As Atta's father explains, "I told him we should look for a wife for him. We went to visit a family, and Mohamed met the daughter and they liked each other. The woman's parents also liked Mohamed, but their only condition was that their daughter not leave Cairo. So Mohamed got engaged to her and then went back to finish his Ph.D."[124]

Although this should have been a positive development in Atta's life, it may have actually increased his feelings of hopelessness. Again, Atta was living a lie, the clock was ticking, and it was only a matter of time before he would be exposed as a fraud.

For one thing, Atta had agreed to live in Cairo with his future wife, based on her parents' orders. However, as mentioned earlier, Atta actually believed that this was impossible for him, because in Egypt he would be persecuted as an Islamic fundamentalist.[125] Furthermore, Atta may have reasonably feared that when everyone found out the truth about his phony Ph.D. program, he would be left disgraced, alone, and without any future prospects. Finally, if the marriage were somehow saved, Atta would be forced to confront his sexual shame and insecurities, which had plagued him since adolescence and had steadily grown more severe.

Given the growing weight of these lies and pressures, Atta must have felt that his day of reckoning was inevitable—one way or another.

NO ORDINARY SOLDIER

For more than a decade, the experts have gotten it wrong. You've been told that Mohamed Atta was not socially isolated, that he was not depressed, and that he was psychologically normal. You've been told that he was just like an ordinary soldier and that he was purely motivated by his powerful ideological beliefs.[126]

Enough of that gibberish. This psychological autopsy has revealed that Atta's struggles with social isolation, depression, guilt and shame, and hopelessness were very similar to the struggles of those who commit conventional suicide and murder-suicide. For those who wish to retrace Atta's path to suicide visually, that material has been modeled in Figure 4.1. Of course, Figure 4.1 is not a complete summary of this chapter—it

Figure 4.1 Modeling Mohamed Atta's Path to Suicide

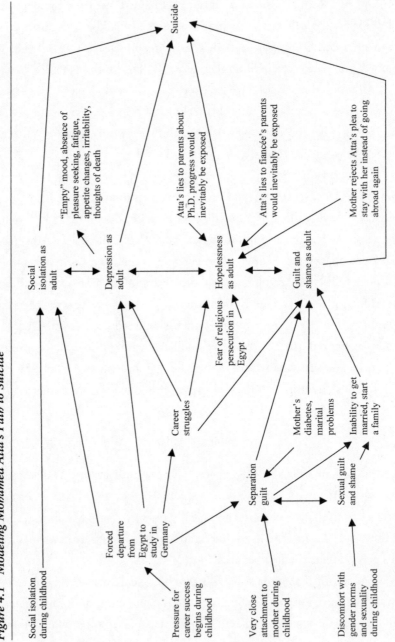

©Adam Lankford, 2013

is merely a basic visual representation of some of the key conceptual points.

The details from Atta's life show why individual psychology is so critical in assessing events like the September 11 attacks. They explain why Atta behaved so differently from the millions of Islamic fundamentalists and tens of thousands of terrorists and terrorist leaders who have not carried out suicide attacks—and never will.

Normal soldiers and terrorists have not struggled with social isolation since childhood, and they do not claim that "joy kills the heart," avoid laughing whenever possible, condemn fun, music, and delicious food, complain about needing to eat to stay alive, write an angry last will and testament at age twenty-seven, act ashamed of normal sexual desires, and hopelessly lament wasting most of their lives.

Atta's religion and politics affected the form of his suicide and the target for his rage, but they were not the underlying cause of his behavior.

THE OTHER 9/11 HIJACKERS

If for more than a decade experts misunderstood the most infamous and influential suicide terrorist in human history, what else have they missed?

A preliminary review indicates that, much like Atta, many other 9/11 hijackers had significant personal problems, and that it may have been these personal struggles, more than ideology, that served as the primary reason for their suicide attacks.

For instance, one of the original suicide terrorists selected for the "planes operation" was Tawfiq bin Attash, also known as Khallad. When he was just fifteen years old, Khallad left home to fight in Afghanistan, but his transformation from traditional warrior to suicide terrorist did not occur until three years later. In one terrible battle, he was severely injured, lost his lower right leg, and saw his brother killed.[127] After this traumatic series of events, Khallad volunteered to carry out a suicide mission. As luck would have it, he could not gain entry into the United States and could not participate in 9/11, but these events help explain why he wanted to die. As an Afghan man who lost his legs in a land-mine explosion suggests, after the injury, "there is complete loss of hope in being able to live a normal life . . . In a culture like ours, disability and the possibility of being out on the street are equated with great shame. . . . He might find it easier to die."[128] In turn, as a former assistant to famed Afghan warrior Ahmad Shah Massoud explains, committing a suicide attack makes the most sense for those who are disabled and can no longer keep up with their comrades. "As long as you can fight, why blow yourself up?"[129]

In addition, 9/11 pilots Marwan al Shehhi, Hani Hanjour, and Ziad Jarrah all struggled with a range of personal problems that could help explain their suicidal intent. Al Shehhi—who crashed the second plane into the World Trade Center towers—had been very close to his father. But when he was studying abroad at age nineteen, he received the devastating news that his father had unexpectedly died.[130] In the aftermath, he began having major difficulties at school, had to repeat several courses, and then barely passed them. Al Shehhi also grew distant from the rest of his family, who worried about him as he became increasingly radical and began considering a suicide attack.[131] He eventually called home and "told his family he had been going through a tough time, but that things were improving. . . . He could, he said, see a light at the end of the tunnel."[132] Little did they know that at that point he was actually looking forward to his suicidal escape.

Hanjour—who crashed into the U.S. Pentagon—appears to have been the most timid and insecure of the 9/11 pilots. As a family friend whom he lived with in the United States recalls, "He was like a little mouse around the house. . . . He really didn't make any friends . . . [and] he would pretty much stay holed up in his room."[133] Before he ever got involved in terrorism, Hanjour had actually wanted to become a flight attendant, but his brother pushed him to become a pilot instead. Taken with the idea, he became obsessed with studying—which may have been a way to escape social interaction. As a former roommate explains, "I'd tell him 'Let's go see a movie.' He'd say 'No.' I'd tell him 'Let's go play basketball.' He'd say 'No.' He just stayed home and studied his books for flight school."[134] Despite this fixation, Hanjour was an embarrassingly terrible student: he was repeatedly rejected from aviation training programs, and when finally admitted, he was repeatedly failed by his flight instructors and discouraged from continuing.[135] In addition,

Hanjour was being pressured by his family to get married, despite showing no inclination to do so. Given his shyness, one of Hanjour's big problems was his poor language skills: they stifled his opportunities for relationships, friends, and a successful career. Overall, as McDermott summarizes, "The failure depressed him."[136] Hanjour finally got a chance to become a pilot the only way he could: for a suicide mission where he would crash and burn.

Finally, even more blatant suicidal signs appear in the life of 9/11 pilot Ziad Jarrah, who intended to strike the U.S. Capitol Building but crashed outside Shanksville, Pennsylvania, instead. Most directly, he complained about being "dissatisfied with his life" and insisted that he "didn't want to leave Earth in a natural way."[137] And he apparently had dramatic mood swings. Jarrah had nearly flunked out of high school and had dropped out of college. In addition, he had a very stressful and tumultuous relationship with his wife or girlfriend, Aysel Senguen, who had previously attempted suicide herself.[138] Jarrah also had family problems, and they became so extreme that at one point, his father feigned a heart attack in hopes that it would get Jarrah to come home. It didn't work. Overall, the evidence strongly indicates that Jarrah was not simply a terrorist ideologue, motivated by politics or religion, and that something else, such as suicidal urges, must have been the critical factor. Even when filming his own "martyrdom" video, he could not maintain a serious tone and was scolded by terrorist handlers for not displaying any passion.[139] And Jarrah almost backed out of the entire 9/11 terrorist plot at the last minute, so his commitment to the cause could not have been particularly strong.[140] Instead of acting like a well-trained soldier, he displayed the wavering and indecision typical of many suicidal people.[141]

As these brief anecdotes show, we still need to dig deeper. To a large extent, the almost universally held view that suicide terrorists could not be suicidal led commentators to misdiagnose Atta. Let's not make the same mistake again.

In the future, detailed psychological autopsies of the other 9/11 pilots and hijackers should be conducted in order to shed more light on their personal motives. Initial evidence suggests that hijackers Wail al Shehri and Ahmed al Nami both struggled with mental health problems.

Al Shehri reportedly "fell into a deep depression" in late 1999 that was so bad that he had to leave his job and seek medical treatment: "His friends say it was not just depression, but perhaps even a suicidal tendency."[142] Similarly, in 1999, al Nami's behavior apparently became so strange that his family feared a "bipolar disorder."[143] And there are other hijackers who are still unaccounted for, so who knows what we might find?

Past research on "suicide pacts" suggests that every member of a group need not be suicidal—at least in the conventional sense—for them all to kill themselves.[144] It is thus possible that given Atta's leadership position, his own suicidal drive—combined with the personal problems and weaknesses of the others—helped propel the rest of the group to their deaths. Another possibility is that the pilots who deliberately crashed their planes were suicidal in the conventional sense, while the muscle hijackers who just secured the planes were suicidal in some indirect way. (Indirect suicidality will be discussed in Chapter 7).

These are just a few of the questions future studies should attempt to answer—and soon. Because, ultimately, if we want to prevent the next 9/11, we need to make sure we accurately understand the psychology of suicide terrorists.

We need to know how to recognize the next Mohamed Atta—before it's too late.

FIVE

WHAT REAL HEROES ARE MADE OF

n 1938, the first issue of *Action Comics* was released, featuring Superman, who is considered by many to be the greatest superhero ever.

At the time, Americans were increasingly anxious about Nazism and the possibility of World War II. So perhaps it was only natural that they embraced this fictitious savior. Along with a wildly successful comic book franchise, Superman would eventually inspire multiple movies, a television series, and a Broadway musical, becoming a cultural icon and symbol of unparalleled strength.

However, in those early years, Superman's creators ran into a dilemma. Things were becoming too easy for the "Man of Steel," who was portrayed as "faster than a speeding bullet, more powerful than a locomotive, and able to leap tall buildings in a single bound." Superman was essentially invincible, and that made it hard to be a true hero. Sure, he saved lives, and the people who benefited were eternally grateful. But for Superman himself, lifting a train to rescue a damsel in distress was no more dangerous than picking up some dirty socks from the bedroom floor. And there's nothing heroic about that.

The solution was simple: Kryptonite. By creating something that would instantly rob Superman of his powers and make him incredibly vulnerable, the authors paved the way for true heroism. Instead of simply saving others without breaking a sweat, Superman now had to risk his life to fight the forces of evil. And that made all the difference.

THE ULTIMATE SACRIFICE

We see the same thing in the real world. Heroism and personal risk almost always go together. If you have nothing to lose, you can still help people. You can be generous and charitable. But you can't be a great hero.

That's why it's so hard for psychologists to study heroism in controlled experiments. Most other behaviors can be tested and analyzed in the lab. For instance, researchers often ask college students to participate in some artificial situation that will create hunger, excitement, frustration, or some other feeling, and then they can study the response in more depth. But you cannot put volunteer test subjects in situations where they have the opportunity to be truly heroic unless you also convince them that they are facing serious personal risk. And that becomes unethical.

Fortunately, we can still learn about heroism by looking around us. For thousands of years, people have saved their loudest praise for individuals who made "the ultimate sacrifice." Our most celebrated heroes are almost always figures who died—or were willing to die—for some other person, principle, or cause.

The historical evidence is abundant. Jesus Christ is worshipped and revered, at least in part, because he selflessly gave his life to "save his people from their sins."[1] Joan of Arc became a national hero and Catholic saint because, despite the risks, she insisted that it was her religious duty to support the French war effort—and then she was captured and burned at the stake.[2] George Washington, Thomas Jefferson, Benjamin Franklin, and America's other founding fathers were heroic not because of their political acumen, but because they were willing to risk having their neck in a noose for the principle of independence. As Franklin famously remarked, "We must indeed all hang together, or most assuredly we shall all hang separately."[3] And Abraham Lincoln, Mohandas Gandhi, and Martin Luther King Jr. are all considered heroes because they pushed for justice despite tremendous criticism and personal risk, and were eventually assassinated as a result. The fact that they paid the ultimate price somehow makes them more heroic.

There are countless examples of sacrificial heroes in popular culture as well. For instance, the final sentence of Charles Dickens's *A Tale of Two Cities* is spoken by a man who chose to switch places with someone who was about to be executed, in order to help the woman he loved. As this character's fatal moment with the guillotine draws close, he famously explains that "It is a far, far better thing that I do, than I have ever done; it is a far, far better rest that I go to, than I have ever known."[4]

J. K. Rowling's tremendously popular Harry Potter series, which has sold more than four hundred million books worldwide, is also largely based upon sacrificial heroism.[5] A recent analysis titled *Jesus Potter Harry Christ* explores the many parallels between the two figures over nearly five hundred pages.[6] From the beginning, Harry is known as "The Boy Who Lived" because his mother sacrificed her life to cast a magic spell that would protect her son from being murdered. As the series progresses, Harry repeatedly risks everything to fight the forces of evil. And then in the final book, the enemy gives him an ultimatum: save yourself—or save your friends. Naturally, he chooses the latter. As Rowling writes, "Harry understood at last that he was not supposed to survive. His job was to walk calmly into Death's welcoming arms."[7]

A GROSS OVERSIMPLIFICATION

The problem is that in recent years, many people have oversimplified the relationship between risk, death, and heroism. They have jumped to the conclusion that in order to be a great hero, like these famous figures, you have to make the ultimate sacrifice.

The U.S. government has supported this misconception by reserving its highest military award for those who died on the battlefield. From 1975 to 2009, the United States did not issue the Medal of Honor to a single living member of the armed forces. Technically, the award criteria state that an individual must show "gallantry and intrepidity at the *risk* of his life above and beyond the call of duty."[8] But for nearly a quarter century, risk wasn't enough. You had to die to qualify.

Of course, the distinction between those who live and those who die is not necessarily a matter of courage or character. It's often the product of pure luck in the midst of whizzing bullets and ticking grenades. Fortunately, American leaders have now seen the error of their ways, and in 2010, military personnel who displayed sufficient heroism and *survived* once again began to receive the Medal of Honor.

But the same misconception directly contributes to the myth of martyrdom, and it has not yet been corrected. In fact, it goes even further. In the contexts where suicide terrorism is popular, "the ultimate sacrifice" has been redefined as requiring more than just death. If people who fight for the cause and survive unharmed are making a minimal sacrifice (of time and effort), those who are wounded in battle are considered to have given more. A still greater status is bestowed upon the sacrifice made by those who die in battle. But the highest honor is reserved for those who voluntarily embrace death, like suicide bombers.

In these contexts, people often assume that the relationship between risk and heroism is strictly linear, as represented below:

Risk with a 100 percent chance of survival = no courage or heroism

Risk with a 95 percent chance of survival = minimal courage and heroism

Risk with a 50 percent chance of survival = major courage and heroism

Risk with a 10 percent chance of survival = extreme courage and heroism

Risk with a 0 percent chance of survival = unsurpassed courage and heroism[9]

If you buy into this reasoning, then you would consider suicide terrorists to be extraordinarily heroic. After all, there are very few activities with a smaller chance of survival than strapping a bomb to your chest and pressing the detonator.

But of course, many risky behaviors are not heroic at all. Some are just reckless, and others are blatantly suicidal. Reckless and suicidal behavior while attacking one's enemies is still reckless and suicidal behavior. It's not heroism.

In addition, risk, courage, and sacrifice are relative concepts. For many suicide terrorists, blowing themselves up is actually easier than continuing to live. For them, the risky thing would be to face their uncertain future. The courageous thing would be to tackle their problems one day at a time. The ultimate sacrifice would be to swallow their pride and ask for help.

But as we're about to see, there are many other factors that matter too. Sometimes those who take the greatest risks really are the greatest heroes. Sometimes they're not even close.

A MATTER OF INTENT

In May 2009, six months before Major Nidal Hasan killed thirteen people and wounded thirty-one more at the Fort Hood base in Texas, he tried to convince himself that he was not suicidal. Although he intended to die during his attack, Hasan needed to be sure that it would constitute "martyrdom," not suicide, since the latter is explicitly condemned by Islam and guarantees the offender an eternity in hell.[10] On an internet forum, Hasan posted that almost all scholars agree with him about this suicide/sacrifice distinction. Unfortunately, as we saw in Chapter 2, he was correct.[11] The consensus among the so-called experts has been almost universal.

Piggybacking on their arguments, Hasan tried to equate suicide terrorists with others who sacrifice their lives for the greater good:

There was a grenade thrown amongst a group of American soldiers. One of the soldiers, feeling that it was too late for everyone to flee, jumped on the grave with the intention of saving his comrades. Indeed he saved them. He intentionally took his life (suicide) for a noble cause i.e., saving the lives of his soldier[s].

To say that this soldier committed suicide is inappropriate. It's more appropriate to say he is a brave hero that sacrificed his life for a more noble cause. Scholars have paralleled this to suicide bombers whose intention, by sacrificing their lives, is to help save Muslims by killing enemy soldiers. If one suicide bomber can kill 100 enemy soldiers because they were caught off guard, that would be considered a strategic victory. Their intention is not to die because of some despair. . . .

So the scholars main point is that "IT SEEMS AS THOUGH YOUR INTENTION IS THE MAIN ISSUE" and Allah (SWT) [may He be glorified and exalted] knows best.[12]

Hasan also suggested that suicide terrorists were the modern equivalent of the kamikaze pilots from Japan, who he similarly insisted were not suicidal. We'll expose the flaws in that assumption in Chapter 7.

But what about the soldier who jumps on a grenade? Is Hasan correct? If so, then maybe there really isn't a behavioral difference between the American soldiers we've considered heroes in the past and the suicide terrorists who have been celebrated as heroic "martyrs" by their supporters.

If Hasan and those scholars are right, that would also mean that the 9/11 hijackers were essentially the psychological equivalent of the firefighters and policemen who died on September 11, 2001, while pulling people from burning buildings. After all, at least at first, it would seem that they all shared the same *intent*: to save the people they cared about, even though they had to make "the ultimate sacrifice" to do so. The 9/11 hijackers were genuinely trying to save fellow Muslims from Western infidels, weren't they? If so, shouldn't this legitimately make them heroes to the people who share their views?

No sir. There are fundamental differences between the true heroes and the fakers. You just need to know where to look.

FOUR SCENARIOS

In order to expose the behavioral and motivational differences between those who make heroic sacrifices and those who commit suicide, we should investigate some real-life cases:

1. A woman wearing a bomb vest blows herself up at a café.
2. A pilot deliberately crashes a hijacked jet into a skyscraper.
3. A Secret Service agent steps in front of the president to take a bullet.
4. A soldier jumps on a grenade that was thrown at his unit.

Since we are well acquainted with suicide terrorism, there's no need to reexamine the first two scenarios. It should suffice to say that they represent real cases. Examples include Hanadi Jaradat's suicide bombing at an Israeli restaurant (see Chapter 3) and Mohamed Atta's 9/11 attack on the World Trade Center (see Chapter 4).

Now let's take a closer look at the third and fourth scenarios, so that we can make informed comparisons.

A Secret Service agent steps in front of the president to take a bullet.

The U.S. Secret Service has come to symbolize sacrificial heroism. Secret Service agents are widely praised for their willingness to give up anything, including their lives, to protect the president of the United States.

This selfless pledge captivates the imagination and has led to a series of books and films on the subject. Perhaps most notable is the 1993 movie *In the Line of Fire,* which stars Clint Eastwood as agent Frank Horrigan, who had failed to prevent the Kennedy assassination and now gets a second chance, thirty years later, to take a bullet for the new president.

The inherent challenges of being willing to sacrifice your life for someone else are a constant theme in the film. At one point, Frank is mocked by an assassin, who questions whether his failure to save President Kennedy was based on a lack of courage and commitment. "If you'd reacted to that first shot, could you have gotten there in time to stop the big bullet? And if you had—that could've been your head being blown apart. Do you wish you'd succeeded, Frank? Or is life too precious?"[13] Later, Eastwood's character jokes with a colleague about having second thoughts. "I normally prefer not to get to know the people

I'm protecting. . . . You might decide they're not worth taking a bullet for."[14]

In real life, there has been only one case where a Secret Service agent deliberately took a bullet for the president. On March 30, 1981, Tim McCarthy was one of several agents responsible for protecting President Ronald Reagan. When Reagan exited the Washington Hilton Hotel after giving a speech, he began walking toward his armored vehicle, surrounded by agents.

And then, as McCarthy explains, the unexpected happened. "Just before the president got to the car, John Hinckley pushed himself forward and fired six rounds in about one and a half seconds."[15]

Video evidence shows that McCarthy immediately threw his body in front of the president and took a bullet in the chest. But by that point, Reagan had already been hit by one bullet that stopped a half inch from his heart. A police officer and Reagan's press secretary, James Brady, were also wounded by the gunfire. Fortunately, all four men survived, although Brady was left partially disabled.[16]

At some underlying level, were McCarthy's actions similar to the behavior of suicide terrorists? We shall see. But first, let's take a look at the other scenario.

A soldier jumps on a grenade that was thrown at his unit.

You've probably heard stories about soldiers who jump on a grenade to save their comrades. In the Western world, it is considered the quintessential act of courage, self-sacrifice, and heroism. That's why screenwriters used it in the 2011 blockbuster film *Captain America*. There was no better way to show what young Steve Rogers was made of than to have him throw his body on a live grenade while everyone else runs for cover. Fortunately for the comic book hero, the grenade turned out to be a dud, but by then, his inner strength had been demonstrated for all to see.

Sadly, this is not just the stuff of fiction. On December 4, 2006, in Baghdad's Adhamiyah district, U.S. Private First Class Ross McGinnis is manning a .50 caliber machine gun on the top of a Humvee when he spots an insurgent on a nearby rooftop who is throwing a grenade right at him. McGinnis swings his hand to deflect it, but the grenade falls inside the vehicle.[17]

There isn't much time for conversation. McGinnis yells, "Grenade!" His platoon sergeant yells, "Where?" "In the truck!" McGinnis responds, ducking into the Humvee and pinning the grenade with his body, just before it explodes. The nineteen-year-old boy—the youngest in his unit—is instantly killed, but all his comrades survive. In recognition of his heroic actions, McGinnis is posthumously awarded the Medal of Honor.[18]

Other cases provide a fuller view of this behavior. For instance, on May 26, 2008, U.S. Army Ranger Leroy Petry and his unit attempted to strike a heavily armed insurgent compound in Afghanistan in broad daylight. Normally, this mission would have been considered too risky, but the Rangers wanted to capture a high-ranking Al Qaeda commander who was believed to be hiding inside.[19]

Immediately upon dropping out of their helicopters, Petry and his comrades face heavy fire from the insurgents' AK-47s. Petry suffers bullet wounds in both legs but continues to fight on. At one point, the Rangers take cover behind a chicken coop, where they radio for support. An enemy grenade lands nearby and explodes, wounding two of Petry's comrades. And then another one lands a few feet from Petry, who lunges toward it, picks it up, and cocks his arm to throw it back. As he's in the process of throwing the grenade back, it explodes. Fortunately Petry survives, having only lost his right hand, which is eventually replaced with a prosthetic. And in 2011, Petry receives the Medal of Honor.[20]

Let's look at one last case. On February 9, 2008, British Lance Corporal Matthew Croucher's Royal Marine unit was sent to investigate a suspected Taliban bomb-making factory. As he walks through the building, Croucher steps on a trip-wire booby trap, which automatically flips a live grenade right at him. He dives toward the grenade, rolls over on the floor, and covers it with the backpack he is still wearing on his back. When the grenade explodes, Croucher is thrown into the air, but he only suffers a broken nose and some cuts and bruises, and his comrades are virtually unscathed. He later recalls that "It took 30 seconds before I realized I was definitely not dead."[21] Croucher eventually receives the George Cross award, which recognizes "acts of the greatest heroism or of the most conspicuous courage in circumstances of extreme danger."[22]

The question is whether McGinnis, Petry, and Croucher were the Western equivalent of suicide terrorists, as Hasan and many scholars have claimed.

SUICIDE OR SACRIFICE?

A woman wearing a bomb vest blows herself up at a café. A pilot deliberately crashes a hijacked jet into a skyscraper. A Secret Service agent steps in front of the president to take a bullet. A soldier jumps on a grenade that was thrown at his unit. According to terrorist propaganda and many presumed experts, all four actions constitute sacrifice, not suicide, and all four are motivated by the same underlying desire to save lives.

At some gut level, we may "know" that these claims seem absurd, but that's not good enough. We need specific ammunition—in the form of undeniable factors and variables—to support our position. So let's identify some of the fundamental differences.

Difference #1: Amount of decision time.

Time does not heal all wounds. Sometimes it makes them worse. And the road to suicide is no exception: the majority of people who kill themselves do so after a significant amount of premeditation.[23] Over time, their desire to die evolves along the continuum of suicidality, from suicidal thoughts to a suicide plan to a suicide attempt.[24]

Similarly, when a suicide bomber finally presses that detonator, it has almost always been preceded by days, weeks, months, or years of thoughts and plans for that final act.[25] Even when the attacker's behavior is triggered by an unexpected personal crisis, many days usually pass while the individual first tries and fails to cope with the trauma, then eventually seeks death as a way out. For instance, 9/11 ringleader Mohamed Atta had suicidal thoughts as early as 1996, even though his specific suicide plan and suicide attempt came much later.[26]

On the other hand, the sacrificial decisions made by McCarthy, McGinnis, Petry, and Croucher were in the heat of the moment. These individuals had no plans to throw themselves in harm's way and potentially die that day. And unlike the suicide terrorists, they did not have days, weeks, months, or years to weigh the options and look for a better solution. These sacrificial acts were split-second responses to unexpected threats that suddenly appeared before them. As McCarthy recalls, he barely had the chance to think before jumping in front of Reagan: "Quite frankly, it probably had little to do with bravery and an awful lot to do with the reaction based upon the training," he humbly insists.[27]

Difference #2: Intention of dying.

Now think back to the definition of suicide from Chapter 1. For an act to constitute a completed suicide, it requires the (1) death of the actor, (2) intention of dying, and (3) self-orchestration of that death.[28] It is the second and third factors that are most relevant here.

Suicide bombers who blow themselves up and suicide terrorists who deliberately crash hijacked jets into buildings clearly intend to die. Although some bomb vests malfunction and some suicide terrorists are arrested before they can strike, it's not clear that any of those who attempt their attacks actually expect to survive. In fact, they often explicitly clarify their intention of dying in suicide notes and "martyrdom" videos.

Commentators often assume that the Secret Service agent who takes a bullet for the president or the soldier who jumps on a grenade similarly intends to die. But that's actually not true. In fact, Secret Service agents specifically wear bulletproof vests to protect themselves in the extremely unlikely event that they do get shot.

And we know that Petry did not intend to die, because he tried to throw the grenade back. But things could have turned out very differently. If the insurgent had waited another second between pulling the pin and throwing the grenade, Petry would have taken the full blast with his body as he lunged toward it. He would have been killed in action—just like PFC Ross McGinnis. If the insurgent had thrown the grenade a second sooner, he would have been greeted by an unwanted surprise coming back over the wall, and Petry would have kept his hand. But regardless of the insurgent's timing, Petry wanted to survive.[29]

Similarly, we know what Croucher intended because he lived to tell the tale. "I thought, 'I've set this bloody thing off and I'm going to do whatever it takes to protect the others,'" Croucher recalled. But he hoped that his backpack of supplies would somehow smother the blast and minimize the shrapnel it expelled. Looking back, Croucher remembers that he "fully expected" to lose a limb, but that he was willing to make that sacrifice "if I could keep my torso and head intact." Of course, he also realized that the selfless action could have cost him his life. "I'm constantly reminded how lucky I am," he recalls, to "beat the grim reaper."[30]

And what about McGinnis? It's likely that his thoughts and intentions were similar to Petry's and Croucher's—only the outcome was different. McGinnis took a very serious risk by ducking back inside the Humvee toward the grenade—but he still had a chance to survive, as they did. It just wasn't his day.

Difference #3: Self-orchestration of one's death.

The third component of suicide is self-orchestration of one's death. This factor is partially related to the previously discussed issue of time: it's hard to orchestrate anything in a few seconds, but suicide terrorists have plenty of time to plan and arrange their own deaths. Most of them are orchestrating their suicides from the moment they volunteer to carry out "martyrdom" attacks. As a career choice, suicide terrorism is an unambiguous statement that you're trying to die.

By contrast, those who become Secret Service agents or soldiers are certainly not just signing up to die. Of course, it's entirely possible for Secret Service agents, soldiers, or anyone else to be suicidal. But the critical point is that these specific scenarios—taking a bullet for the president or jumping on a grenade—are so rare within their respective professions that it would be absurd for suicidal people to try to orchestrate their deaths that way.

In the hundred-plus-year history of the U.S. Secret Service, only one agent has been shot and killed while protecting the president. And what made McGinnis's actions worthy of the Medal of Honor is how unusual they were. Unlike most suicide terrorists, McCarthy, McGinnis, Petry, and Croucher did not orchestrate their situations. These deadly threats—the bullet, the grenade—found them, not the other way around.

Difference #4: Direct result of the action: does it save or harm?

What also made McCarthy's, McGinnis's, Petry's, and Croucher's actions heroic was that they directly saved lives, despite great personal risk. You don't have to be a psychic to see that if McCarthy had not shielded Reagan with his body, the bullet that hit the Secret Service agent would have struck the president instead. Similarly, as McGinnis's sergeant later explained, as soon as the grenade landed in their Humvee, they all faced "certain serious injury or death."[31] McGinnis "had time to jump out of the truck. He chose not to."[32] In turn, Petry had just seen two fellow soldiers wounded by a grenade blast moments earlier, so he wasn't about to run away and let the second grenade do the same. And Croucher's actions also directly saved lives. As he recalls, "I knew a grenade like this has a killing circumference of about five meters. . . . It was a case of either having four of us as fatalities or badly wounded—or one."[33] Even though, at a minimum, he fully expected to lose a limb, Croucher did everything he could to save his comrades.

By contrast, suicide terrorists do not directly save anyone. In general, the further the gap between one's actions and the desired payoff, the less likely those benefits will ever occur. Even if we give suicide terrorists the benefit of the doubt, the indisputable fact remains that a tremendous number of dominoes would have to fall between their attacks and any lives being saved. All they know for sure is that their self-destructive acts will kill themselves and probably others.

In fact, suicide terrorists often make things worse for their own people. Unlike taking a bullet for the president or jumping on a grenade to save your comrades, carrying out a suicide attack often leads to retaliatory violence from the enemy, and thus more deaths on all sides. For instance, Palestinian suicide bombers surely realize that decades of previous suicide attacks haven't gotten Israel to simply surrender or disappear. And the 9/11 hijackers appear to have known that their attacks would lead to *more* deadly violence between the West and the Islamic world, not less.[34]

Whether you're a drunk guy at a bar or a suicide terrorist, there's nothing heroic about picking a fight if you won't be around to settle it. That's not courageous or selfless. That doesn't save anyone.

THE TROLLEY PROBLEM

Deep down, most people know that the direct results of their actions matter. They understand that if you do something bad, it's not heroic—even if it somehow saves lives.

The consensus on this matter has been successfully demonstrated in the lab. In 2008, three Italian scholars conducted a series of experiments to test a famous moral dilemma known as the trolley problem.[35] (Images of the trolley problem are easy to find online). But on this side of the ocean, let's think of trains instead of trolleys. Subjects were asked to evaluate two scenarios, one at a time:

Scenario 1:
A train without passengers and without conductor is traveling at full speed down a track. On the track there are five people, who will surely be killed if the train keeps riding on the actual path. There is also a side-track, on which there is one person.

A passer-by could pull a lever next to the track, and this way deviate the train onto the side-track. The passer-by realizes that, if he does not pull the lever, the five people will be killed. If he pulls the lever instead, the five people will be saved. The passer-by is aware, however, that by pulling the lever the person on the side-track will be killed.[36]

When responding to this scenario, nearly 90 percent of people say that it's acceptable to pull the lever and divert the train to the sidetrack.[37] In doing so, they would be condemning the person on the sidetrack to death, but they would also be saving five other people. They're okay with this tradeoff. Then they're given the second scenario:

Scenario 2:

A train without passengers or conductor is traveling at full speed down a track. On the track there are five people, who will surely be killed if the train keeps riding on the actual path.

A passer-by stands next to the track, and he could push a very fat stranger on the train's path, halting its ride. The passer-by realizes that, if he does not push the stranger, the five people will be killed. If he pushes the stranger instead, the five people will be saved. The passer-by is aware, however, that by pushing him, the stranger will be killed.[38]

When responding to this scenario, the majority of people say that it's *not acceptable* to push the fat stranger in front of the train. Furthermore, 90 percent say that pushing the stranger in front of the train would constitute deliberate murder.[39]

If we just focused on the end results, it would be easy to claim that these scenarios are essentially the same. In both cases, one person would be sacrificed to save five others.

So why are many people willing to pull the lever to divert the train, but not to push the fat stranger in front of the train? Perhaps it's because actions matter. Pulling a lever and diverting a train is not an inherently violent act. But pushing an innocent bystander in front of an oncoming train is horribly cruel—regardless of the reason.

In Germany, a similar experiment was conducted to test the moral differences between what researchers loosely referred to as "throwing a bomb on a person versus throwing a person on a bomb."[40] Participants were asked to evaluate the following scenarios:

Scenario 1:

In a restaurant, a bomb threatens to kill 9 guests. The bomb could be thrown onto the patio, where 1 guest would be killed.

Scenario 2:

In a restaurant, a bomb threatens to kill 9 guests. One guest could be thrown on the bomb, which would kill this 1 guest.[41]

Not surprisingly, the first scenario was rated as much more acceptable than the second one, even though they yield the same end result, in terms of lives lost. Again, actions matter. Throwing yourself on a grenade, like McGinnis did, is selfless and heroic. Grabbing a grenade or bomb and throwing it away, like Petry tried to do, is heroic, too. But throwing an innocent bystander on a bomb is a savage act of murder, regardless of your reason.

When it comes to what they will and won't do, our real heroes always draw a line in the sand. Sacrificing your own life is one thing. But sacrificing another person's life—against his or her will—is something else. If you would really do *anything* to succeed, anything for the cause, or anything to save a life, that's not a sign of courage or commitment. It's a sign that you lack the character and principles required for true heroism, and that you're in desperate need of some perspective.

Would you be willing to rape someone to save a life? How about rape an entire village? Torture the elderly? Slaughter babies? Blow up a café of families with children? True heroes, as well as the civilized people they try to protect, realize that even survival itself isn't worth that kind of moral sacrifice.

At some point, when the costs get too high, it becomes more heroic to risk the possibility of becoming a tragic victim yourself than to coat your hands in other people's blood. That's one of the things that made Christ, Gandhi, and Martin Luther King Jr. so inspiring.

Of course, sometimes the ends really do justify the means. Sometimes lives must be taken. But in those rare cases, good people don't celebrate or pat themselves on the back. They realize that it's a dirty job, but somebody has to do it. It may be necessary, but it's not mankind at its best. It's not how real heroes are made.

THE FOG OF WAR

Terrorist leaders argue that in the long run, suicide terrorism saves lives, because every enemy killed brings their people a step closer to victory.[42] For instance, even if suicide attacks lead to an increase in violent conflict and Muslims dying, this will be offset by the millions who are saved by the eventual defeat of infidel powers.[43]

Armed conflict is often justified in this manner—by all sides. And sometimes it's true that aggression can be appropriate and wars can be just. But regardless of the context or provocation, nothing can change the fact that there is a fundamental difference between taking a life and saving one.

That's why our greatest killers are not celebrated as our greatest heroes. If they were, J. Robert Oppenheimer, who is known as "the father of the atomic bomb," would be one of America's finest. He made it possible for the United States to end World War II with two devastating nuclear attacks that left between 150,000 and 246,000 people dead.[44] Some commentators argue that Oppenheimer's bombs may have indirectly saved many American lives because the alternative—invading Japan—would ultimately have been so costly. But the man himself never received an award for heroism, because all we know for certain is that he helped us *kill*.

Along these same lines, Gunnery Sergeant Carlos N. Hathcock did not receive military honors for being the most effective sniper in the history of the United States Marine Corps. No—although he risked his life for his country and registered a record ninety-three confirmed kills during the Vietnam War, Hathcock did not receive a prestigious military award until he directly saved lives. In 1969, he pulled seven Marines from a burning vehicle, despite being severely wounded and burned himself. It was only after that heroic act that Hathcock received the Silver Star for Valor.[45]

Even in the context of war, where killing is widely rationalized, our greatest heroes are not just killers. It takes far more than that.

YOU ARE WHAT YOU EAT

We are defined by our actions. If you rob someone, then you're a robber. If you torture someone, then you're a torturer. If you kill someone, then you're a killer.

Some people try to claim otherwise, based on excuses, explanations, or extenuating circumstances. "Yes, I missed the meeting, but I'm not someone who misses meetings." Eventually they end up on their death-beds, still clinging to the illusion that they were someone else their entire lives.

Of course, most people have multiple identities. A single individual can be father, lover, gardener, policeman, Nazi. Or sister, wife, lawyer, Muslim, terrorist. Heroic figures like McGinnis, Petry, and Croucher may have also been killers. And some suicide terrorists may have legiti-mately done heroic things during their lives.

But the key is that carrying out a suicide attack wasn't one of them. Even if you believe in their God, their cause, and their right to fight, the act of killing itself is not heroic—for any reason. And when it's done out of pain, desperation, and the desire to die, that just adds layers of heart-break to an already sad situation.

True heroes walk among us. They face each challenge that comes their way and try to do the best they can. And then in fleeting moments of grace, they risk their lives to save people from a tragic fate. It may require the ultimate sacrifice. Or it may not. But live or die, it represents the highest possible caliber of human action. And it defines them forever.

SIX

MURDER-SUICIDE
THE NATURAL COMPARISON

What's the easiest way to become famous?

Hard work? Don't be naïve. Abraham Lincoln once said, "You can be anything you want to be, do anything you set out to accomplish if you hold to that desire with singleness of purpose."[1] But we know better. No amount of desire or hard work will make you a brilliant scientist or a famous basketball player unless you have certain God-given abilities.

Even then, social recognition of your talent largely depends on luck: being born in the right place, at the right time, where your skills are celebrated. Albert Einstein would have been just another caveman in prehistoric days, and Michael Jordan would never have become a global icon if he was born in sixteenth-century Africa. Hard work can help you build a meaningful life full of satisfying accomplishments, but it's no sure bet to make you famous.

Paris Hilton or Kim Kardashian might tell you to release a sex tape. It certainly worked for them. After the news of their illicit behavior spread worldwide, both scored modeling gigs, starred on television shows, and released music albums. But the truth is that they were always different from the rest of us: they benefited from their looks, their riches, and their well-known family names. Lacking those advantages, amateur sex tapes are increasingly common and increasingly ignored.

YouTube offers more egalitarian opportunities. Anyone with an idea and access to a video camera can potentially become an instant, worldwide sensation. For instance, a video diary from crying nineteen-year-old Britney Spears fan Chris Crocker received more than four million views in just two days.[2] "Leave Britney alone!" he sobbed with mock tears, and people couldn't help but tune in and laugh. And a recording of Andrew Meyer's attention-grabbing confrontation of U.S. senator John Kerry, which ended in a police struggle and Meyer yelling "Don't tase me, bro," received more than five million internet hits.[3] Other videos, capturing everything from clever pet tricks to stupid music parodies, have produced immediate online celebrities. However, it is nearly impossible to predict what will become popular and what will not. Millions of people who've tried the YouTube path to success have gotten absolutely nowhere.

No—the cold hard fact is there's only one surefire way for an average person to become famous. Kill innocent people. The more random your victims, the better, because it sends the message that no one is safe. And when they're scared, people pay attention.

DELUSIONS OF "GRANDEUR"

For instance, there is nothing I could do—no matter how skilled I am or how hard I work—that would get me more attention for this book than committing mass murder. That's a fact. And like many law-abiding people, I find the fantasy of fame, and everything that comes with it, incredibly alluring.

So why wouldn't I consider grabbing a semiautomatic and engaging in the best PR move of all time? Well, for one thing, there's the morality issue: we have been told that killing people is wrong. I agree with that principle. On the other hand, when it comes to rationalizing their actions and numbing their consciences, human beings can be remarkably creative.[4] Surely, given the thousands of people who die around the world every day, there must be some way I could convince myself that the ends justify the means. However, there's also the other issue: the punitive consequences. Even if I could rationalize killing and then sleep soundly at night, I have no interest in a firsthand experience with society's wrath.

FAME AND GLORY

But suicidal killers get to have their cake and eat it, too. They combine the only surefire way for an average person to become famous with the only foolproof way to kill people and get away with it. By committing acts of *murder-suicide* that strike random, innocent victims, these individuals get immediate attention and fame that will last far beyond their own deaths. At the same time, they do not have to suffer arrest, detainment, or criminal punishment. They also avoid the psychological costs of killing: the guilt and shame that can result from having to live with the memories of slaughtering helpless men, women, and children.

The desire to acquire fame and glory through killing, and then escape the consequences, is a critical similarity between certain suicide bombers, rampage shooters, and school shooters. In general, when it comes to violent crime, fame is an extremely rare motive. There have been some serial killers who directly sought fame in the past, but they were far and few between.[5] The fact that this otherwise unusual motive is so common for both suicide terrorists and other perpetrators of murder-suicide suggests an underlying connection between them.

Prior research indicates that for many suicide terrorists, the fame and glory that comes with "martyrdom" in the Middle East appeal as compensation for their personal failures and insecurities.[6] Such individuals become fixated on the idea that after their death, they will be elevated to the highest levels of social status—as will their families. Thus, for suicidal people who feel like failures, losers, victims, or outcasts, the path to fame and glory is extraordinarily enticing. As psychologist Arie Kruglanksi and his colleagues explain, despite suicide terrorists' attempts to portray their deaths as noble sacrifices, many are actually engaging in a "quest for personal significance."[7] Other scholars have made similar findings. In a deeper sense, many suicide terrorists' desperation for fame and glory is a desire for what Mohammed Hafez refers to as "redemption" and the "salvation of self," what Post describes as "significance for the insignificant," and what Larry Pastor summarizes as "self-fulfillment . . . status advancement, [and] conspicuous demonstration of bravery."[8] Instead of being remembered as the unmarried girl who became pregnant, the boy who contracted HIV, the woman who committed adultery, or the man who struggled with mental health problems, these suicidal individuals have a chance to redefine their social identity—once and for all.

Recruiters of suicide terrorists capitalize on these selling points with their production and distribution of martyrdom videos, murals, calendars, key chains, posters, postcards, and pennants.[9] This is one of those times when the terrorist organization's priorities are the same as the suicidal individual's. Both want attention. The terrorist organization benefits from publicity because their strategy is based on reaching as many hearts and minds as possible, then rallying them to the cause. And the suicide bombers become convinced that after death they will be eternally famous as heroic "martyrs," even though they will not get to experience their glory in the physical world.[10]

For instance, the aforementioned suicide bomber Shadi Nassar is an extreme, though fitting, example of this phenomenon. As you may recall from Chapter 3, he suffered from a permanent disability and chronic epileptic episodes, was constantly rejected, humiliated, and mocked by his peers, and was insulted and abused by enemy soldiers. When he ultimately sought an escape from his painful life, suicide terrorism was far more appealing than conventional suicide because it could provide him with the attention and respect he so desperately craved. Sure enough, soon after he blew himself up, there were posters with Nassar's image on every wall and corner of his village.[11] He achieved far more fame in death than he ever could in life.

Many suicidal rampage killers and school shooters also carry out their attacks for fame and glory. Sociologist Ralph Larkin identifies this as a critical motive for Virginia Tech killer Seung Hui Cho, Columbine killers Eric Harris and Dylan Klebold, Nebraska mall shooter Robert Hawkins, and Red Lake High School shooter Jeffrey Weise, among others.[12] He labels it "killing for notoriety" and explains that "The body count, almost always innocent bystanders, exists primarily as a method of generating media attention."[13] This is remarkably similar to the strategy behind suicide terrorism. And much like suicide terrorists, these shooters appear to be compensating for their lack of social status. As school shooting expert Katherine Newman explains, "they are searching for a way to retire their public image as dweebs and misfits, exchanging it for something more alluring: the dangerous, violent man."[14] Much like suicide bombers, these shooters often leave behind letters, manifestos, and videos so that their new identity will live on.

For instance, after Hawkins was fired from his job at McDonalds, arrested by police for underage alcohol possession, and dumped by his girlfriend, he resorted to lethal violence to increase his status.[15] Before he opened fire at a mall—killing eight and wounding four, then shooting himself in the head—Hawkins wrote in his suicide note, "I've been a piece of shit my entire life; it seems this is my only option . . . just think tho, I'm gonna be fuckin famous."[16]

Similarly, in videotapes, Harris and Klebold discussed the publicity that would result from their Columbine attack. As Harris exclaimed, "Isn't it fun to get the respect that we're going to deserve?"[17] They also talked about their expectations that a movie would be made about their lives. Klebold claimed that "Directors will be fighting over this story," and he and Harris argued about whether it would be better to have Steven Spielberg or Quentin Tarantino in charge of the movie's production.[18] Harris hoped that their future film would include "a lot of foreshadowing and dramatic irony."[19] And sure enough, Harris and Klebold received a tremendous amount of media attention for their attacks, including countless articles, books, movies, and documentaries. They even got their faces on the cover of *Time* magazine. There was virtually nothing else these teenage boys from a small Colorado town could have done to become so famous. And as we will see later on, their desperate craving for social recognition was directly linked to their suicidal urges.

A NATURAL COMPARISON

Of course, the desire for fame and glory is not the only underlying connection between suicide terrorists and other perpetrators of murder-suicide. Not by a long shot.

Unfortunately, most scholars have assumed that suicide terrorists have nothing significant in common with suicidal rampage, workplace, and school shooters.[20] In fact, previous research comparing these various types of killers is virtually nonexistent.[21] When these different types have been discussed in the same context, it has primarily been to emphasize the apparent differences and quickly dismiss any similarities.[22] In large part, this is because of the common misconceptions discussed in Chapter 2. Since the so-called experts insist that suicide terrorists are not suicidal, why would they bother to compare them with other types of killers who clearly want to die?

On the surface, perhaps the most significant difference between suicide terrorists and suicidal rampage, workplace, and school shooters is the role of organizations: suicide terrorists usually work with them, while the others almost always act on their own. However, as reviewed earlier, many suicide terrorists are self-selected, have their own primary goals distinct from the organization, and decide for themselves that they're ready to die. For these individuals, the organization may provide rationalizations for violence, suggested targets, and the explosive device. At the same time, those who act alone—whether they're suicide terrorists or other types of suicidal killers—usually receive these same things, just from different sources. They may get their rationalizations for violence from radical websites, their ideas for targets from news coverage of previous attacks, and their weapons from local shops. Of course, context usually influences human behavior, but these different types of perpetrators still share an underlying desire to kill and be killed.

Nowhere is the overlap between suicide terrorists and other perpetrators of murder-suicide more evident than in the aforementioned case of Ali Hassan Abu Kamal (see Chapter 3). He was the suicide terrorist who attacked the Empire State Building using the strategy of a mass shooter, which included shooting himself in the head.

There is also evidence of the reverse: rampage, workplace, and school shooters who both act and attack like typical suicide terrorists. For instance, past school shooters have referred to themselves as "martyrs," the same self-glorifying term used by suicide bombers.[23] Some have also claimed to fight for an ideological cause, whether it's neo-Nazism, eugenics, masculine supremacy, or an antigovernment revolution.[24] In addition, suicide bombers commonly target public buses; a week before George Sodini went on a murder-suicide rampage at a Pittsburgh gym, he brought a grenade on a public bus.[25] And when Sebastian Bosse was found after shooting five people at his high school and then killing himself, he had explosive devices strapped to his body.[26]

Columbine killers Harris and Klebold essentially used suicide terrorist tactics as well. Before they killed themselves and others with guns, they planted numerous large-scale propane bombs, which were intended to blow up the cafeteria and everyone inside, including nearly five hundred students.[27] It was only after these bombs failed to explode that they began shooting and throwing homemade pipe bombs.

Furthermore, three years before 9/11, Harris wrote that he and Klebold would like to "hijack a hell of a lot of bombs and crash a plane into NYC with us inside."[28] It is no mere coincidence that Harris envisioned almost the exact same attack that Al Qaeda's nineteen hijackers eventually carried out. They were attracted to the similar attack methods because at some deeper level, they had far more in common than we've ever realized before.

THE WORST KIND OF MIDLIFE CRISIS

A powerful comparison can be made between two attackers who both struck in 2009: forty-eight-year-old rampage shooter George Sodini and thirty-nine-year-old suicide terrorist Nidal Hasan.

Many experts would claim that Sodini was crazy, suicidal, and someone who killed for personal reasons, while Hasan was ideologically motivated, a "martyr," and someone who killed for strategic reasons. And based on these misconceptions, government investigations into Hasan's behavior have focused almost exclusively on his radicalization and embrace of Islamic extremism.[29] However, as noted earlier, more than two hundred thousand Americans believe that suicide bombings are justified to defend Islamic interests, yet only a very few actually carry out attacks.[30]

It's true that Hasan had radical beliefs, but what made him different from other radicals was his personal problems. As we will see, Sodini was also abnormal—*for almost the exact same reasons.* Islamic extremism influenced Hasan's choice of target and where his suicidal rage would explode, but it was not the underlying cause of his behavior. If Hasan had been Christian or Jewish, he would have still had severe personal problems and the inability to handle them. He just would have attacked somewhere else instead.

The details from these two suicidal killers' lives tell the full story. Let's do a side-by-side comparison of their paths to murder-suicide.

First of all, both were socially isolated:

George Sodini	*Nidal Hasan*
Sodini explained in his online blog that "I haven't met anybody recently (past 30 years) who I want to be close friends with OR who want to be close friends with me. . . . [This] makes me realize how TOTALLY ALONE—a deeper word is ISOLATED—I am.[31]	Hasan's aunt recalled that he "did not make many friends" and his landlord reported that Hasan "pretty much kept to himself—never had any visitors."[32] By some accounts, Hasan's best friend was actually a pet parakeet whom he used to chew food for and let eat from his mouth. Unfortunately, one day he rolled over while sleeping and actually crushed the bird to death, leaving him—once again—all alone.[33]

As a way out of their loneliness, both desperately sought wives. But despite the urgency of their advanced age and closing window for romance, both failed to do so:

George Sodini	*Nidal Hasan*
Sodini lamented that he hadn't had a girlfriend for twenty-four years, hadn't had sex for nineteen years, and saw no hope for the future. As he explained, "A man needs a woman for confidence. He gets a boost on the job, career, with other men, and everywhere else when he knows inside he has someone to spend the night with and who is also a friend. . . . [But] 30 million women rejected me."[34]	Hasan had been searching for a suitable wife for years, and even resorted to personal ads, with no success.[35] As discussed earlier, this pressure can become particularly tough for Muslim men, given that marriage is a religious duty. But for even longer than Mohamed Atta and Hani Hanjour, Hasan struggled to find a bride. As a local imam from Hasan's mosque recalled, "He wanted a woman who prayed five times a day and wears a hijab, and maybe the

women he met were not complying with those things."[36]

Both were also having difficulties at work:

George Sodini	Nidal Hasan
Sodini was afraid of budget cuts and layoffs. As he explained, "When I began 10 years ago, this used to be a nice place to work. . . . [But] the big problem on my mind now is that my job will end soon. One project is being transitioned to another. The other one I am solely responsible, but is being fast tracked to production. I estimate maybe a month. I am not ready for the job market."[37]	A U.S. Senate committee investigation concluded that Hasan was a "barely competent psychiatrist" and "a chronic poor performer during his residency and fellowship . . . ranked in the bottom 25 percent. He was placed on probation and remediation and often failed to meet basic job expectations such as showing up for work."[38]

Like many perpetrators of murder-suicide, Sodini and Hasan both felt like victims who had been bullied by others:

George Sodini	Nidal Hasan
Sodini pointed the finger at his family. As he wrote, "Brother was actually counter-productive and would try to embarrass me or discourage my efforts when pursuing things. . . . Useless bully . . . He calls only when he wants something."[39] His mother was apparently even worse: "Don't piss her off or she will be mad and vindictive for years. She actually thinks she's normal. Very dominant. Her way and only her way with no flexibility toward everyone in the household. A power and control thing . . . Why are people vicious with their closest ones?"[40]	Hasan's parents had both died by 2001. Of course, that was also the same year as the September 11 attacks, which led Hasan to feel like an instant target for many newly racist and prejudiced Americans. Hasan complained to relatives that due to his ethnicity and Islamic beliefs, fellow soldiers were harassing him and calling him a number of slurs, including "camel jockey."[41] The relatives claim that this unfair persecution made Hasan begin to look for a way out of the military.

Another link between these suicidal killers is that both seemed to be pushed over the edge by impending or anticipated crises:

George Sodini	Nidal Hasan
As Sodini wrote, "I predict I won't survive the next layoff. That is when there is no point to continue. . . . The paycheck is all I have left. The future holds nothing for me. . . . Also unlikely to find another similar job. I	For Hasan, the last straw was his belief that he was about to be deployed to Iraq or Afghanistan. As his cousin explained, "that was probably his worst nightmare. . . . He was mortified by the idea of having

guess then is when I take care of things."[42]

to deploy. . . . He had people telling him on a daily basis the horrors they saw over there."[43]

Ultimately, due to some combination of individual, social, and situational factors, both Sodini and Hasan developed severe mental health problems:

George Sodini	Nidal Hasan
Sodini summarized on his blog that "I know I will never enjoy life. This is an over 30 year trend. Some people are happy, some are miserable. It is difficult to live almost continuously feeling an undercurrent of fear, worry, discontentment and helplessness. . . . Life is over."[44] He further admitted that he had been planning to commit suicide for at least nine months, and that he had somehow fooled "99% of the people who know me well [and] don't even think I was this crazy."[45]	Hasan's mental health problems are slightly harder to document, but only because he tried more to hide them. Naturally, given his struggles with social isolation, failure to find a wife, work problems, perceived victimization, and an impending crisis, we would expect Hasan to have an altered state of mind. In addition, the psychiatrists and supervisors who oversaw Hasan's training had expressed concerns about his psychological competency, and some even thought he might be "psychotic."[46]

Both killers became angry, suicidal, and desperate for a way out. Sodini began to plot his attack against a local gym, and Hasan made preparations to strike a military base. Much like Sodini, Hasan now took to the internet to express his thoughts. In an online post nearly six months before his attack, Hasan tried to clarify the precise differences between suicide and "martyrdom" so that he could be sure to commit the latter.[47]

At this point, the biggest difference between the two suicidal attackers was their honesty and self-awareness. While Sodini acknowledged that his goals were personal, Hasan depicted himself as a selfless "martyr" motivated by politics and the desire to save other Muslims.[48] And while Sodini acknowledged his suicidal desires, Hasan tried to mask his death wish as something much more heroic.

And then they struck:

George Sodini	Nidal Hasan
On August 4, 2009, Sodini walked into an aerobics class and placed a duffel bag with four guns on the ground. He flipped off the lights, reached into the bag, and began shooting. His targets were all unarmed women: he killed three of them and wounded nine more before shooting himself in the head.	On November 5, 2009, Hasan walked into a military building, shouted "Allahu Akbar!" ["God is Great!"], and began shooting soldiers. He killed thirteen and wounded thirty-one. He was attempting "suicide by cop" and expected to be killed by military police.[49] However, they shot him in the spine, leaving him paralyzed.

As should be expected, given his military training, Hasan was the better-armed and more efficient killer. He fired more than two hundred bullets, while Sodini got off approximately fifty shots.[50]

Notably, in both cases, the attackers did not hunt down a specific list of people who had insulted them or done them wrong. Instead, both killers' rage erupted against seemingly random victims—people they did not personally know or have any specific vendetta against:

George Sodini	*Nidal Hasan*
Sodini attacked the symbolic source of his pain and despair: young, attractive women in an aerobics class who represented the "millions" of potential wives and girlfriends who had rejected him over the years.	Hasan attacked his own symbol of pain and victimization: American soldiers who represented the bullies who had supposedly persecuted him for his ethnicity and religious beliefs.

Overall, Sodini and Hasan were remarkably similar perpetrators of murder-suicide. Anyone who gets too hung up on their respective labels—"rampage shooter" versus "suicide terrorist"—is clearly missing the underlying connections. These desperate killers had a tremendous amount in common, and one of the most significant areas of overlap is that they were both suicidal.

THE BIGGER PICTURE

In-depth case studies reveal a lot, but we should also look at the bigger picture. This book presents the first combined quantitative assessment of suicide terrorists and rampage, workplace, and school shooters who attempt suicide. By comparing these different perpetrators of murder-suicide across key variables, it shows both where there are statistically significant differences and where they appear almost identical.

Since these attacks are quite rare, the goal was to analyze all qualifying cases that occurred in the United States between 1990 and 2010, not just a sample. Focusing on attacks in just one country helps control for cross-cultural differences in data availability. Also, in order to eliminate more conventional murder-suicides, attacks were excluded if they involved fewer than two victims or were primarily domestic in nature (targeting family members or significant others).[51]

The resulting dataset thus includes eighty-one suicide attacks: twelve terrorist strikes, eighteen rampage shootings, sixteen school shootings, and thirty-five workplace shootings.[52] Although eighty-one cases may not seem like a lot, it is much larger than the previous seven best studies of school shooters, all of which used sample sizes of fewer than forty-two attackers.[53]

Categorizing the attackers was straightforward. The school shooters were all current or past students attacking at their school or university; the workplace shooters were all current or past employees attacking at their work. The rampage shootings included all public attacks that did not fall into another category and involved some symbolic or random victims. And the Federal Bureau of Investigation's definition was used to assign attacks to the suicide terrorism category: "The unlawful use of force or violence against persons or property to intimidate or coerce a Government, the civilian population, or any segment thereof, in further-ance of political or social objectives."[54]

Of course, since there are more than one hundred different defini-tions of terrorism around the world, categorizing attacks as suicide ter-rorism naturally depends on the specific standard used. However, the attacks in this dataset all unambiguously targeted the U.S. government, and Table 6.1 outlines the perpetrators' attempts "to intimidate or co-erce . . . in furtherance of political or social objectives."

Overall, seventy-six of the attacks were committed by lone offend-ers; five involved leaders and supporters or followers. To avoid skewing the quantitative analysis toward the few attacks with larger numbers of support personnel, the lead perpetrators in each joint attack were ana-lyzed, but not those who played supporting roles. By limiting this study to the eighty-one offenders who were the driving force behind their re-spective eighty-one suicide attacks, we ensure that their cases get equal comparative weight. See Appendix B for a full list of offenders, attack designations, and attack locations.

If the conventional wisdom about suicide terrorists is true, there should be very few similarities between suicide terrorists and these other perpetrators of murder-suicide. On the other hand, if suicide terrorists are in fact suicidal, like these other killers, we should see a number of important similarities.

Table 6.1 Suicide Terrorism Attacks in the United States, 1990–2010

Target	Date	Political Objective
CIA Headquarters, Langley, VA	January 25, 1993	to stop the U.S. government and CIA's involvement in Muslim countries[a]
Empire State Building, New York, NY	February 23, 1997	to stop the U.S. government's use of Israel as "an instrument" against Palestinians[b]
Riverside City Hall, Riverside, CA	October 6, 1998	to stop the U.S. government's "public dishonor and ritualized humiliation of African people and particularly African-American school children"[c]
World Trade Center, New York, NY; U.S. Pentagon and U.S. Capitol Building, Washington, DC[d]	September 11, 2001	to stop the U.S.'s government's "oppression, lies, immorality and debauchery," support of Israel, and involvement in Muslim countries[e]
Bank of America, Tampa Bay, FL[f]	January 5, 2002	to support Osama bin Laden and the September 11, 2001, terrorist attacks[g]
Los Angeles Airport, Los Angeles, CA	July 4, 2002	to influence U.S. policy in the Middle East, particularly regarding its support of Israel[h]
Kirkwood City Council, Kirkwood, MO	February 7, 2008	to "get people's attention" and fight against the U.S. government's violation of constitutional rights to free speech[i]
Knoxville U.U. Church, Knoxville, TN	July 27, 2008	to "kill Liberals," "stop the downfall of this great nation," and "encourage other like-minded people to do what I've done"[j]

Target	Date	Political Objective
Fort Hood Army Base, Fort Hood, TX	November 5, 2009	to protest U.S wars in Muslim countries and "help save Muslims by killing enemy soldiers"[k]
IRS Offices, Austin, TX	February 18, 2010	to make people "wake up and see the pompous political thugs and their mindless minions for what they are"[l]

a. "Mir Aimal Kasi," *Clark County Prosecuting Attorney,* 2002, accessed February 24, 2011, http://www.clarkprosecutor.org/html/death/US/kasi807.htm.

b. Tom Hays, "N.Y. Killer Carried Political Note," *Associated Press,* February 25, 1997.

c. Jose Arballo, "City Hall Shooter Recalled as 'Very Intelligent Man,' *Press-Enterprise,* October 5, 2008, accessed February 22, 2011, http://www.pe.com/reports/2008/cityhall/stories/PE_News_Local_S_neale05.2eb926.htm.

d. Hijacked United Airlines Flight 93 never reached its target, crashing near Shanksville, Pennsylvania.

e. Osama bin Laden, "Letter to the American People," *Guardian,* November 24, 2002, accessed March 12, 2011, http://www.guardian.co.uk/world/2002/nov/24/theobserver.

f. Since this attack harmed no one except the offender himself, it did not qualify for the quantitative analysis.

g. "Police: Tampa Flyer Voiced Support for Bin Laden," *CNN,* January 6, 2002, accessed December 3, 2011, http://articles.cnn.com/2002–01–06/us/tampa.crash_1_plane-charles-j-bishop-crash?_s=PM:US.

h. Charles Feldman, "Federal Investigators: L.A. Airport Shooting a Terrorist Act," *CNN,* September 5, 2002, accessed March 11, 2011, http://archives.cnn.com/2002/US/09/04/lax.shooting/index.html.

i. "Six Dead in Missouri City Council Shooting," *CBS News,* February 8, 2008, accessed March 14, 2011, http://www.cbsnews.com/stories/2008/02/07/national/main3805672.shtml.

j. Jim Adkisson, "To Whom It May Concern," *Knoxville News Sentinel,* February 10, 2009, accessed March 14, 2011, http://web.knoxnews.com/pdf/021009church-manifesto.pdf.

k. "What Nidal Hasan Said About Suicide Bombers."

l. Stack, "Raw Data: Joseph Stack Suicide Manifesto."

WHAT THE STATS SHOW

A series of statistical tests—including ANOVA, Chi-Square tests, and multinomial logistic regression—were conducted in order to determine whether there were any significant differences between the four types of attackers.[57]

Overall, findings squarely support the evidence that suicide terrorists are suicidal.[58] As expected, the suicide terrorists were very similar to the suicidal rampage shooters and school shooters. In fact, if there was a type of killer that stood out as most different from the others, it was actually the workplace shooters, not the suicide terrorists.

Much like suicidal rampage killers and school shooters, the suicide terrorists struggled with social marginalization, family problems, work or school problems, mental health problems, and precipitating crises. When it came to these problems, *there was not a statistically significant difference between the three types of offenders*. These variables are particularly meaningful because they have been identified as risk factors for both conventional suicide[59] and murder-suicide.[60] In addition, all types of offenders were overwhelming male and (with the exception of the younger school shooters) of similar average ages.

Furthermore, suicide terrorists, rampage shooters, and school shooters were almost equally likely to prepare an explanation or suicide note before striking, and they were almost equally likely to successfully end up dead as a result of their attacks. In the case of rampage and school shooters, experts accurately differentiate between the perpetrators' self-aggrandizing rhetoric, which may include claims of acting "for the greater good," and the true psychological root of their actions. It's time to similarly look beyond the rhetoric of suicide terrorists and recognize the true causes of their behavior.

With the exception of the September 11, 2001, attacks, suicide terrorist attacks in the United States from 1990 to 2010 were actually *less lethal* than rampage, workplace, and school shootings involving suicide attempts over the same period. This directly contradicts the conventional wisdom that suicide terrorists are rational political actors who sacrifice their lives to maximize the destructive effects of their attacks, while rampage, workplace, and school shooters are mentally unbalanced individuals who simply "snap" and begin shooting.[61]

The similar frequency of suicide terrorist attacks and suicidal rampage and school shootings is another indicator of their underlying connection. In the United States from 1990 to 2010, there were twelve suicide terrorism attacks, eighteen rampage shootings, and sixteen school shootings that met the criteria for this study (see Table 6.2). It's no mere coincidence that these attacks occurred at similar rates. These perpetrators were all driven by the same types of homicidal-suicidal desires. If previous scholars were correct that suicide terrorists were completely different than these other killers, we would expect far more variation in the number of cases in the United States, per year, per type, especially considering the variation in world events that could trigger politically minded killers.

Again, as it turns out, it was the workplace shooters, not the suicide terrorists, who stood out from the rest. Their attacks were about twice as common as the others, but caused only about half as many casualties.

Table 6.2 Comparison of Different Types of Suicide Attackers in the United States, 1990–2010

Variable	Suicide Terrorists n = 12	Rampage Shooters n = 18	School Shooters n = 16	Work- place Shooters n = 35
Sex (% male)	100%	100%	94%	97%
Age (mean)	41.42	37.11	20.22	41.66
Social marginalization	50%	44%	75%	37%
Family problems	41%	56%	56%	23%
Work/school problems	75%	50%	88%	97%
Mental health problems	75%	78%	94%	43%
Precipitating crisis event	58%	56%	63%	80%
Suicide note or written explanation	67%	56%	50%	11%
Successful suicide	67%	89%	69%	91%
Fatalities per attack (excluding 9/11 outlier)	3.25	5.67	5.19	3.26
Casualties per attack (excluding 9/11 outlier)	12.38	10.56	12.81	5.94

Workplace shooters were significantly less likely to have struggled with family or mental health problems before their attacks, and their actions were more commonly linked to specific crisis events.

In quite a few cases, the workplace shooters got suspended, reprimanded, or fired by their employers, and they seem to have just "snapped." Some barely stopped to think. Instead of carefully planning their acts of murder-suicide—like the others usually do—the workers just grabbed a gun and went back for revenge.

A closer look suggests that the workplace shooters may actually be the most "normal" of the four types of attackers, from a cultural, motivational, and behavioral standpoint. For instance, relatively ordinary frustrated employees sometimes joke about "going postal" and ending it all. And this behavior has been casually depicted as an almost natural response to work strains in numerous forms of popular culture, including television shows like *Seinfeld* and *The Simpsons*. But at least in the United States, there does not appear to be a parallel mainstream fantasy of killing strangers in a public place or shooting students at a school, much less committing an act of suicide terrorism.

TWO ROADS TO HELL

Let's get back to the Columbine killers, because there is something else they can show us about suicide terrorists.

If variety is the spice of life, Harris and Klebold demonstrate the darker side of diversity. Like snowflakes and fingerprints, no two suicidal killers are identical. But the differences between these young men were not subtle. In fact, from a psychological standpoint, they were almost polar opposites. Nevertheless, they eventually shared the same desire to kill and be killed.

Klebold fits the classic stereotype of a suicidal person. He was painfully shy and insecure as a child. He started school a year early, which meant he was younger and smaller than his peers, and his parents enrolled him in a "High Intellectual Potential" program, which actually sheltered and isolated him further. In sports, he was afraid to lose. With family and friends, he was desperate for hugs and reassurance. He felt so vulnerable that when kids laughed at him during normal social interactions, he would start screaming and freak out.[62]

As he grew older, Klebold made friends, but he remained a social outcast. Despite his intelligence, he often felt inferior, and this manifested as self-loathing. As he explained in his journal, "I don't fit in here. . . . I don't know what i do wrong with people, it's like they are set out to hate & insult me, i never know what to say or do."[63] He dreaded the constant pattern that dominated his life: "go to school, be scared & nervous, hoping that people can accept me."[64] Klebold soon became obsessed with a girl named Harriet who didn't even know him. He wrote her a love letter, then threw it out, ever frustrated by his own insecurity. "She in reality doesn't give a good fuck about me," he lamented, "no LOVE."[65] Later, his anger settled into despair. "A dark time, infinite sadness. I want to find love."[66]

The teenage Klebold eventually began self-medicating by drinking vodka alone in his room. More than two years before the Columbine attack, he explained that "Thinking of suicide gives me hope that i'll be in my place wherever i go after this life—that i'll finally not be at war w. myself, the world, the universe."[67] But his thoughts of a conventional suicide eventually gave way to murder-suicide, based largely on the urgings of Harris. Klebold began to direct his self-hatred outward, blaming others for his pain.

Meanwhile, Harris was a full-blown psychopath. This diagnosis was confirmed by the world's leading psychologists at an FBI summit, three months after the attacks.[68] However, to this day, major misconceptions remain about Harris's psychology and motives. Esteemed journalist Dave Cullen wrote the authoritative book on Columbine. As he explains, "Ten years afterward, Eric still baffled the public, *which insisted on assessing his motives through a 'normal' lens. Eric was neither normal nor insane. Psychopathy represents a third category.*"[69] This should sound very familiar: as we saw in Chapter 2, commentators have been making a very similar "normal" versus "insane" oversimplification with suicide terrorists that has led them to dismiss the third category of "suicidal."

In any case, psychopaths are different from the rest of us in two major ways. First, they lack the normal range of human emotions, including empathy and compassion. To fill this void, they "act big." They are usually thrill seekers and risk takers, and they enjoy provoking big reactions from other people—even if they have to make them suffer. Second, they are terrific liars and manipulators. Despite their shortcomings, they are extremely skilled at faking empathy and convincing others that they're relatively normal. Not surprisingly, this ability to act without conscience and do what others are afraid to do—then get away with it—is extremely empowering. It often breeds arrogance and the belief that they are superior to everyone else.

Harris was a classic case, right down to the risk taking, manipulation, and arrogance. He broke his parents' rules, led Klebold on vandalism "missions," made death threats against other students, hacked into school computers, and eventually got caught stealing electronics equipment from a parked van. But ever the skilled liar, Harris talked his way out of any serious punishment, which only left him more emboldened.[70]

Unlike Klebold, Harris did not feel inferior—but he was still extremely bothered by insults from fellow students. As past research on self-esteem has shown, people with inflated egos can be particularly sensitive because they have further to fall.[71] If you think you're a perfect "10," anyone who calls you a "9" is essentially insulting you. Harris believed he was better than everyone else and that all of humanity should bow down to him. When that didn't happen, he became enraged. "If you got a problem with my thoughts, come tell me and i'll kill you," he posted online. "DEAD PEOPLE DON'T ARGUE! God DAMMIT I AM PISSED!!"[72] So he plotted his revenge.

Harris's top priority was murder, not suicide. As he wrote in his journal, "I have a goal to destroy as much as possible. . . . God I want to torch and level everything in this whole fucking area."[73] It was Harris, not Klebold, who was the first to make propane bombs, pipe bombs, and Molotov cocktails—Harris, not Klebold, who pulled the strings to get them guns. Without the push from his best friend, Klebold would have almost certainly killed only himself, if that. On the other hand, Harris primarily considered suicide as an exclamation point to murder. After punishing his enemies, he expected to go out in a blaze of glory, whether that involved a bullet from a cop or blowing himself up inside the school.[74]

As Harris posted on his website, for everyone to see, "I will rig up explosives all over a town and detonate each one of them at will after I mow down a whole fucking area full of you snotty ass rich mother fucking high strung godlike attitude having worthless pieces of shit whores . . . i don't care if I live or die in the shootout, all I want to do is kill and injure as many of your pricks as I can!"[75]

The differences between the two Columbine shooters suggest that similar variation must exist among suicide terrorists as well. Some will be depressed, insecure, and self-loathing, while others will be arrogant, risk-taking psychopaths. And there may be other types as well.

Even if they all end up in the same place—hell—that doesn't mean they all get there the same way.

SEVEN

THE FOUR TYPES OF SUICIDE TERRORISTS

D on't drink the Kool-Aid.

Don't drink it in the figurative sense, when jihadist leaders and presumed experts try to convince you that suicide terrorists are not suicidal. And certainly don't drink it in the literal sense, if you're getting instructions from a radical cult leader and there's a strong smell of poison coming from your cup.

That's exactly what hundreds of people did in Jonestown, Guyana, in 1978, as part of the largest mass suicide in human history. The images are harrowing. At first glance, it looks like hundreds of people simply lay down and fell asleep. They seem peaceful: a multicolored collage of T-shirts, jeans, and dresses—men, women, and children—black, white, and Asian.[1] But then we realize that they're never waking up. We see some on their stomachs, faces in the grass; others on their sides, arms draped over loved ones. We see short little kid legs—far too small to have run their last race, stepped their last steps.

More than nine hundred people committed suicide that day, due to their radical beliefs and blind obedience to cult leader Jim Jones. Or so we've been told. *Time* magazine and *Newsweek* both proclaimed the Peoples Temple congregation to be "The Cult of Death."[2] And Jones himself tried to portray his community as a tight-knit, ideologically committed group of people willing to sacrifice their lives to serve "the will of Sovereign Being."[3] He claimed that they were performing a "revolutionary" act of "protesting the conditions of an inhumane world": "We lay down our lives to protest in what's being done. The criminality of people, the cruelty of people."[4]

The truth is far more complex. Jones was a charismatic speaker, but also a drug addict with serious psychological problems and a history of suicidal behavior.[5] On that fateful day, he needed everyone dead to preserve the illusion of total commitment and uniformity. However, there was actually a wide variety of motives among his followers.

Some people were suicidal in the conventional sense. They had been desperately searching for answers to their own problems, which is why the cult appealed to them in the first place. When it failed to meet their expectations, and Jones failed to be the true savior they so badly needed, they lost all hope. Considering what they'd been promised, their struggles at Jonestown only made things worse. As former member Dianne Scheid explains:

> Peoples Temple and Jonestown did not come close to being a "Heaven on Earth" or a socially egalitarian community. Sleep deprivation, long meetings into the night, working from dawn to dusk (including the children), "white night" sirens blaring at any time day or night . . . [Many people] were just plain tired, tired of being oppressed, tired of feeling there was no hope of ever being able to get out, just tired of being tired. So like a wolf that will gnaw off its leg to free itself from a trap, many chose the only option before them.[6]

Many of these people drank the Kool-Aid because they genuinely wanted to die—just like suicide terrorists. In fact, some of the cult members had previously volunteered *to carry out suicide bombings*. For instance, one wrote a letter to Jones explaining that "I am again willing to go and get our enemies. I will make sure that each time I get one, I will be ready to blow myself up."[7] Another suggested that "If I could get to a conference of traitors, I could detonate myself in their midst."[8]

Other cult members were pressured and coerced into committing suicide. They decided they would rather kill themselves than disappoint

Jones and their fellow members, risk the unknown consequences of trying to escape, or refuse and face a violent confrontation with the Jonestown security team.[9] For these people, a painless death was preferable to a frightening and uncertain life. Given the alternative—which may have been awkward, embarrassing, traumatic, or even hopeless— they chose suicide. Jones pleaded for them to "die with respect, die with a degree of dignity. Lay down your life with dignity."[10] And sure enough, instead of trying to escape, they just gave in and drank the Kool-Aid. It was easier for them to die.

There were also cult members who became suicidal because they wanted to avoid an impending military assault by the Guyana Defense Force. The community had just been visited by U.S. congressman Leo Ryan, who was conducting an investigation of human rights abuses within the cult. When Ryan attempted to board a plane to leave, he and four associates were shot and killed by the Jonestown security team. Jones used the news of this attack to get many members to commit suicide before the legal authorities arrived. As he explained over a loudspeaker, "The Congressman's dead . . . please get us some medication . . . please get it before it's too late. . . . The GDF [Guyana Defense Force] will be here. . . . They'll torture our people, they'll torture our seniors. We cannot have this. . . . Hurry, hurry my children, hurry. All I say, let's not fall into the hands of the enemy."[11] For these people, it was the immediate crisis Jones had orchestrated, combined with their fear of retribution from outsiders, that made them want to die.

But not everyone at Jonestown was suicidal. Some people were unwilling to kill themselves and managed to escape. Before the final day, there had been a number of red flags that led the healthier members of the community to leave for good. For example, at one point, Jones had passed around red wine and told everyone to drink. After they complied, he informed them that it contained poison, and that they would all be dead in a matter of minutes. He soon admitted that this was simply a rehearsal and he had just been testing their commitment, but this raised major concerns among those who truly valued their lives.[12] In addition, just three weeks before the mass suicide, Jones had a number of cult members stand up and publicly proclaim their willingness to die.[13]

Again, this was a sign of things to come, and in the name of self-preservation, some people took the opportunity to get away.

In fact, more than twenty individuals left the premises that final day, never intending to return. Some left with the congressman; others fled under the guise of going on a picnic.[14] These people were perfectly willing to be labeled "traitors" or "defectors," as long as they survived.[15] In addition, several members who were still in Jonestown at the time of the mass suicides took actions that specifically demonstrated their desire to live: fleeing into the jungle, hiding until it was safe to come out, or lying down among the other bodies and pretending to be dead.[16]

THE FOUR TYPES

As with the Columbine killers, the variation among the Jonestown cult members is a sign of what we should expect with suicide terrorists.

Overall, there are four primary types of suicide terrorists: (1) conventional, (2) coerced, (3) escapist, and (4) indirect. In brief, conventional suicide terrorists become suicidal for the same reasons other people become suicidal, and they exhibit the same risk factors. Coerced suicide terrorists become suicidal because they fear the organizational consequences of not carrying out a suicide attack. Escapist suicide terrorists become suicidal because they fear being captured or punished by the enemy. And indirect suicide terrorists become suicidal at an unconscious level: they orchestrate their own deaths in ways that disguise their desire to die, even from themselves.

Despite the differences among them, these four types of suicide terrorists are all suicidal. Each one demonstrates at least a few behaviors on the continuum of suicidality, such as suicide ideation, a suicide plan, or a suicide attempt.[17] And each successful suicide attack involves (1) the death of the actor, (2) the intention of dying, and (3) the self-orchestration of that death.[18]

So far, this book has primarily focused on the first type: conventional suicide terrorists like Qari Sami, Joe Stack, Wafa al-Biss, Rafik, and Zuheir. Since there are over one hundred years of research on conventional suicide, this type of suicide terrorist is the easiest to understand. Like other suicidal individuals, their desire to die may be the product of individual traits, social forces, situational factors, or any combination thereof. Common risk factors include a previous suicide attempt, social isolation, depression, low self-worth, guilt, shame, hopelessness, rage, post-traumatic stress disorder, exposure to the suicidal behavior of others, perceived loss of security, perceived victimization, a traumatic brain injury, a precipitating crisis event, and a multitude of other variables.[19] And as we saw in Chapter 3, suicide terrorists have struggled with divorce, adultery scandals, financial problems, job problems, poor health, physical disabilities, and the death of a loved one.

But now it's time to explore the other types. It's time to connect the dots between suicide terrorism and other extreme behaviors, including the kamikaze missions of Japan, the bunker suicides of the Nazis, and the deadly game of Russian roulette.

COERCED SUICIDE

A man with a gun orders you to commit suicide.

Would you do it? Or would you disobey?

Your answer probably depends on the specific details of the situation and the value you attribute to your own life. How close is the man with the gun—if he shoots, could he miss? Is there a chance you could run away and escape? If you stall for time, will new options present themselves? How does he want you to kill yourself? If it's with a gun or knife, could you use that weapon against him? If it's with pills or poison, could you fake your own death and possibly escape when he's gone? What are the consequences of disobeying? A messier death? A more painful death? What exactly do you have to lose?

No matter what your calculations, if you kill yourself to avoid being shot, that constitutes suicide. Although your decision may seem more rational than a teenage girl with an unwanted pregnancy or an elderly man ravaged by disease, at the core, all three of you would be killing yourselves to escape a crisis and the anticipated consequences of continuing to live.

The key difference is that with coerced suicides, those who kill themselves are more clearly the victims of someone else. Their decisions are often made "under duress," which is a legal phrase defined as "unlawful pressure exerted upon a person to coerce that person to perform an act that he or she ordinarily would not perform."[20] These individuals' actions become abnormal primarily because of the abnormal pressures upon them. However, in the exact same situation, many other people would try almost anything to survive.

Examples of coerced suicides are many. As we saw earlier, some cult members at Jonestown killed themselves because they were coerced. If they hadn't been pressured by their peers or surrounded by armed guards, they would not have drunk the Kool-Aid. Instead, they chose to "die with dignity," as Jones called it, rather than object or try to escape.[21] In other cases, people have become suicidal because they were treated brutally. For example, the Nazis intentionally coerced suicides from many concentration camp prisoners. There were reports of between six and seven suicide attempts per week at the Dachau concentration camp and evidence of similar suicide prevalence elsewhere.[22]

THE KAMIKAZE

Another powerful example of coerced suicide comes from the kamikaze pilots of Japan. Despite common misconceptions to the contrary, the *tokkōtai* program was not stocked with courageous warriors who boldly sacrificed their lives for the good of their country. That is a total fabrication.

As renowned kamikaze expert Emiko Ohnuki-Tierney explains, when the *tokkōtai* program was instituted, "*none* of the professional soldiers who had graduated from the naval and army academies volunteered."[23] Why not? It's simple—because they valued their lives. They were too mentally healthy to carry out suicide attacks. As one pilot explained, "There is no more hope for Japan, if it has to kill such a skillful pilot as myself. I can hit an aircraft carrier with a 1,102 lb. bomb and return alive, without having to make a suicidal plunge."[24] He was worth more alive than dead, and he damn well knew it. (As a reminder from

Chapter 2, this is the same explanation given by many regular terrorists and organizers of suicide attacks, who insist that they are too important to blow themselves up.)

Lacking volunteers, Japan drafted four thousand boys and university students for suicide missions, then systematically broke their wills with regular beatings and abuse.[25] As one would-be kamikaze recalls, "'training' took place day after day. I was struck on the face so hard and frequently that my face was no longer recognizable. . . . [My commander] hit my face twenty times and the inside of my mouth was cut in many places. I had been looking forward to eating. . . . Instead, I was swallowing blood."[26] Another survivor remembers similar trauma:

> I felt little desire to rush out and die gloriously for some great cause. Like all the others, I was overwhelmingly demoralized and intimidated. . . . Anxiety had left me exhausted yet too nervous for sleep. . . . By the first month's end, many in our group were breaking emotionally, beyond remedy. Continual pain, continual humiliation, continual pressure. Endless stress! It could not be endured forever.[27]

This is exactly what Japan's military leaders intended, but coercive measures can also have dangerous side effects. For instance, in one unit, nine of sixty recruits *actually killed themselves during training*.[28] These individuals didn't bother to disguise their psychological pain as heroic sacrifice—they just took the quickest way out. However, the majority of recruits carried out their kamikaze missions as planned. Deeply traumatized and threatened with torture, execution, and the punishment of their families if they disobeyed, they concluded that they were ready to die.

COERCED SUICIDE TERRORISM

Coerced suicide terrorists similarly decide to kill themselves because they fear the consequences of not carrying out suicide attacks. These consequences may be explicit threats of punishment for disobedience, made by terrorist leaders, or implicit assumptions about what would happen if they backed out, made by the suicide terrorists themselves.[29] For instance, the Tamil Tigers of Sri Lanka apparently threatened to harm individuals' families if they did not carry out suicide attacks, and similar tactics have been used in Chechnya.[30]

If the anticipated consequences were not weighing on them, these individuals may not have complied. Ultimately, however, they chose to kill themselves "for the cause" rather than risk the uncertainty of disobedience or escape. This makes them fundamentally suicidal, because regardless of the pressures, many others would grasp at any chance to survive. Furthermore, in some cases, the coercive force may be largely a matter of perception, whereby the suicidal individual imagined more pressure on him- or herself than actually existed.

The most glaring example may come from Afghanistan and Pakistan, where teenage boys have been kidnapped by the Taliban for suicide missions.[31] Interviews of some who were rescued before they could blow themselves up revealed that much like the kamikazes, they were beaten and abused by their captors from their very first day in captivity.[32] Psychiatrist Fareeha Peracha identified signs of depression and other psychological disorders among these "lost souls," who, not surprisingly, appeared willing to do whatever their captors ordered.[33]

In less extreme cases, people have volunteered to *fight,* but were then coerced to carry out suicide attacks instead. Consider the following examples:

- A sixteen-year-old boy named Ghulam left his madrassah in 2007 and traveled to Afghanistan. When he arrived, he was told that if he did not carry out a suicide attack, one of the mission organizers would chop his head off and he would go to hell. He was drugged to increase his compliance, forced to put on a suicide vest, and then driven to the target police station, where he was dropped off and watched from afar. When Ghulam still refused to blow himself up, the terrorist organizers grabbed him and pulled him back into their car. Fortunately, he was arrested before they could execute him.[34]

- A young man named Saleh met with several members of a terrorist organization and eventually agreed to carry out a strike against Israel. However, he explained that he did not want to die and would only try a conventional attack. The commander saw things differently, and offered to pay $25,000 to Saleh's family if he would carry out a suicide bombing. Saleh agreed to *consider* the offer, but from that point on, the terrorist organization acted as though he had already committed to blow himself up. After repeated insistence and pressure from numerous members of the terrorist organization, Saleh eventually gave in.[35]

- A young woman named Nazima volunteered for weapons training with a terrorist group, but she never wanted to carry out a suicide bombing. However, the men in charge had other plans. They tricked her into signing a commitment document, then steadily pressured her until she cracked. As Nazima explains:

> There was an older man there, and other, younger men in the same room. . . . He said, "You prepared yourself, you trained, you know who we are, who the operatives in the organization are, and you have to do it."
>
> I told him I only came for the training, not to carry out a suicide bombing attack . . . and then we argued. I told him I wasn't strictly observant when it came to religion, I didn't wear traditional clothing or cover my hair, didn't pray at all the prescribed times and actually sometimes I prayed and sometimes I didn't. . . . I also said that I watched television and listened to songs, things devout Muslims usually don't do, and that I hadn't planned on becoming a *shaheeda* [martyr], otherwise I would have been more scrupulous in my religious behavior.
>
> I found myself screaming at him. . . . I asked him if I could start all over from the beginning, to forget that there had ever been a connection between us. I would forget them and they would forget me. They refused, naturally, and said "You know

everything about us and we aren't sure of what will happen
once you leave this room."[36]

Ultimately, she gave in. "I began counting the days until I was going to
die, because they forced me. I hate the idea of dying, I like living . . . [but]
I didn't have the courage to tell my father."[37] Nazima decided she would
rather blow herself up than face the shame of backing out and asking
her family for help. Fortunately, she was arrested before the fateful day
arrived.

In other cases, individuals agree to carry out suicide bombings without really planning to go through with it, and then are too scared to
withdraw. In various scenarios, they may volunteer because they give in
to the inflamed passions, lofty boasts, or peer pressure of the moment—
or because they seek social recognition, fame and glory, money, luxury
goods, or a range of other tangible and intangible benefits.[38] The Taliban
have even gotten some people to volunteer for suicide bombings simply
by offering them motorcycles and cell phones.[39]

When reality sets in, some of these volunteers are overcome by buy-
er's remorse. But at that point, it may seem too late, and the prospect
of backing down may become too intimidating to bear. Despite their
true desires, despite the fact that they might not be remotely suicidal in
another context, and despite the fact that they would prefer not to carry
out a suicide attack, they come to feel so much pressure that they choose
death over life.

For instance, a teenage boy named Majed was approached by a local terrorist commander whom he already knew and was asked to carry
out a suicide attack. As he explains, "I was confused because of our
previous acquaintance and I did not know how to avoid him. I was
stressed and thought a lot about how to refuse his request."[40] Instead of
flatly rejecting the idea, Majed agreed, but he secretly planned to leave
town to study abroad, and thus avoid following through. To his dismay,
the commander quickly arranged the attack, and Majed soon found
himself making a martyrdom video and preparing to blow himself up,
rather than trying to escape. He was suicidal only because of these pressures—because of the terrible crisis of the moment. As luck would have

it, Majed was arrested two days before his suicide bombing would have taken place.[41] Of course, many others are not so fortunate—and they don't live to tell the tale.

REMOTE DETONATION

Sometimes terrorist leaders realize that coercion is not enough. Sometimes they see that no matter what they do, no matter what mind games they play or what pressures they levy, their victim will not give in. Other times, gaining the individual's consent and cooperation is deemed unnecessary.

In such cases, terrorist leaders may resort to more devious tactics such as remote detonation. There have been a number of cases in the past in Afghanistan, Iraq, and Palestine in which individuals have been tricked into carrying explosives that were then detonated by remote control, against their will.[42] The types of people exploited in this fashion vary widely, from adult males to eight-year-old girls to people with Down's syndrome.[43] In other scenarios, people have been handcuffed to the steering wheels of bomb-laden vehicles and then blown up when they drove by enemy targets.[44]

It must be emphasized that these people are *not* suicide terrorists. They are more like the aforementioned donkeys that were strapped with explosives and then detonated, or like one of us would be, if someone slipped a bomb into our luggage without us knowing. Of course, after the bombs explode, it can be hard to distinguish these individuals from real suicide terrorists, but they are fundamentally different at a behavioral level. Unlike coerced suicide terrorists, who give in and then choose to kill themselves, these people do not have suicidal intent. They don't get a choice in the matter.

ESCAPIST SUICIDE

If you were surrounded by an approaching enemy and knew that it was only a matter of time before they got to you, would you kill yourself?

To some degree, it probably depends on your expectations of what the enemy would do. If they're just going to question or detain you,

you'd be a fool to commit suicide. If they're going to torture and kill you, the decision becomes more difficult.

Escapist suicides occur when people fear seemingly inevitable arrest, punishment, or slaughter at the hands of others. If they could be magically transported to another place, these individuals would probably not commit suicide, but lacking that possibility and facing an impending confrontation, they choose death. The key difference between coerced and escapist suicides is that with the former, there is someone actively pressuring the attackers to kill themselves, but with the latter, the approaching enemy has no such agenda. In most cases of escapist suicide, the enemy would actually discourage the self-imposed death; it is the individual who makes the personal decision to end it all.

People who commit escapist suicides are still fundamentally suicidal, because in the exact same circumstances, regardless of the odds or options, many others would fight to survive. Even in the most desperate of situations, human beings have an amazing capacity for hope. The most vile enemies can sometimes be talked out of murder, decide to show mercy, or make mistakes that provide a way out. And even when cornered by an angry grizzly bear—whose propensity for mauling you and feasting on your innards far outweighs its desire to negotiate—victims don't slit their wrists with their pocketknives. They run or fight until the very last breath.

As we saw with the Jonestown case, sometimes people commit escapist suicides without full knowledge of how the enemy will treat them. Cult leader Jim Jones largely exaggerated the threat of the impending assault by the Guyana military, which certainly would not have tortured people in the wholesale fashion he claimed. For the vast majority of cult members, their suicidal solution was far more severe—and permanent— than any external punishment would have been. Similarly, a wide range of criminals have committed suicide when surrounded by police because they had exaggerated expectations of the consequences they would face. If they had just surrendered, they would have only received short-term punishment before they were eventually released to live freely.

When trapped by an approaching enemy, why do some people kill themselves while others choose to live? The difference is most likely a matter of individual psychology and suicidal tendencies. It's easy to jump to the conclusion that these suicidal people are just doing what anyone else would do, given the same difficult circumstances. But the evidence suggests otherwise.[45]

Those who commit escapist suicides are not always making hasty decisions in the heat of the moment. In many cases, they had already considered the option of suicide before the emergency situation arose. For days, weeks, months, or years, they counted on the knowledge that if they were ever cornered and trapped, death would become their self-imposed exit strategy.

HITLER AND THE NAZIS

There are numerous examples of escapist suicides in Nazi Germany at the end of World War II. Many Nazi leaders killed themselves when defeat became certain and unpleasant consequences loomed. However, despite the desperate circumstances, those who committed escapist suicides were still the minority.[46] Less than 15 percent of the upper echelon killed themselves: 8 of 41 party regional leaders, 7 of 47 high-ranking SS and police leaders, 53 of 554 army generals, 14 of 98 Luftwaffe generals, and 11 of 53 admirals.[47]

Adolf Hitler also killed himself at the end of the war, but the possibility of suicide as an exit strategy was present in his consciousness much earlier. In September 1931, Hitler's niece shot herself and died. In November 1932, Hitler's girlfriend Eva Braun attempted suicide but survived. One month later, while frustrated with the Nazi Party's slow rise to prominence, Hitler exclaimed, "If the Party falls to pieces, I shall end it all in three minutes with the pistol."[48] Then in a speech given the following year after Hitler assumed control of the armed forces, he proclaimed that "I now wish to be nothing other than the first soldier of the German Reich. Therefore, I have put on that tunic which has always been the most holy and dear to me. I shall not take it off again until after victory is ours, or—I shall not live to see that day!"[49]

Hitler's suicidal tendencies became so well known that two years before the leader's death, psychoanalyst Walter C. Langer wrote, "Not only has he frequently threatened to commit suicide, but from what we know of his psychology it is the most likely possibility."[50] In August 1944, Hitler glorified the self-destructive act, explaining, "It's only (the fraction) of a second. Then one is redeemed of everything and finds tranquility and eternal peace."[51] Eight months later, with defeat finally inevitable and Soviet troops swiftly advancing, Hitler formally married Braun in a brief bunker ceremony. Then he killed her and shot himself in the head.

It is not particularly surprising that Adolf Hitler committed suicide, given the treatment he would have received at the hands of the Soviets upon capture. His decision could almost be viewed as rational. However, most leaders do not take this same path, no matter what their crimes. Hitler's actions cannot simply be explained by the circumstances: they were also a product of his own personal weaknesses. As fellow Nazi leader Hermann Göring explained during his own interrogation, "We always knew that the Fuehrer would kill himself if things were coming to an end. We always knew that. There is not the least doubt about it."[52]

Notably, Hitler insisted that the Nazis' self-orchestrated deaths *would not actually constitute suicide.* He claimed that they were heroic and honorable self-sacrifices, made by those who courageously refused to negotiate or surrender, because only cowards would cling to life.[53] Of course, it is hard to see how these acts could have possibly been "sacrificial," because their deaths helped no one but themselves. This sounds eerily like the absurd rationalizations used by suicide terrorists and their leaders. When Hitler killed himself shortly before the enemy arrived, it was not out of courage—it was out of fear.

ESCAPIST SUICIDE TERRORISM

Like Hitler, Osama bin Laden also considered an escapist suicide. Of course, bin Laden was not a typical suicide terrorist—which makes his behavior particularly informative about how some terrorists may change under certain strains. In the aftermath of the September 11, 2001, attacks and the United States' invasion of Afghanistan, the Al Qaeda leader was essentially running for his life, and he was very concerned about being caught. As his former chief bodyguard Nasser al-Bahri explained, bin Laden commanded his followers to kill him if capture seemed imminent.[54] "He said: 'If we are besieged, do it. . . . I'd rather be shot in the back by the bodyguards than be arrested alive by the Americans.'"[55]

Remarkably, al-Bahri insisted that this self-orchestrated death would not constitute suicide, and would instead be "martyrdom." Much like Hitler, he mocked the cowardice of surrender: "Saddam Hussein was not willing to die in the days preceding his capture, but Osama bin Laden never considered the possibility of being captured. Being captured was not even an option."[56] But the truth is that killing oneself to escape punishment is neither courageous nor heroic. In fact, unlike his bodyguards, bin Laden would not have died fighting. And unlike suicide terrorists, his death would not have killed even a single member of the enemy population.

Sure enough, when bin Laden was ultimately killed in May 2011, he did not harm a single U.S. operative, despite having approximately thirty minutes to react while American special forces landed helicopters and cleared the two floors beneath him.[57] Interestingly enough, he did not try to commit suicide either. Navy SEALs were prepared for the Al Qaeda leader to be strapped with bombs or armed with automatic weapons, ready to go out in a blaze of glory. But he just sat there, waiting for them to arrive. Perhaps he lost his nerve. After nearly a decade of successfully avoiding an international manhunt, he was no longer willing to pull the trigger.

There are other, more direct cases of escapist suicide terrorists. For instance, in 2002, security forces tracked 9/11 facilitator Ramzi bin al-Shibh to a safe house in Karachi, Pakistan, where he and several co-conspirators were surrounded. During a four-hour standoff, al-Shibh and two others held knives to their own throats and threatened to kill themselves rather than surrender.[58] Eventually they gave in and were captured. In similar scenarios, terrorists have killed themselves to escape arrest in Iraq, Afghanistan, and Uzbekistan,[59] and it seems likely that this type of suicide has occurred in many other countries as well. Anywhere the enemy gets too close and the odds are overwhelming, some terrorists with suicidal leanings may choose death as their easy way out.

DO "HEROES" HIDE IN THEIR APARTMENT?

The most powerful example of escapist suicide terrorism comes from Madrid, Spain, where on April 3, 2004, seven men blew themselves up in their apartment after they were cornered by police. Approximately three weeks earlier, the men had helped carry out one of the most destructive terrorist attacks in European history. During the morning rush hour, they used cell phones to detonate ten backpack bombs that had been left on four different commuter trains, killing 191 people and wounding more than 1,800.[60]

The fact that the Madrid terrorists did not blow themselves up during their train attacks shows that suicide was not their top priority—at least at that point. By contrast, when four other jihadists struck the London transportation system one year later, they chose to die, even though they could have simply dropped off their bombs and walked away.[61] That behavioral difference suggests a corresponding difference in the perpetrators' psychology. On the other hand, a total of twenty-nine suspects were eventually charged and tried for their role in the Madrid attacks, but only seven killed themselves.[62] There must have been some fundamental difference between the majority, who allowed themselves to be arrested and then took their chances in court, and the minority, who preferred to die. In addition, there were some suspects who apparently left the country and escaped altogether, rather than hang around and tempt fate.[63] These latter individuals may have actually had the strongest survival instinct.

Biographical details from those who ultimately blew themselves up in their apartment suggests that they may have had suicidal tendencies. Many of them had been involved with drug trafficking, and some were addicts as well. And many had previously served time in prison, which may explain their desperation to avoid going back. Furthermore, as scholars Rogelio Alonso and Fernando Reinares summarize based on their close investigation, in terms of job prospects, "Most of them could be described as under-achievers with few or no qualifications."[64]

Consider the following:

- Allekema Lamari reportedly never had a girlfriend and was literally a forty-year-old virgin. He had a history of radical behavior, and his brother, also a militant, had died in Algeria. In addition, he had previously served five years in prison for terrorist activities, where his lawyer suggested he developed a mental disorder. After his release, Lamari had told a friend that he would never be caught alive again.[65]
- Jamal Ahmidan had a tumultuous background. He had arrived in Spain as an illegal immigrant, married a drug addict to obtain civil status, and had personally used heroin, cocaine, and alcohol, despite his religious beliefs. Ahmidan had repeatedly been in trouble with the law and had served numerous years in prison.[66]
- Abdennabi Kounjaa, who also had a criminal record, wrote a final letter to his family in Morocco that sheds some light on his state of mind. Although Kounjaa was in Spain voluntarily, he called it "hell" and warned his children to never follow him there. He also lamented that "I can't put up with this life living like a weak and humiliated person under the scrutiny of infidels and tyrants," adding that "this life is the path towards death" and that he preferred "death instead of life."[67]

Given this brief sample of personal problems and hopelessness, it makes sense that some of the Madrid terrorists chose to commit escapist suicides rather than be arrested. But notably, even when they were surrounded, not all the terrorists in the room were suicidal. One apparently tried to survive the blast by hiding under a bed.[68]

It is also important to emphasize that these suicide terrorists' primary goal was to kill themselves to avoid capture, not to harm the enemy. Although their explosion killed one Spanish police officer and wounded others,[69] the seven terrorists could have almost certainly killed more "infidels" if they had mounted an all-out attack. However, this would have put them in jeopardy of being wounded and apprehended—a risk they were unwilling to take, even for "the cause."

INDIRECT SUICIDE

What's the most dangerous thing you've ever done? Perhaps you had a night when you pushed your speedometer to its limit, went too far with drugs or alcohol, jumped off a cliff into unknown waters, or went ice-skating on a thinly frozen pond. We all do some dangerous things in our lives—particularly when we're young. But there are two questions that can help distinguish people who are indirectly suicidal from everyone else. First, were you fully aware of the risks at the time of your behavior? And second, at any deeper level, did you secretly hope you would fail?

In general, indirectly suicidal people may engage in a wide range of risk-taking and self-destructive behaviors, including high-stakes gambling, high-risk recreation, substance abuse, deviant sexual behavior, erratic driving, and even self-mutilation.[70] However, some people engage in similar acts without being suicidal at all. For instance, some teenagers ride motorcycles at 120 miles per hour based on youthful ignorance: they genuinely feel they are invincible, they overestimate their competency and control, and they underestimate the risks. These teenagers are not suicidal, they're just naïve.

But others ride motorcycles at 120 miles per hour and claim that they don't care about the risks, that they like to "live dangerously," and that whether they wake up tomorrow should be in "God's hands" or left up to fate.[71] In reality, this is a desperate overcompensation. They act invincible to mask their vulnerability, and they emphasize maximizing the pleasures of the moment because they fear the uncertainties of the future.[72] Previous research suggests that whether they realize it or not, these indirectly suicidal people actually want to die, and they are likely either to orchestrate an "accidental" death or eventually commit suicide by their own hand.[73]

The most extreme example of indirectly suicidal people may be those who play Russian roulette. This game of death has captured imaginations since the 1930s and is still played today.[74] In its standard form, players insert a bullet into a six-chambered revolver and leave the other five chambers empty. Then they spin the chamber so that the bullet's placement is determined by chance. The first player aims the gun at his own head and pulls the trigger, taking an approximately 16 percent chance of death. He either lives or dies, and then the gun is passed to the next person who spins the chamber again. Russian roulette players often claim that they genuinely want to win, and that "the goal of the game is to experience the rush of excitement in cheating fate."[75] But in reality, these individuals are almost always suicidal, and it comes as little surprise that their lives have often been filled with depression, substance abuse, and a range of high-risk and self-destructive behaviors. In addition, many are under the influence of alcohol or drugs when they play the game, which helps them hide their suicidal intentions from themselves.[76]

INDIRECT SUICIDE TERRORISM

Indirect suicide terrorists are suicidal at an unconscious level: they orchestrate their own deaths in ways that disguise their desire to die, even from themselves. Not surprisingly, this subterfuge makes them particularly hard to recognize: the same lies and rationalizations they use to convince themselves that they are not truly suicidal often successfully deceive those around them as well.

Perhaps the most common form of indirect suicide terrorism involves those who attempt "suicide by cop." Instead of spinning the chambers of a revolver, these suicide terrorists mount attacks on hard targets where they will almost certainly be greeted by a hail of bullets. But although their chances of death are much greater than the 16 percent odds offered by Russian roulette, their suicidal intentions are much more easily camouflaged by the nature of the act. After all, much like with the different types of reckless motorcycle drivers, it can be extremely difficult to differentiate between someone who engages in a high-risk terrorist mission and wants to survive and someone who mounts the exact same attack and wants to die.

There are many possible examples of these indirectly suicidal terrorists. For instance, in 2009, four terrorist suspects plotted to storm an

Australian military base and attack with automatic weapons until they were killed.[77] Fortunately, they were arrested before they could carry out the strike. Other indirectly suicidal terrorists may include Mir Aimal Kasi, who attacked CIA headquarters in 1993, Hesham Mohamed Hadayet, who attacked the Los Angeles airport in 2002, and Nidal Hasan, who attacked the Fort Hood army base in 2009. These attackers were all struggling with serious personal problems that may explain their suicidality.[78] Of course, whether they were indirectly suicidal or suicidal in another way would require much deeper psychological analyses, and it is possible that they were some combination of types.

For instance, as reviewed in Chapter 6, Hasan displayed risk factors for conventional suicide, but he was also in denial about his suicidal motivations and claimed that he was motivated by "martyrdom," not the desire to die. He both planned an attack that he was certain would end in his death, and also ducked behind physical barriers for protection while exchanging gunfire with military police. Like many indirectly suicidal people, he was drawn toward high-risk activities and fully planned to fail, but he was also unwilling to take the final step of directly stepping into a bullet.

What stands out is that in all these "suicide by cop" scenarios, the terrorists could have picked much softer targets elsewhere and would have almost certainly killed more of the enemy. Instead, they chose riskier targets that offered an increased likelihood of their own deaths—and that was probably part of the appeal.

A significant percentage of terrorist hostage takers may be indirectly suicidal as well. After all, their attacks are not only high risk, but they often end with deadly assaults by government security forces against the hostage takers. For instance, the 2008 Mumbai terrorists almost certainly expected to die as a result of their attacks, which explains why they didn't make any real attempts to negotiate.[79] As it turned out, all but one of them accomplished this suicidal objective, and the "unlucky" surviving terrorist still managed to get sentenced to death. In an interesting parallel to the Russian roulette players who need drugs and alcohol to elicit their suicidal desires, these Mumbai attackers reportedly used steroids, cocaine, and even LSD as part of their suicidal rampage.[80]

Similarly, many of the Chechen terrorists who mounted the 1995 Budennovsk hospital attack, 2002 Moscow theater attack, and 2004 Beslan school attack appeared to have been suicidal, despite not directly killing themselves by suicide bombing or similar means.[81] For instance, during the first attack, tactical leader Shamil Basayev, who was understandably distraught after the death of his wife and family just two weeks earlier, told journalists that "It does not matter to us when we die."[82] Much like many other indirectly suicidal people who gamble on death but survive, Basayev and some of his fellow terrorists lived through that first attack, but nevertheless found a premature end. Many were later killed by Russian security forces. And Basayev died in a mysterious bomb explosion at the ripe old age of forty-one.[83]

Other indirect suicide terrorists may carry out high-stakes suicide bombings. For these individuals, simply joining a terrorist organization was a gratifying risk, but death failed to come quickly enough to satisfy their self-destructive urges. Because indirectly suicidal people often pride themselves on taking chances, showing no fear, and doing what others are unwilling to do, these individuals may find suicide bombings against seemingly impenetrable targets particularly alluring. If they decide to end it all by blowing themselves up, it is likely to be at hard target sites where government officials, security officers, or police chiefs are waiting.

Overall, these indirect suicide terrorists should be expected to carry out the most risky, daring, and elaborate attacks. They may be more likely to go on wild shooting sprees with automatic weapons, engage in hostage taking, or attempt to blow up high-value targets—simply because they lust for the challenge. Some may be psychopaths like Columbine shooter Eric Harris, while others may have different mental disorders. At some deeper level, they know that their high-risk behavior will eventually end their lives, and they are comforted by this fact. However, since their suicidal intentions are often unconscious, they leave their immediate fate—be it arrest, injury, death, or anything in between—up to chance.

Being willing to *not die* makes them far less predictable than the other types of suicide terrorists. And in many cases, far more dangerous.

THE OVERLAP

Answers are sexy, and true enlightenment can be almost orgasmic. But the world's best criminal profilers know that they must fight the temptation to oversimplify human nature. As forensic scientist Brent Turvey explains:

> The fact is that different offenders can exhibit the same behaviors for completely different reasons. . . . You've got a rapist who attacks a woman in the park and pulls her shirt up over her face. Why? What does that mean? There are ten different things it could mean. It could mean he doesn't want to see her. It could mean he doesn't want her to see him. It could mean he wants to see her breasts, he wants to imagine someone else, he wants to incapacitate her arms—all of those are possibilities. You can't just look at one behavior in isolation.[84]

A similar principle applies to the behavior of suicide terrorists. Just because they all end up killing themselves, that doesn't make them all the same. As we have seen, there is a great deal of variation among these perpetrators. Even conventional suicide terrorists may have a wide range of psychological triggers that push them over the edge. And among the other types, various individual, social, and situational factors combine to produce their final acts.

This chapter has presented four distinct types of suicide terrorists, and it is useful to examine attackers according to these categories. The typology provides a valuable guide for quickly assessing an individual suicide terrorist and pinpointing his or her primary motive for seeking death, be it personal problems, pressure from others, fear of an approaching enemy, or hidden self-destructive urges. A chart with detailed behavioral expectations and security countermeasures for each type is presented as Appendix C.

At the same time, human psychology is so complex that we should recognize the likelihood of interaction and overlap across the four types. For instance, in Jonestown, there were cult members whose suicidal motives fit the conventional, coerced, and escapist types. However, there must also have been some who were a combination: they had personal problems and suicidal tendencies, they felt tremendous pressure from Jones and their peers, and they also feared an impending assault by the Guyana military. If you pressed the cosmic "pause" button right before they drank the Kool-Aid and asked them why they were committing suicide, they could have given you an answer. But considering the storms raging inside their heads, they may not have known for sure.

The same must be true of some suicide terrorists. For centuries, philosophers have challenged their pupils to "know thyself," but that's easier said than done. In some cases, we may understand suicide terrorists better than they understand themselves.

Which means we should be able to stop them.

EIGHT
MISSION IMPOSSIBLE?
HOW TO STOP SUICIDE TERRORISM

These days, self-preservation requires the ability to see the future. You need to see the job market trends, see the next technological breakthrough, see the deadly threat that looms around the corner and could leave you and your family devastated. Or you can trust your leaders to see it for you—but they better know what they're doing. Because when it comes to suicide terrorism, the experts have consistently gotten it wrong, and once a suicide attack occurs, the terrorists win that round. As we've learned the hard way, nothing can undo the damage and destruction they cause.

Of course, no one has a crystal ball—but some people have better foresight than others. More than two years before Osama bin Laden was killed in Pakistan, I outlined the possible counterterrorism strategies for dealing with the terrorist leader and identified the best one. At the time, one U.S. president had suggested that it didn't really matter if we killed bin Laden, and other experts were saying similar things.[1] Some high-ranking officials had even claimed that killing him would make him a "martyr" and thus be counterproductive.[2]

My research said otherwise, and I wrote that "the best scenario might be if he is killed by soldiers in a surprise attack, leaving a clearly identifiable corpse. It would be quick, degrading of his lofty image, and could shake Al Qaeda terrorists' confidence in their system and its goals."[3]

Looking back, these words appear prophetic. If bin Laden wanted to see what was coming before the helicopters were circling overhead, maybe he should have read my book.

EXPLAINING, PREDICTING, AND PREVENTING SUICIDE TERRORISM

Knowledge is power. Disagree? Just ask Bill Gates, Warren Buffett, Mark Zuckerberg, or any other modern tycoon who forged a billion-dollar empire from an idea. Or think back to 9/11. It wasn't military might that made those terrorists so powerful—it was the fact that they outsmarted us.

But it's time to turn the tables. Now that we understand the psychology of suicide terrorists, we should be able to explain, predict, and prevent their attacks better than ever before.

Why are suicide attacks so common in certain international hot spots? Why are they so rare in the United States? And will these trends continue? How can we find suicide terrorists and stop them before it's too late? How can we destroy the myth of martyrdom once and for all? There are compelling answers to each one of these questions, if we're ready to put our minds to work.

But life is determined by much more than just psychology, so our knowledge can't stop there. Human beings are often shaped by the forces and factors around them, and suicide terrorists are no exception.

At the bare minimum, there are three main requirements for suicide attacks: (1) suicidal intent (whether it's conventional, coerced, escapist, or indirect), (2) access to weapons, and (3) access to enemy targets. If these factors are present, a suicide attack can be launched. It may be limited in sophistication or magnitude, but it can occur. On the other hand, if one of these variables is missing or successfully neutralized, security officials can sleep more soundly at night, knowing a suicide attack will not occur in that specific setting.[4]

Beyond the minimum, there are additional facilitators for the most deadly suicide attacks and prolonged suicide terrorism campaigns. These include: (4) homicidal intent, (5) a sponsoring terrorist organization, (6) social stigmas of conventional suicide, and (7) social approval of suicide terrorism.

Homicidal intent often increases the severity of attacks. For instance, unlike attackers in the mold of Qari Sami—who had been taking antidepressants and deliberately walked away from a crowd in Kabul, Afghanistan, before blowing himself up[5]—truly homicidal suicide terrorists are motivated to maximize enemy casualties.

A sponsoring terrorist organization may increase suicidal and homicidal intent, provide access to weapons and enemy targets, and boost social approval of suicide terrorism through its use of propaganda. As we've seen, suicide attacks can be essentially manufactured by terrorist organizations, instead of being left to occur organically.

Social stigmas surrounding conventional suicide and social approval of suicide terrorism often work together. When a community strongly condemns conventional suicide as a certain path to hell, it virtually disappears as a potential escape route. And when a significant percentage of people believe that suicide terrorism is justified, a new door opens for desperate individuals.

THE MAN IN THE MIRROR

Anders Behring Breivik did not die in a hail of bullets. And he did not blow himself up. In fact, most people do not even classify his July 2011 behavior as an attempted suicide attack—although they are wrong about this, as we shall see. In fact, Breivik's case can teach us several important things about the requirements and facilitators for suicide terrorism.

After a rough childhood characterized by his parents' divorce, his father's abandonment, bullying, social isolation, and delinquency, Breivik decided, at some point in his twenties, to carry out a suicide attack.[6] In 2009, he bought a farmhouse in Norway and started what he claimed was a "Geofarm" company. However, the business actually served to camouflage his purchase of six tons of highly explosive fertilizer for the purpose of making bombs.[7]

Breivik also began writing a fifteen-hundred-page manifesto that would eventually reveal his suicidal intent. In the rambling document, he writes that "Europe is heading towards cultural and demographical suicide. . . . The book 'Prozak Nation' illustrates quite well that the cultural Marxist model is failing miserably and is leading to millions of people with psychological problems and tens of thousands of suicides."[8] "Over the next 5 decades," he asks, "How many of our brothers and sisters will commit suicide . . . How many more conservatives will be persecuted, ridiculed and pushed towards suicide before they capitulate?"[9] Breivik explains that "Many single people live in small flats or in segments of apartments. Many are lonely and some commit suicide."[10]

It doesn't take a rocket scientist to see that Breivik was not diagnosing Europe's suicidal tendencies—he was diagnosing his own. This is a classic example of "psychological projection": the act of denying one's own undesirable traits and instead attributing them to others.[11] Breivik even tried to claim that "Individual flaws are very often related to the flaws of society."[12]

For comparison's sake, in his own manifesto, the Unabomber Ted Kaczynski engaged in a very similar type of psychological projection. Kaczynski was a brilliant mathematician who had gone from a professorship at the University of California, Berkeley, to an isolated cabin in Montana. Would you like to guess what he thought some of society's most serious problems were? "Lack of goals whose attainment requires effort . . . [b]oredom . . . frustration . . . tendency to depression."[13] Along these same lines, if I started ranting about young professors being severely underpaid, would that tell you more about what's wrong with this country or more about what's on my mind?

Instead of trying to prevent Europe's "cultural and demographical suicide," Breivik should have listened to the King of Pop. As Michael Jackson explained in his critically acclaimed song "Man in the Mirror," sometimes the best way you can help others is to "take a look at *yourself,* and then make a change."

PREPARATIONS FOR DEATH

It's obvious that the requirements for suicide terrorism were present in Breivik's case. That's the easy part. He had (1) suicidal intent, (2) access to weapons, and (3) access to enemy targets.

It's also easy to see that Breivik developed (4) homicidal intent. He wrote that "Innocent people will die, in the thousands" and "let there be no doubt whatsoever; I would be the first person to pull the trigger, given the opportunity."[14]

In his manifesto, Breivik also revealed that the combination of (6) social stigmas against conventional suicide and (7) social approval of suicide terrorism paved the way for his deadly attack:

Justiciar Knights, Martyrdom vs. Suicide

There is normally absolutely no justification or excuse to commit suicide. It is a shameful, selfish and cowardly act which normally can and should never be justified. According to the canon laws of the Catholic Church; any individual who commits suicide will forever burn in hell as suicide is considered the gravest of sins.[15]

If Breivik ever considered just shooting himself—as his father later said he should have—this stigma and religious prohibition must have gotten in the way.[16] So with one escape route closed, Breivik tried to convince himself that a so-called "martyrdom" attack would not actually constitute suicide:

So, in regards to Catholic canon law, the question is; will Justiciar Knights be rejected in heaven as they martyr themselves for the cause or have to "self terminate" during or after an operation, for various reasons?

There are several distinctions that have to be made in this regard:

1. A Justiciar Knight martyring himself for the cause and dies from wounds inflicted by system protectors (police/regime agents)
2. A Justiciar Knight martyring himself for the cause and dies non-intentionally from wounds inflicted by his own actions (explosion etc.)
3. A Justiciar Knight martyring himself for the cause and dies intentionally from wounds inflicted by his own actions (explosion etc.) in order to prevent capture . . .
4. A Justiciar Knight self terminates after apprehension to escape torture and murder/execution

Points 1–3 are considered standard martyrdom deaths, under canon law, which guarantee an abundance of grace and the entry to heaven.

Point 4, however, is not a clear case of a martyrdom death but must be seen in perspective to the circumstances. In point 4, a Justiciar Knight would have fulfilled his pact with God. . . . As such, if he chooses to self terminate (not suicide) for logical reasons, or to prevent torture and certain death (this is a likely scenario in many Western European prisons as Muslims dominate a majority of them), it is not considered suicide. . . . As such, this final act of sacrifice is added to the amount of good deeds and grace generated by the individual.[17]

Here Breivik essentially maps out the possibilities for his upcoming suicide attack. He could die by provoking suicide by cop. He could kill himself in the midst of his attack, through his own actions. He could kill himself after his attack, to avoid being captured. Or he could kill himself after he is arrested and put in prison, in order to escape abuse, torture, and society's wrath. Remarkably, Breivik insists that *all* these actions would constitute martyrdom, not suicide.

This kind of distorted logic is what the myth of martyrdom is built on. Believe it or not, Islamic terrorists detained at the Guantánamo Bay prison in Cuba have similarly claimed that slitting their own throats, overdosing on pills, or hanging themselves in their cells constitutes martyrdom, not suicide.[18] Of course, the psychiatrists who examined them found the opposite: the terrorists who become suicidal in prison are usually those already struggling with depression and despair.[19]

THE RECORD HOLDER

Breivik did not complete his manifesto until the day he attacked. "I believe this will be my last entry. It is now Fri July 22nd, 12:51. Sincerest regards," he wrote.[20] Then he posted a YouTube video that called for others to "embrace martyrdom," and sent out his entire manifesto to thousands of people on Facebook.[21]

For the next step, Breivik drove to Oslo, where he parked his truck in front of a government building and walked away shortly before it exploded, leaving eight people dead. If he had just wanted to end his life in a "martyrdom" attack, this is where he would have done it. But like many suicidal killers, Breivik also wanted to maximize casualties. So when these initial acts did not spark a confrontation with police, he traveled twenty-five miles to a Workers' Youth League summer camp on Utøya island.

There Breivik launched the second stage of his suicide attack. Disguised as a police officer and carrying ten thirty-round ammunition clips, he opened fire with a high-powered rifle, fatally shooting sixty-nine people and wounding sixty-six more.[22] More than half his victims were teenagers, some as young as fourteen.[23]

But there was still one big problem. After fifty minutes of victims screaming, crying, bleeding, and dying, the police had not arrived, and Breivik remained uncomfortably alive.

In his manifesto, he had written that "I know I will die fighting the overwhelming cultural Marxists/multiculturalist forces in phase 1 and that's not a problem for me at all. I have prepared mentally for a very long time and I will gladly sacrifice my life."[24] And he later admitted that he had expected to be shot and killed by police officers during his attack.[25] But death had not come as anticipated, and standing in the midst of the bodies, with his suicidal rage beginning to cool, Breivik found himself at a loss for what to do next. So he reached for his cell phone and called the police.

The audio recording is chillingly devoid of emotion. "Hello, my name is Anders Behring Breivik of the Norwegian anti-communist resistance movement. I'm on Utøya at the moment and I wish to surrender."[26] When police eventually arrived, he raised his hands above his head in a sign of submission. They almost shot Breivik anyway, because they feared he might be wearing an explosive belt, but he was successfully arrested without further incident and taken into custody.[27]

For the simple reason that Breivik surrendered, most commentators have assumed that he was not suicidal and was not attempting a suicide attack. This is patently absurd. In fact, shortly after he was booked by police, Breivik was put on suicide watch.[28] He is not the first suicidal person to change his mind at the last minute—not by a long shot.[29] By comparison, an in-depth study of school shooters from 1974 to 2001 revealed that even though 55 percent of them were suicidal, only 30 percent actually attempted suicide during their attacks, and just 15 percent wound up dead.[30] Similarly, there are many would-be suicide terrorists who are undeniably suicidal, yet do not end up killing themselves. In many cases, we never learn what changed their minds.

Subsequent investigations confirmed that, although he shared the ideology of some radical groups and had even tried to reach out to them, Breivik acted alone.[31]

In doing so, he gained the infamous distinction of committing the most deadly solo terrorist strike in human history. But we can be certain that Breivik won't be the record holder forever. As computers and cell phones continue to get more sophisticated and more effective, so will bombs and guns. Our only chance to stop the next suicidal killer is to be better, faster, smarter.

A FALSE SENSE OF SECURITY

Breivik's case provides a very important cautionary tale.

If we put ourselves in the shoes of Norway's security officials the day before Breivik struck, it's easy to imagine why they might have felt safe. In their entire history, there had been only one person killed on their soil by a terrorist attack, and that was back in 1987.[32] In addition, given the terrorist anger focused on prime "infidel" powers like the United States and Israel, analysts had determined that Al Qaeda viewed Norway as a "low-priority target."[33] Sure, there had been rumors of a failed plot a year earlier.[34] But without the major threat of a terrorist organization that wanted to do them harm, why should they worry?

It's very simple. No matter how much progress is made in other areas of the broader counterterrorism struggle, as long as the minimum *requirements* for suicide terrorism are present, the threat remains. Security officials in Norway may have been comforted that some of the *facilitators,* such as a sponsoring terrorist organization or social approval of suicide terrorism, were not a major factor in their country. But as Breivik shows, that didn't matter. He had everything he needed.

The distinction between requirements for suicide terrorism and facilitators for suicide terrorism is critical, because counterterrorism officials who focus solely on the latter can create a dangerous false sense of security.

Imagine that a ferocious lion is fifty feet away, charging you at full speed. You have a firearm and a few seconds to react. Do you shoot at a body part *required* for the lion to keep charging, like its vital organs? Or do you shoot at a body part that just *helps* the lion run fast—like its foot? The only way to ensure that the lion doesn't tear you limb from limb is to counter the features it *requires* to attack you. Reducing its ability to operate at full capacity might be a step in the right direction, but that does not eliminate the threat.

WHY ARE SUICIDE ATTACKS SO COMMON IN CERTAIN INTERNATIONAL HOT SPOTS?

Ron Paul wants you to shoot the lion in the foot.

For years, the congressman and presidential candidate has insisted that suicide terrorism is caused by foreign occupation. As recently as 2011, Paul made the following claims:

> Though it is hard for many to believe, honest studies show that the real motivation behind the September 11 attacks and the vast majority of other instances of suicide terrorism is . . . primarily occupation. If you were to imagine for a moment how you would feel if another country forcibly occupied the United States, had military bases and armed soldiers present in our hometowns, you might begin to understand why foreign occupation upsets people so much.[35]

Of course, Paul is correct in observing that suicide attacks have been quite common in countries beset by foreign occupation, such as Iraq and Afghanistan. Anyone could tell you that, simply by scanning the newspaper headlines. But the relationship between foreign occupation and suicide terrorism is not simply the product of anger against foreigners—it's much more complex than that.

By considering the requirements and facilitators reviewed earlier, we can better analyze how foreign occupation affects suicide terrorism rates. For starters, foreign occupation should be expected to increase suicidal intent, due to the psychological consequences of war. For instance, during the first two years of the Iraq War, more than sixty-seven thousand civilians were documented as killed or wounded, and many more went missing.[36] Others lost their jobs and homes. This is not solely the fault of the United States—in fact, the majority of those killed, wounded, and displaced had local fighters and criminals to blame.[37] But either way, it was almost inevitable that this kind of chaos and turmoil would increase the number of suicidal people. (In fact, the psychological consequences of war also increased suicidality among American military personnel. It is no mere coincidence that over the same post-9/11 period when suicide terrorism attacks suddenly increased, U.S. military suicides rose dramatically as well.[38])

In addition, occupation generally increases access to weapons.[39] It also increases access to enemy targets, due to the local presence of a large military force.[40] And foreign occupation generally leads to a rise in both homicidal intent and social approval of suicide terrorism, due to widespread victimization and desires for revenge.

Ultimately, in contexts where (1) suicidal intent, (2) access to weapons, (3) access to targets, (4) homicidal intent, and (7) social approval of suicide terrorism have suddenly spiked—and where (6) strong stigmas against conventional suicide are already present—we would expect (5) sponsoring terrorist organizations to surface. For them, the opportunity is just too damn good to resist. From there, setting up operations and beginning to crank out regular suicide attacks are a relatively straightforward business. And if they need to use coercive measures to increase suicidal intent, they have shown the ability to do that, too.

These factors help explain what has been happening in Iraq and Afghanistan, as well as in other hot spots around the world.

A PROBLEM OF PRIORITIES

The problem is that by claiming that 95 percent of suicide attacks are caused by foreign occupation,[41] Paul is confusing an indirect cause with a direct cause. And that's a very dangerous mistake.

"Why should I care if it's the Snickers candy bar that's making me fat, or if it's the *sugar* in the Snickers candy bar that's making me fat?"

Some may argue that the distinction between direct and indirect causes doesn't matter, but it is easy to see why they're wrong. First, because it may be possible to create a Snickers bar without sugar (blegh!). If so, weight-conscious consumers around the world could have their Snickers and eat them, too. Second, because if people stop eating Snickers bars, and instead start eating something else that has similar levels of sugar, they'll make no dieting progress whatsoever. When predicting whether you'll get fat from eating certain foods, understanding the *direct causes* of weight gain is absolutely critical.

The same is true for predicting suicide terrorism attacks.

Just like sugar-free Snickers, there can be suicide-terrorism-free foreign occupations. People have been forcibly occupying each other's lands for thousands of years, but suicide terrorism is a relatively new phenomenon. History has shown that across a wide variety of cultures, the vast majority of foreign occupations have not produced a single suicide attack.

And just as the removal of Snickers from one's diet does not guarantee a halt in weight gain, the removal of foreign occupying troops does not guarantee a stop to suicide terrorism. For instance, much like foreign occupation, sectarian violence and civil war should be expected to increase suicidal and homicidal intent, due to their psychological consequences on local inhabitants. These types of conflict will likely boost social approval of suicide terrorism against nearby enemies as well.[42]

This helps explain why many suicide attacks in Iraq and Afghanistan have been launched against other Muslims—*not just the foreign occupiers.*[43] A 2011 study published in the leading British medical journal *The Lancet* found that from 2003 to 2010, suicide bombings in Iraq killed a horrific 12,284 civilians—but just 200 coalition soldiers.[44] So claims that these attacks are primarily motivated by anger against foreigners are simply not credible. Anecdotal evidence supports this data. In August 2011, a suicide bomber exploded inside Baghdad's largest Sunni mosque, killing twenty-nine and wounding thirty-eight more.[45] In December 2011, a suicide bomber detonated in front of a Shiite mosque in Afghanistan, leaving sixty dead.[46] Suicide attacks like these have been occurring for years, and are likely to continue whether U.S. forces are present or not.

Along these same lines, *anything* that provides potential attackers with access to one hundred thousand new enemy targets is likely to increase attack rates—not just foreign occupation. Whether American forces are in Iraq or Afghanistan for political purposes or humanitarian ones, their presence alone would increase the number of suicide attacks sponsored by local terrorist organizations who have sworn to strike. Try setting up an American vacation resort on the Gaza Strip and watch what happens—even if the tourists mean well. There are plenty of would-be suicide terrorists who are willing to attack if their enemies are close by, but not if they have to travel thousands of miles to seek them out. Unfortunately, as the world gets "smaller"—because transportation gets cheaper, faster, and easier—suicide attackers' access to targets could certainly grow.

In the short term, whenever the United States removes its military from foreign lands, American forces will be attacked less frequently because access to them will be reduced. The most basic type of foreign suicide terrorist—one who becomes suicidal, is given a bomb by a local sponsoring organization, and then blows him- or herself up at a nearby target—will no longer harm U.S troops.

But that does not mean that in the long term, the American people will be any safer. In fact, U.S. officials may be tempted to pat themselves on the back for reducing the threat and begin to fall back asleep, lulled by the same false sense of security that preceded 9/11. Meanwhile, the threat of a catastrophic suicide terrorist attack in New York, Chicago, or Los Angeles could remain just as serious and just as deadly.

WHY ARE SUICIDE ATTACKS SO RARE IN THE UNITED STATES?

Many leaders have been baffled by the scarcity of suicide terrorism attacks on American soil, because they personally predicted otherwise. After 9/11, U.S. Vice President Dick Cheney declared that "It's not a matter of *if*, but *when*."[47] FBI Director Robert Mueller suggested that suicide bombers would begin to attack the United States on a regular basis, as they had done in Israel. "There will be another terrorist attack; we will not be able to stop it," he warned.[48] Homeland Security Secretary Tom Ridge insisted that Americans had to "prepare for the inevitability" of suicide bombings in the United States.[49]

Not a pretty picture. And yet, from 1990 to 2010, there were just thirteen attacks in the United States that met the definition of suicide terrorism.[50] Even more shockingly, as of this writing, Americans have yet to see a single suicide bombing on U.S. soil.

The question is, why? The answer is compelling.

First, the simple stuff. Social approval of suicide terrorism is very low in the United States. Despite significant domestic turmoil and anger toward the government, more than 93 percent of Americans describe themselves as at least "somewhat patriotic."[51] Most of these people are simply unwilling to commit acts of terror that would harm their own country.

Second, although there is a significant minority who would like to see the United States suffer, very few of these individuals have suicidal intent. Pew Research Center surveys indicate that more than two hundred thousand Americans believe that suicide attacks are "often" or "sometimes" justified.[52] But the national suicide rate suggests that on average, only twenty-two of these two hundred thousand would commit suicide each year.[53] Of these twenty-two, some percentage would kill only themselves. It's the relatively small remainder who might even consider carrying out suicide attacks.

But additional barriers exist. First, most potential suicide terrorists in the United States don't have the bombs they need. Historically, the vast majority of suicide bombers have been provided with ready-made bombs by sponsoring terrorist organizations.[54] In the United States, those organizations have not been present, which means that the bomb vests and explosive belts haven't gotten into the hands of the few individuals with the intent to use them.

In theory, these people could construct their own explosive devices. Suicidal people are certainly capable of this, as Columbine killers Harris and Klebold demonstrated in 1999 and the London suicide bombers did in 2005.[55] But the risk of non-detonation may give them second thoughts. For instance, Harris and Klebold had to adjust their exit strategy after their bombs failed to explode, so they eventually shot themselves in the head. However, if Islamic suicide terrorists construct bombs that fail to explode, they would be up the creek without a paddle, because shooting themselves in the head clearly constitutes suicide, and that leads directly to hell. This risk might be too great to proceed.

If potential suicide terrorists in the United States don't have access to bombs, they could certainly carry out gun-wielding suicide attacks, like Breivik's "phase 2" or Nidal Hasan at Fort Hood. Firearms are very easy to obtain, and mass-shooting attacks are much simpler to prepare for than elaborate bombings or hijackings. Furthermore, given the prevalence of soft targets—such as public schools, shopping centers, and malls—attackers have no shortage of potential places to wreak death and destruction.[56]

So why don't more suicide terrorists use this gun-wielding method? There are a few reasons. First, some would-be attackers lack the level of homicidal intent it requires. Psychologically, most people would find it far easier to kill by pressing a detonator button than by gunning down civilians in cold blood.[57] And second, some may fear the uncertainty of a successful suicide. If they rely on suicide by cop and the bullets do not strike just right, they may end up wounded and in enemy custody. For instance, Hasan was shot in the spine and paralyzed, and a series of other attackers have been shot in the face, groin, leg, and so on—and then lived to face the consequences.[58] For some suicidal people, the prospect of surviving one's attack—perhaps in agonizing pain—can be the ultimate deterrent.

THE NIGHTMARE SCENARIO

In the United States, murder-suicide rates have stayed constant for nearly a century.[59] Rampage, workplace, and school shootings have increased, but they are still extremely rare. On average, suicide terrorism attacks occur less than once a year. And there has never been a suicide terrorist bombing within national borders.

Will it stay this way? Hard to say. But there are several possible changes that could turn things bad in a hurry.

The first would be an increase in the access potential suicide terrorists have to reliable bombs. If it becomes easier for terrorists to purchase or construct explosive devices that would guarantee them a successful suicide, attacks would almost certainly increase. In the past, terrorists in the United States caught in FBI stings have almost always sought assistance with weapons acquisition. But if they didn't need the help, they might not have been stopped.

The second dangerous change would be an increase in the access foreign suicide terrorists have to targets on American soil. Although there are more than two hundred thousand Americans who believe that suicide attacks are "often" or "sometimes" justified, this number is dwarfed by the more than ninety million people around the world who share this same view.[60] The vast majority of them are not suicidal, but they are the huge pool from which most suicide attackers come.[61] Right now, their biggest obstacle is a lack of access. But this may not last forever.

The third potential change would be an increase in Americans' social approval of suicide terrorism. If a significant percentage of them began to support suicide attacks as a legitimate form of political resistance, far more suicidal individuals would seriously consider this deadly path. Currently, most Americans dislike suicide bombing because they see it as a tactic employed by their enemies. But that doesn't mean that they would condemn it if it was being used by people they like. For instance, in August 2009, American crowds happily cheered two suicide bombers in Quentin Tarantino's blockbuster movie *Inglourious Basterds*. Why?

Because the bombers were members of the U.S. military and they were killing Nazis with their attacks. For years, Hollywood movies have been glorifying characters who choose to "go out in a blaze of glory" for some noble cause, and many Americans still believe that a suicide bomber is not that different from a heroic soldier who jumps on a grenade. So a shift to more positive opinions about suicide tactics is far from impossible, since some of the underlying values are already present.

The fourth possibility is perhaps the most frightening: the presence of a sponsoring terrorist organization on U.S. soil. Regardless of its ideology—Islamic fundamentalist, neo-Nazi, left-wing, or right-wing—it could take advantage of all the benefits enjoyed by Hamas in Palestine, the Taliban in Afghanistan, and Al Qaeda in Iraq. The raw materials for prolonged suicide terrorism campaigns are virtually all here. In the United States, approximately thirty-four thousand people commit suicide each year.[62] So there is plenty of suicidal intent to harness, along with the tens of thousands of people who could be coerced into becoming suicidal. A sponsoring organization could easily train bomb makers to provide ready-made explosive vests. The local targets would be easy to access, and it is impossible to guard them all. And organizational leaders could use propaganda to inflame homicidal intent and social approval of suicide terrorism among their supporters. This could really develop into a nightmare scenario.[63]

Fortunately, the future is not set in stone—one way or the other. The steps we take in the years to come may be what ultimately determines our fate.

IDENTIFYING SUICIDE TERRORISTS BEFORE THEY STRIKE

Where's Waldo? You remember him, right? He's that tall, skinny guy from the children's books. Red-and-white-striped shirt, red-and-white hat, black-rimmed glasses. He's always hiding in a crowd. Sources say he may have a bomb strapped to his chest, so we need to find him—and find him fast.

Unfortunately, when it comes to blending in, most suicide terrorists are far better than Waldo. This puts a tremendous amount of pressure on security officials, and the odds are stacked against them. In their version of the game, the picture has millions of people, no one stands still, and the wanted individual isn't conveniently dressed like a human candy cane. It might seem almost impossible for them to figure out who is a threat, and who isn't, before it's too late.

But starting right now, much more can be done to identify future suicide terrorists before they strike. This book is the first step in that direction. There has been more than one hundred years of research on conventional suicide and murder-suicide, and many scholars before me have identified the many common risk factors and warning signs.[64] In the preceding chapters, we have seen how personal problems and suicidal tendencies dominate the lives of many suicide terrorists and directly explain their behavior. It is time for counterterrorism officials to extend these findings, increase their precision, and narrow their sights. When it comes to identifying suicide terrorists, they need to stop looking for just radicalized individuals—and start looking for radicalized individuals who match these specific profiles. And they need to use every resource they can.

A Terrorist in the Family

"I don't remember a time when I wasn't aware that my brother was 'special,'" David Kaczynski recalls.[65] "I was probably seven or eight years old when I first approached Mom with the question 'What's wrong with Teddy?' . . . he doesn't have any friends . . . he doesn't seem to *like* people."[66]

Things got worse. Ted moved to an isolated cabin in Montana, where David could tell he became increasingly upset:

> Ted's angry—well, blistering—letters to our parents started arriving in the late 1970s. The gist was that he was unhappy all his life because Mom and Dad had never truly loved him. . . . At first, I thought he had simply lost his temper. After all, he was emotionally intense and spent nearly all his time alone. . . . But when I wrote to Ted, hoping that he would appreciate the pain his letter had caused our parents and apologize, I received a series of increasingly disturbed replies.[67]

Eventually, David's wife read the letters and told him that Ted might be mentally ill. They shared the letters with a psychiatrist, who saw signs of paranoia and schizophrenia. But with Ted thousands of miles away, they felt powerless to do anything.[68]

Finally, in 1995, David's wife confronted him with a very sensitive question. "Have you ever considered the possibility, even the remote possibility, that your brother might be this Unabomber?"[69] "I didn't know whether to scoff, laugh or get angry," David recalls. "At this point, the Unabomber was the most wanted person in America, and here's my wife saying that it's my brother."[70] David began reading the Unabomber's manifesto, which sounded eerily similar to his brother's letters. He contacted the FBI, the FBI arrested Ted, and Ted admitted to the crimes.

The parents of the "Underwear Bomber" had a similar experience. Throughout his adolescence, Umar Farouk Abdulmutallab's life was characterized by social marginalization, family problems, and a growing obsession with Islamic fundamentalism. His parents were aware of this, and they should have gotten him some professional help. Instead, they sent him away to a British boarding school, where the differences between him and other students were further amplified.

Four years before his suicide attack, Abdulmutallab posted online that "i am in a situation where i do not have a friend . . . i have no one to speak too, no one to consult, no one to support me and i feel depressed and lonely. i do not know what to do."[71] This was not just a bad moment—it was indicative of the problems he struggled with for years.

After continued fights with his father, Abdulmutallab eventually left home for good. In one of his final phone calls, he told his father that he was quitting school and moving to Yemen to study Arabic and Islam. When asked how he would support himself financially, Abdulmutallab explained that he was being sponsored. By whom? "That's none of your business."[72] He sent his father three final text messages, and then was not heard from again.

"I've found a new religion, the real Islam."[73]

"You should just forget about me, I'm never coming back."[74]

"Forgive me for any wrongdoing, I am no longer your child."[75]

His father finally got the message. He understood that something was deeply wrong with his son and that a suicide attack might be forthcoming. So on November 19, 2009, he contacted the local authorities, who put him in touch with the CIA field office.[76] Although U.S. security officials took some steps to address the threat, as it turned out, they did not do nearly enough. It was pure luck that Abdulmutallab's Christmas Day bomb on Northwest Airlines Flight 253 failed to explode. The Underwear Bomber was arrested and charged with eight counts, including terrorism and attempted murder.

Mobilizing Family and Friends

As these cases have shown, the family and friends of future terrorists could potentially be mobilized to help identify attackers before they strike.[77] No one sees potential suicide terrorists more often or knows them more intimately than their own friends and family. Because of his inside information, David Kaczynski was able to accurately identify the bomber who had baffled the FBI, criminal psychologists, and law enforcement experts for seventeen years. And Abdulmutallab's father sensed that his son might carry out an attack *five weeks* before he actually tried to blow himself up.

These friends and family members are a valuable untapped resource. After all, the desire to keep one's loved ones alive is a human universal. It's just as strong in Nigeria and Yemen as it is in London and New York. Once a suicide attack occurs, families of suicide terrorists may fiercely defend their loved ones' actions, labeling them "martyrs" and "heroes"—no matter what they did. But while the future perpetrators are still alive, all their parents, siblings, spouses, and friends care about is keeping them that way.[78] Most have the exact same goal as security officials: preventing the suicide attack.[79]

Of course, counterterrorism experts already know that they must rely on the eyes and ears of the public. And in the past, they have done a good job of encouraging community members to report suspicious activity. For instance, U.S. Homeland Security Director Janet Napolitano launched the public awareness campaign called "If You See Something,

Say Something," making it easy for people to call the cops or log on to the FBI website to submit tips.[80]

However, most people assume that this mandate applies to the suspicious behavior of strangers—*not to their own friends and family.* So we need to make sure that they understand their responsibility and exactly what is at stake. When it comes to saving their loved ones from making an irreversible mistake, they are the last line of defense. Members of the public should be educated about the critical risk factors and warning signs for suicide terrorism so that they can recognize suicidal people in their midst and get them the help they so desperately need.

Internet Monitoring and Surveillance

Identifying suicide terrorists before they strike also depends on improved internet monitoring and surveillance. Past "experts" who have downplayed the value of this resource simply don't know what they're talking about. For instance, in December 2010, a professor with twenty-eight years of experience working for the CIA declared that "A real terrorist who is going to blow up the Washington Metro wouldn't put an advertisement on Facebook. He'd just do it."[81] Unfortunately, this is a very shortsighted and potentially dangerous assumption. Was there anything "unreal" about Nidal Hasan, who posted online about suicide bombings six months before he launched a suicide attack at the Fort Hood base in Texas?[82] And in other cases, suicide terrorists have stopped short of explicitly revealing their intentions, but they left a series of obvious clues online that a skilled analyst could easily piece together.

The internet is a particularly good place for identifying future suicide terrorists because many cannot help but give themselves away. They are not purely rational—they are also psychologically conflicted, emotionally compromised, and deeply consumed by pain. Before they attempt suicide—which is often referred to as a "cry for help"—they may literally cry out by posting online. In addition, suicide terrorists are often socially isolated and desperate for attention, which makes internet forums, online communities, dating websites, and social networking platforms especially attractive for fulfilling their needs. And if they have bottled-up anger that they cannot share with those around them, they may be particularly likely to vent it online, where users still feel essentially anonymous and free to say whatever is on their minds.[83]

Once tentatively identified, suicide terrorists could be lured by government sting operations. The key is to customize the "bait" to the motives and psychology of suicidal people who are also willing to kill. Past FBI stings have almost exclusively targeted nonsuicidal terrorists, who are largely driven by anger and ideology. As we've seen, suicide terrorists are psychologically different, so the strategies to trap them should be different, too.

The Latest Scientific Breakthroughs

We could use a little magic on our side. Maybe a wand-wielding wizard with some wacky and wonderful spells. Or the next best thing. As British writer Arthur C. Clarke explains, "Any sufficiently advanced technology is indistinguishable from magic."[84]

In this case, our magic may come from 2011 MacArthur Fellow Matthew Nock. He and his colleagues recently discovered that a five-minute computer test can distinguish individuals who have previously attempted suicide from those who have not.[85] The same computer test also has *predictive powers,* showing which individuals are most likely to attempt suicide sometime in the next six months. Amazingly, the test was actually better at predicting whether people would attempt suicide than the test takers themselves—or their psychiatrists.[86]

In other words, no human being—regardless of information or qualifications—could apparently see the future as accurately as this simple, five-minute test. The test works by measuring implicit associations between the self and concepts of death or suicide at an unconscious level. For instance, subjects were asked to match words representing constructs of "death" (die, dead, deceased, lifeless, suicide) or "life" (alive, survive, live, thrive, breathing), with either attributes of "me" (I, myself, my, mine, and self) or attributes of "not me" (they, them, their, theirs, and other).[87] By timing people's reactions and thus tapping into the human unconscious, it is possible to get them to reveal things that they are genuinely unaware of, along with things they consciously want to keep hidden.[88] Previous versions of this test have successfully exposed racial bias, gender bias, and religious bias among test takers.

This could be an incredibly powerful security screening tool for identifying anyone who is contemplating a suicide attack. It could be employed by officials who are running security checkpoints, conducting interrogations, interviewing sources in the field, and so on. It could even become an iPhone app. And airports could use it to test departing passengers before they board their flights.

Naturally, we'd need more trials to make sure that test takers could not find a way to cheat. But Nock and his research team were using the most basic version of the test, so there is plenty of room for improvement. Increasing its complexity in measuring suicide-related signs could further enhance its validity and accuracy.

Of course, there would be some false positives. Some suicidal individuals who have no terrorist inclinations whatsoever would also be flagged. But encouraging them to get help wouldn't be a bad thing either. And overall, this tool could significantly help counterterrorism officials narrow their search to those who are actually suicidal, at which point other threat assessment measures could be employed.

DESTROYING THE MYTH OF MARTYRDOM

Even if this book were a work of fiction, and everything it said was wrong, it would still be a valuable weapon against suicide terrorism. As a form of psychological warfare, it could be used to smear the reputations of suicide terrorists by portraying them as weak, cowardly, and suicidal. It would also be an effective propaganda tool for maligning terrorist organizations and their leaders as immoral vultures who exploit the mentally ill.

But this is no mere fiction. Virtually everything in this book has been documented, vetted by peer-reviewed journals, and corroborated by other sources.[89] That should make it infinitely more valuable for our leaders, who need to stop spreading terrorist propaganda and simply embrace the truth. They need to stop claiming that suicide terrorists are the psychological equivalent of America's Navy SEALs—fully committed, unafraid of death, and willing to do whatever it takes. Stop insisting that terrorist organizations would never use mentally unstable people. And stop suggesting that 95 percent of suicide attacks are caused by foreign occupiers from the West. These misconceptions are not only wrong—they're dangerously wrong. They glorify suicide terrorism and help the cult of martyrdom grow.

Instead, this book should be the first step in a broader effort to correct misunderstandings about suicide terrorism worldwide. Setting the record straight is not just important for educational purposes—it's also the best chance we have to deter future suicide terrorists. As experts have maintained for years, the best way to stop suicide terrorists before they strike is to alter the social perceptions of the practice, so that it is no longer seen as a certain path to fame and paradise.[90] Otherwise, all the armed guards, metal detectors, and body scanners in the world will not prevent individuals who want to kill and die from finding soft targets for their attacks.

By rejecting the myth of martyrdom and helping everyone recognize that suicide terrorists are truly suicidal, we can begin to turn things around. The key is that the attackers themselves fear the stigma and consequences that come from committing "suicide." For instance, as we've seen, short of early identification and arrest, there appears to have been only one thing that could have stopped Nidal Hasan and Anders Behring Breivik from carrying out their murderous attacks: the stigma of suicide. Their own words made this quite plain.[91]

And many other suicide terrorists are similarly desperate to conceal the truth. When the subject of suicide comes up, they immediately become defensive—they protest too much. Instead of helping them convince themselves that they are making a noble "sacrifice," we need to start making their primary rationalization a transparent relic of the past.

Hasan's and Breivik's obsession with not being seen as suicidal is typical: most suicide terrorists believe they will go directly to hell—do not pass "Go," do not collect two hundred dollars—if they commit suicide. And even most terrorist organizations themselves condemn suicidal behavior as "weak," "selfish," and "mentally disturbed."[92] So let's make these values work for us. By spreading the truth about suicide terrorists, the personal crises and pressures that lead them to act, and the motives behind their attacks, we can expose these attackers for what they really are.

Once the truth is widely recognized, a significant percentage of would-be suicide terrorists will begin to think twice. Instead of gaining status as heroic "martyrs," they would risk losing it. Volunteering to carry out a suicide attack would become like raising your hand and saying, "Hi, I have serious mental health problems, which I am trying to mask as something heroic. Please judge me."

That kind of exposure is what many suicide terrorists fear the most, and the last thing they would ever want.

THE BIGGER PICTURE

If suicide terrorism becomes properly stigmatized as the exploitative use of suicidal individuals, terrorist organizations can be expected to adjust. Their leaders are generally rational and perceptive—they will not use a tactic if it is so disreputable that it costs them support among the populations they hope to rally to their cause.[93] Under such circumstances, they would likely turn away volunteers for suicide attacks, and find other ways to deal with the suicidal members within their own ranks. After all, terrorists have a variety of other strategies and tactics at their disposal, and even without suicide terrorism, they could still wreak plenty of destruction. But this is a case where perceptions clearly affect reality. By demystifying these so-called "martyrdom" attacks and exposing the suicidality of those who carry them out, the United States and its allies could strike a significant blow against terrorist organizations worldwide.

But ultimately, stopping suicide terrorism is not just a matter of self-preservation. It's much bigger than that. We would do almost anything to prevent the next 9/11 attack, because we don't want to lose our colleagues, friends, or loved ones to a tragic fate. And that's reasonable. But we should also care about preserving human potential on all sides.

People who were suicidal at some point in their lives include Isaac Newton, Ludwig van Beethoven, Leo Tolstoy, Abraham Lincoln, Kurt

Vonnegut, and J. K. Rowling.[94] Walt Disney, Frank Sinatra, Sammy Davis Jr., Johnny Cash, Tina Turner, Oprah Winfrey, and George Clooney were each suicidal as well.[95] Fortunately, these individuals all survived their moments of darkness, and they all went on to make valuable contributions to society. The same could be true of the desperate people who are out there somewhere, wondering if they should blow themselves up.

In the long run, we should strive to save us *and* save them. So they can one day return the favor.

APPENDIX A

PARTIAL LIST OF SUICIDE TERRORISTS WITH RISK FACTORS FOR SUICIDE[1]

FROM CHAPTER 1

JOSEPH STACK: Compared himself to suicidal 1929 Wall Street Crash window jumpers, given his recent loss of retirement savings during an IRS tax audit. Admitted his own mental health problems, lamenting that "There isn't enough therapy in the world that can fix what is really broken [with me]."
SUCCESSFUL SUICIDE? Yes

QARI SAMI: Took antidepressants but had complained they weren't working. Described by friend as a depressed and brooding loner.
SUCCESSFUL SUICIDE? Yes

FROM CHAPTER 2

WAFA AL-BISS: Had tried to throw herself out a window but lost her nerve; later tried to set herself on fire, but was saved after third-degree burns. Had been regularly beaten by her father. Expressed guilt about being so difficult for her parents.
SUCCESSFUL SUICIDE? No

FROM CHAPTER 3

ALI HASSAN ABU KAMAL: Clearest form of *suicidal* terrorism: shot himself in the head after shooting seven people at the Empire State Building.
SUCCESSFUL SUICIDE? Yes

RAFIK (PSEUDONYM): Suicidal tendencies identified through direct psychological assessment. Almost slit his own wrists after father's fatal heart attack, but was interrupted. Had also threatened to kill the hospital

doctor. Was shy and insecure, had almost no friends at school during his childhood. Stockpiled painkillers for potential suicide attempt in prison.
SUCCESSFUL SUICIDE? No

ZUHEIR (PSEUDONYM): Suicidal tendencies identified through direct psychological assessment. Explained motive for suicide attack as "I reached such a state of despair that I wanted to kill myself. . . . I wanted to get rid of my life in this world. That's it." Had tried getting in front of Israeli tanks and hoping they would shoot him, to no avail. History of physical abuse during childhood, family problems, and social isolation.
SUCCESSFUL SUICIDE? No

HAMED (PSEUDONYM): Very low self-esteem identified through direct psychological assessment. Struggled with social marginalization, parental disapproval, and difficulties in school, from which he had dropped out.
SUCCESSFUL SUICIDE? No

SABRI (PSEUDONYM): Depressive tendencies identified through direct psychological assessment. Expressed pain over brothers leaving for school and father being hospitalized after car accident. Apparently traumatized by death of close friend's eldest brother: "My friend's tears froze my own tears in my eyelashes."
SUCCESSFUL SUICIDE? No

AYAT AL-AKHRAS: Unmarried eighteen-year-old girl had unwanted pregnancy.
SUCCESSFUL SUICIDE? Yes

ANDALIB TAKATKA SULEIMAN: Unmarried twenty-one-year old girl had unwanted pregnancy. Expressed desire to escape: "We are suffering; We are dying while we are still alive."
SUCCESSFUL SUICIDE? Yes

NICKY REILLY (AKA MOHAMAD ABDULAZIZ RASHID SAEED): Had made several previous suicide attempts, which included a drug overdose and stabbing himself in the stomach. Had IQ of 83 and had been diagnosed with severe mental illness.
SUCCESSFUL SUICIDE? No, suffered serious facial cuts and burns

MURIEL DEGAUQUE: Dropped out of school at age sixteen; often ran away from home; engaged in substance abuse and promiscuity. Devastated by brother's fatal motorcycle accident in her early twenties, overwhelmed by sadness and survivor's guilt. Married Moroccan extremist, who was shot and killed the same day she launched her suicide attack.
SUCCESSFUL SUICIDE? Yes

WAFA IDRIS: Socially marginalized and shamed after she had been divorced because she could not have children.
SUCCESSFUL SUICIDE? Yes

BILAL FAHS: Legally prohibited from marrying his fiancée due to his invalid civil status; had been abandoned by his father as a child.
SUCCESSFUL SUICIDE? Yes

REEM RAIYSHI: Sought forgiveness for her sin of adultery; may have feared the growing rumors and social stigma.
SUCCESSFUL SUICIDE? Yes

SHADI NASSAR: Suffered severe head trauma as a child and epileptic episodes ever since. Mocked and humiliated by peers for seeming insane, he became lonely and depressed and quit school.
SUCCESSFUL SUICIDE? Yes

MURAD (PSEUDONYM): Suffered from degenerative eye condition; expressed desire to die rather than live as a handicapped person.
SUCCESSFUL SUICIDE? No

ARIEN AHMED: Father died when she was a child; loved one recently killed, "So I lost all my future." Had nasty argument with aunt before leaving home, which may have been the trigger for her actions.
SUCCESSFUL SUICIDE? No

HANADI JARADAT: Fiancé, brother, and cousin killed; she was strained by father's deteriorating health. Recurring nightmares and trouble sleeping suggest PTSD.
SUCCESSFUL SUICIDE? Yes

THENMOZHI RAJARATNAM (AKA DHANU): Gang-raped by soldiers; four brothers killed.
SUCCESSFUL SUICIDE? Yes

FROM CHAPTER 4

MOHAMED ATTA: Struggled with social isolation, depression, guilt, shame, and hopelessness for years. Made pleas that he "be forgiven for what I have done in the past," assertions that "Joy kills the heart," and lamentations like "How much time have we wasted in our lives?" Seemed unwilling or unable to express positive emotions, condemned fun, music, and delicious food, complained about needing to eat to stay alive, exhibited signs of life weariness, wrote a bitter last will and testament at age twenty-seven.
SUCCESSFUL SUICIDE? Yes

ZIAD JARRAH: Expressed dissatisfaction with his life and intent to not die in "a natural way." Nearly flunked high school, dropped out of college. Had dramatic mood swings and a stressful relationship with his family and his girlfriend, who had previously attempted suicide herself. Scolded by handlers for not caring enough during filming of his martyrdom video; almost backed out of entire 9/11 plot at the last minute.
SUCCESSFUL SUICIDE? Yes

MARWAN AL SHEHHI: Father's death when he was nineteen was a major psychological blow. Had difficulties as a student.
SUCCESSFUL SUICIDE? Yes

HANI HANJOUR: Socially isolated, very shy, "meek and quiet." Rarely left his home. Was being pressured by family to get married. Had difficulties as a student, even at flight school.
SUCCESSFUL SUICIDE? Yes

TAWFIQ BIN ATTASH (AKA KHALLAD): Lost his lower right leg in combat; his brother was also killed.
SUCCESSFUL SUICIDE? No

AHMED AL NAMI: Behavior apparently became so strange that his family feared a "bipolar disorder."
SUCCESSFUL SUICIDE? Yes

WAIL AL SHEHRI: "Fell into a deep depression" in late 1999 that was so bad that he had to leave his job and seek medical treatment. "His friends say it was not just depression, but perhaps even a suicidal tendency."
SUCCESSFUL SUICIDE? Yes

FROM CHAPTER 6
NIDAL HASAN: Struggled with social marginalization, work problems, mental health problems, personal crises, perceived bullying, and failures to find a wife despite urgency of being middle-aged. Was reportedly "mortified" about impending military deployment and horrors he anticipated.
SUCCESSFUL SUICIDE? No; expected to be shot and killed on-site but was only paralyzed

FROM CHAPTER 7
SALEH (PSEUDONYM): Coerced and pressured by terrorist leaders; originally said no but eventually gave in. Dependent personality identified through direct psychological assessment.
SUCCESSFUL SUICIDE? No

GHULAM (PSEUDONYM): Coerced and pressured by terrorist leaders. Told that if he did not carry out his attack, one of the mission organizers would chop his head off and he would go to hell. Explained, "I was forced to do this."
SUCCESSFUL SUICIDE? No

NAZIMA (PSEUDONYM): Coerced and pressured by terrorist leaders; originally said no but eventually gave in. Explained that "they forced me. I hate the idea of dying, I like living . . . [but] I didn't have the courage to tell my father" about what she'd done or ask for help.
SUCCESSFUL SUICIDE? No

MAJED (PSEUDONYM): Coerced and pressured by terrorist leaders; initially did not want to die, but "did not know how to say no." Became very stressed. Eventually gave in, but hoped to leave town before suicide attack was scheduled. When date was quickly arranged, he decided to go

through with it. Dependent-avoidant personality identified through direct psychological assessment.
SUCCESSFUL SUICIDE? No

ABDENNABI KOUNJAA: Lamented that "I can't put up with this life living like a weak and humiliated person under the scrutiny of infidels and tyrants," adding that "this life is the path towards death" and that he preferred "death instead of life."
SUCCESSFUL SUICIDE? Yes

ALLEKEMA LAMARI: A forty-year-old virgin who had never had a girlfriend. During a five-year prison sentence, he had reportedly developed a mental disorder. His brother had died in Algeria.
SUCCESSFUL SUICIDE? Yes

JAMAL AHMIDAN: Despite his religious beliefs, he was a heroin, cocaine, and alcohol user. He was also married to a drug addict and had been repeatedly in trouble with the law.
SUCCESSFUL SUICIDE? Yes

SHAMIL BASAYEV: Wife and family killed; explained that "It does not matter to us when we die."
SUCCESSFUL SUICIDE? No, but died in mysterious bomb explosion at age forty-one

HESHAM MOHAMED HADAYET: Struggled with marriage problems, business problems. Was reportedly depressed about being left alone on his birthday when his family left the country.
SUCCESSFUL SUICIDE? Yes

MIR AIMAL KASI: Had seizure disorder as a child; described as brooding and introspective loner. Was apparently missing tissue from the frontal lobes of his brain.
SUCCESSFUL SUICIDE? No, expected to be shot and killed but wasn't; later executed

FROM CHAPTER 8

ANDERS BEHRING BREIVIK: Engaged in classic psychological projection, claiming that society's flaws would inevitably produce "millions of people with psychological problems and tens of thousands of suicides." Admitted that he expected to die during his attack, but tried to rationalize his behavior as "sacrifice," not "suicide," to avoid religious punishments.
SUCCESSFUL SUICIDE? No

UMAR ABDULMUTALLAB (UNDERWEAR BOMBER): Wrote that "i am in a situation where i do not have a friend . . . i have no one to speak too, no one to consult, no one to support me and i feel depressed and lonely. i do not know what to do." Struggled with social marginalization and family problems.
SUCCESSFUL SUICIDE? No, suffered serious burns

OTHER CASES FROM CHAPTER 3, TABLE 2

WALID (PSEUDONYM): Suicidal tendencies identified through direct
psychological assessment. Had often wanted to commit conventional
suicide, but did not, due to Islamic prohibitions. Explained motive for
suicide attack as "I wanted to end my life and rest." History of physical
and sexual abuse during childhood, difficulty in school, and social
isolation.
SUCCESSFUL SUICIDE? No

MARYAM: Attempted suicide, which involved slitting her wrist with a razor
blade and led to hospitalization and her getting her stomach pumped,
after she was forbidden from marrying the boy she loved. She was then
essentially abducted and raped by a sixty-year-old man who'd paid to
marry her, at which point she decided to carry out a suicide attack.
SUCCESSFUL SUICIDE? Unknown

ABBY (PSEUDONYM): Considered committing suicide by driving his car off a
cliff after he lost the girl he loved to a forced marriage. He later decided to
carry out a suicide attack instead.
SUCCESSFUL SUICIDE? No

UNIDENTIFIED MALE: Admitted suicidal thoughts in his diary and to police
when arrested; had planned to fill his car with gasoline canisters and blow
up a school as a suicide bomber.
SUCCESSFUL SUICIDE? No

AHMAD GULL: Reportedly had "mental sickness" (possibly PTSD) after
experiencing repeated airplane crashes and "was going through a very
difficult period of time in his life" with financial problems and having to
sell his house.
SUCCESSFUL SUICIDE? Yes

CHARLES BISHOP: Parents had history of suicide attempts and mental illness;
they blamed son's depression on prescription drug use. He was described
by police chief as a troubled loner.
SUCCESSFUL SUICIDE? Yes

MOHAMMED HUSSAIN: During hostage-taking standoff said, "I want to die, I
want police to shoot me right here," pointing to his chest.
SUCCESSFUL SUICIDE? No

SA'ER HUNINEE: Traumatized by witnessing a friend's legs be deliberately
crushed by an enemy soldier who ran over him in a jeep. Had terrible
recurring nightmares and would call out the name of his injured friend
in his sleep, which is a sign of PTSD. Two close comrades had also been
killed. As a youth, he had felt deeply neglected by his father, who had
remarried and essentially abandoned him.
SUCCESSFUL SUICIDE? Yes

UNIDENTIFIED MALE: "Mentally disturbed," according to his brother and a close friend. He had been paid to spy on a local terrorist organization, but was discovered and reportedly forced to "redeem himself by becoming a suicide bomber or face the consequences."
SUCCESSFUL SUICIDE? Yes

JIM DAVID ADKISSON: Was depressed; wrote that "I'm sick and tired of being sick and tired." Struggled with failed marriage and inability to find job.
SUCCESSFUL SUICIDE? No, expected to be shot and killed but wasn't

LORS DOUKAIEV: Mother claimed he was depressed and had admitted he was tired of living, and that he was not motivated by politics or religion. He had only one leg, and as a child had been violently bullied by Russian children, who once broke his arm and his prosthetic leg.
SUCCESSFUL SUICIDE? No

BRYANT NEAL VINAS: Had dropped out of the army after just three weeks because he found it "mentally overwhelming." Later explained that he volunteered for a suicide attack because he was "having difficult time with the altitude [in Pakistan]. I was getting very sick, so I felt that it would be easier."
SUCCESSFUL SUICIDE? No

UNIDENTIFIED MALE: Broke down in tears on a somewhat regular basis, reportedly due to his family's poverty, lack of hot running water, and dependence on secondhand clothes.
SUCCESSFUL SUICIDE? Yes

IBRAHIM NAJI: Fell into a depressed state, according to his parents, following the killing of two friends and the public humiliation of his father.
SUCCESSFUL SUICIDE? Yes

UNIDENTIFIED MALE: Experienced considerable psychological turmoil, according to his parents, after his cousin was betrayed by a family member and then killed.
SUCCESSFUL SUICIDE? Yes

JOSEPH NEALE: Reportedly struggled with mental health problems. Had lost job, then lost lawsuits attempting to get his job back.
SUCCESSFUL SUICIDE? No, shot and seriously wounded but survived

MEDNA BARAYKOVA: Was sick with tuberculosis and was constantly coughing up blood
SUCCESSFUL SUICIDE? Yes

UNIDENTIFIED SIXTEEN-YEAR-OLD BOY: Had recently contracted HIV; was apparently ashamed and feared the social stigma.
SUCCESSFUL SUICIDE? Yes

UNIDENTIFIED MALE: Suffered from tumor that left him partially blind.
SUCCESSFUL SUICIDE? Yes

UNIDENTIFIED MALE: Suffered injury that left him confined to a wheelchair.
SUCCESSFUL SUICIDE? Yes

QARI SAMIULLAH: Suffered physical disability.
SUCCESSFUL SUICIDE? Yes

KOKU KHADJIYEVA: Mental illness.
SUCCESSFUL SUICIDE? Yes

UNIDENTIFIED MALE: Mental illness.
SUCCESSFUL SUICIDE? No

UNIDENTIFIED MALE: Mental illness.
SUCCESSFUL SUICIDE? No

UNIDENTIFIED MALE: Mental illness.
SUCCESSFUL SUICIDE? No

LARISSA (FATIMA) GANIYEVA: Abducted, beaten, tortured, and possibly raped
by Russian soldiers. Her three brothers had been killed and a sister had
disappeared. After returning from abduction, reportedly stated, along with
her sister, that "We are now in shame. We cannot live like this."
SUCCESSFUL SUICIDE? Yes

KHADIZHAT (MILANA) GANIYEVA: Abducted, beaten, tortured, and possibly
raped by Russian soldiers. Her three brothers had been killed and a sister
had disappeared. After returning from abduction, reportedly stated, along
with her sister, that "We are now in shame. We cannot live like this."
SUCCESSFUL SUICIDE? Yes

NIMER (PSEUDONYM): Diagnosed with some PTSD symptoms. Close uncle had
been arrested, beaten, and recently diagnosed with cancer. One extended
family member had been killed and two others had been arrested.
SUCCESSFUL SUICIDE? No

LARISA MUSALAYEVA: Brother had committed suicide.
SUCCESSFUL SUICIDE? Yes

UNIDENTIFIED FEMALE ATTACKER: Claimed that "her whole family had been
killed by the Russians. She had buried all her children and was now forced
to live in the forest. She had nowhere to go and nothing to live for."
SUCCESSFUL SUICIDE? Yes

RAMI GANIM: Psychologically distressed after he was arrested by enemy
soldiers, who broke his hand and nose during interrogations, before
spreading public rumors that he was a traitor.
SUCCESSFUL SUICIDE? Yes

SABRINE AMARA: Brother killed, father had died. She claimed to be happy about the chance to carry out a suicide attack, but broke down and cried when she actually saw her suicide vest.
SUCCESSFUL SUICIDE? No

DJENNET ABDURAKHMENOVA: Husband killed. She was seventeen years old and suspected of being on drugs or mentally ill prior to attack. As a child, her father had abandoned her to the care of an alcoholic uncle.
SUCCESSFUL SUICIDE? Yes

IYAD AL-MASRI: His fourteen-year-old brother, fifteen-year-old cousin, uncle, and four close friends had all been killed, and he had been injured multiple times. He reportedly "developed a strong sense that his days were numbered," and blew himself up just nine days after his brother and cousin were killed.
SUCCESSFUL SUICIDE? Yes

NABIL (PSEUDONYM): Cousin killed. Had lost job and been denied work permit.
SUCCESSFUL SUICIDE? No

ALI (PSEUDONYM): Had been mistakenly shot and wounded by Israeli soldiers; wanted revenge. Brother-in-law had recently died in a suicide attack.
SUCCESSFUL SUICIDE? No

MUSTAFA ABU-SHADUF: Brother and friend killed, close friend disappeared.
SUCCESSFUL SUICIDE? Yes

MUHAMMAD NASSER: Close friend killed.
SUCCESSFUL SUICIDE? Yes

JIHAD TITI: Cousin killed.
SUCCESSFUL SUICIDE? Yes

MAYILLA SOUFANGI: Mother had died; she was struggling with desperate poverty. Had run away from home.
SUCCESSFUL SUICIDE? No

LUIZA GAZUYEVA: Husband and two brothers killed.
SUCCESSFUL SUICIDE? Yes

KAIRA: Husband had died, sixteen-year-old brother had been tortured to death, cousin killed, and family's house destroyed.
SUCCESSFUL SUICIDE? Yes

SHAHIDA BAYMURADOVA: Husband killed.
SUCCESSFUL SUICIDE? Yes

KAWA: Husband tortured to death and mutilated.
SUCCESSFUL SUICIDE? Yes

QIAN MINGQI: Two separate times, his house was seized by the government. The second time, he fought back, and his wife was grabbed and hung upside down by a Chinese demolition team. She died several days later.
SUCCESSFUL SUICIDE? Yes

UNIDENTIFIED ATTACKER: Brother killed.
SUCCESSFUL SUICIDE? Yes

UNIDENTIFIED ATTACKER: Brother killed.
SUCCESSFUL SUICIDE? Yes

UNIDENTIFIED ATTACKER: Brother killed.
SUCCESSFUL SUICIDE? Yes

UNIDENTIFIED ATTACKER: Brother killed.
SUCCESSFUL SUICIDE? Yes

UNIDENTIFIED ATTACKER: Brother killed.
SUCCESSFUL SUICIDE? Yes

UNIDENTIFIED FEMALE: Brother killed; she expressed desire to escape life: "It is a dirty world in which evil reigns—it is difficult to live in this world."
SUCCESSFUL SUICIDE? Yes

UNIDENTIFIED ATTACKER: Family member disappeared after arrest (presumed dead).
SUCCESSFUL SUICIDE? Yes

UNIDENTIFIED ATTACKER: Family member disappeared after arrest (presumed dead).
SUCCESSFUL SUICIDE? Yes

UNIDENTIFIED ATTACKER: Family member disappeared after arrest (presumed dead).
SUCCESSFUL SUICIDE? Yes

UNIDENTIFIED ATTACKER: Family member tortured.
SUCCESSFUL SUICIDE? Yes

UNIDENTIFIED ATTACKER: Father or mother killed.
SUCCESSFUL SUICIDE? Yes

UNIDENTIFIED ATTACKER: Father or mother killed.
SUCCESSFUL SUICIDE? Yes

UNIDENTIFIED ATTACKER: Father or mother killed.
SUCCESSFUL SUICIDE? Yes

UNIDENTIFIED ATTACKER: Father or mother killed.
SUCCESSFUL SUICIDE? Yes

UNIDENTIFIED ATTACKER: Father or mother killed.
SUCCESSFUL SUICIDE? Yes

UNIDENTIFIED ATTACKER: Husband killed.
SUCCESSFUL SUICIDE? Yes

UNIDENTIFIED ATTACKER: More than one family member killed.
SUCCESSFUL SUICIDE? Yes

UNIDENTIFIED ATTACKER: More than one family member killed.
SUCCESSFUL SUICIDE? Yes

UNIDENTIFIED ATTACKER: More than one family member killed.
SUCCESSFUL SUICIDE? Yes

UNIDENTIFIED ATTACKER: More than one family member killed.
SUCCESSFUL SUICIDE? Yes

UNIDENTIFIED ATTACKER: More than one family member killed.
SUCCESSFUL SUICIDE? Yes

UNIDENTIFIED ATTACKER: More than one family member killed.
SUCCESSFUL SUICIDE? Yes

UNIDENTIFIED ATTACKER: More than one family member killed.
SUCCESSFUL SUICIDE? Yes

UNIDENTIFIED ATTACKER: More than one family member killed.
SUCCESSFUL SUICIDE? Yes

UNIDENTIFIED ATTACKER: More than one family member killed.
SUCCESSFUL SUICIDE? Yes

UNIDENTIFIED ATTACKER: More than one family member killed.
SUCCESSFUL SUICIDE? Yes

UNIDENTIFIED ATTACKER: More than one family member killed.
SUCCESSFUL SUICIDE? Yes

UNIDENTIFIED ATTACKER: More than one family member killed.
SUCCESSFUL SUICIDE? Yes

UNIDENTIFIED ATTACKER: More than one family member killed.
SUCCESSFUL SUICIDE? Yes

UNIDENTIFIED FEMALE: One brother killed, three other brothers arrested and
imprisoned.
SUCCESSFUL SUICIDE? No

UNIDENTIFIED FEMALE: Loved one killed.
SUCCESSFUL SUICIDE? No

UNIDENTIFIED FEMALE: Loved one killed.
SUCCESSFUL SUICIDE? No

UNIDENTIFIED FEMALE: Loved one killed.
SUCCESSFUL SUICIDE? No

UNIDENTIFIED FEMALE: Loved one killed.
SUCCESSFUL SUICIDE? No

HUMAM KHALIL ABU MULAL AL-BALAWI: Had been arrested for posting on
extremist websites. Interrogators threatened to end his career, imprison
him permanently, and cause problems for his family unless he agreed
to spy on terrorist groups. His family claimed that "He was always a
loner," but that he became more "strange" and was "a changed person,"
psychologically, after his arrest.
SUCCESSFUL SUICIDE? Yes

ABDALFATAH RASHID: A former police officer, he had accidentally killed
someone during an interrogation and been sent to jail. He escaped
prison, but was apparently fearful that he would be either rearrested and
imprisoned, or attacked by his victim's family.
SUCCESSFUL SUICIDE? Yes

AYMAN (RAJMAN) KURBANOVA: Had been literally thrown out of the house by
her first husband because she was infertile. Family members reported that
this left her devastated.
SUCCESSFUL SUICIDE? Yes

UNIDENTIFIED FEMALE ATTACKER: Missed what she thought was her last chance
for marriage. Explained that "my life wasn't worth anything and my
father wouldn't let me marry the boy I wanted to, so I . . . volunteered, to
get back at my father." Cousin had recently died as well.
SUCCESSFUL SUICIDE? No

ABDALBASIT AWDEH: Was legally prohibited from visiting or marrying the
woman he loved, and she was not allowed to move and join him.
SUCCESSFUL SUICIDE? Yes

SHIFA ADNAN AL-QUDSI: Socially marginalized after being divorced by her
husband; her brother had been arrested while attempting his own suicide
attack.
SUCCESSFUL SUICIDE? No

DARINE ABU AISHA: Socially mocked and marginalized for refusing to marry;
her family was also suffering public shame.
SUCCESSFUL SUICIDE? Yes

IZZ AD-DIN AL-MASRI: Very attached to his mother, who had recently been
diagnosed with diabetes. Very socially isolated: he "wouldn't even look at
people." Struggled at school; considered to be a failure by many.
SUCCESSFUL SUICIDE? Yes

TAIMOUR ABDULWAHAB AL-ABDALY: Troubled childhood. As adult, was described as very confused, overly emotional, and frustrated. Expressed pain about "what happened to me in this life," apart from his wife and children.
SUCCESSFUL SUICIDE? Yes

CHARLES LEE THORNTON: Had been fined thousands of dollars, which he had contested in lawsuits and lost. He had recently been forcibly removed from a city council meeting.
SUCCESSFUL SUICIDE? Yes

NAJIBULLAH ZAZI: Dropped out of high school; got into $51,000 of credit card debt despite having monthly income of only $800. Had filed for bankruptcy and been kicked out of his uncle's house for not paying rent.
SUCCESSFUL SUICIDE? No

MOHAMMED MAHMOUD BERRO: Serious threats had been made against his debt-ridden father and family.
SUCCESSFUL SUICIDE? No

AYAT KMEIL: Came from very strict family; was not allowed to drive or leave home unsupervised. Had recently failed her exams.
SUCCESSFUL SUICIDE? No

ABU MUHAMMAD AL-SAN'ANI: Expressed desire to escape "this transient life"; sought forgiveness from his brothers in the group (spoke in general terms, but may have been covering something more specific).
SUCCESSFUL SUICIDE? Yes

MOHAMMAD SIDIQUE KHAN: Expressed need for "guarantee" of entry into heaven, which implies he may have been struggling with guilt. Lacked tactical reason for not just planting bombs and walking away.
SUCCESSFUL SUICIDE? Yes

UNIDENTIFIED FEMALE: Asked forgiveness for "anything I have done to hurt you" and for the suffering she was causing her mother, whom she claimed had never understood her.
SUCCESSFUL SUICIDE? Yes

UNIDENTIFIED MALE: Asked forgiveness for the pain he had caused his sister and mother, which implies he may have been struggling with some specific guilt.
SUCCESSFUL SUICIDE? Yes

MULTIPLE UNIDENTIFIED ATTACKERS: Mental health problems.
SUCCESSFUL SUICIDE? Sometimes

MULTIPLE UNIDENTIFIED ATTACKERS: Raped or sexually assaulted.
SUCCESSFUL SUICIDE? Sometimes

MULTIPLE UNIDENTIFIED ATTACKERS: Heroin addiction.
SUCCESSFUL SUICIDE? Sometimes

MULTIPLE UNIDENTIFIED ATTACKERS: Suffered physical disabilities.
SUCCESSFUL SUICIDE? Sometimes

MULTIPLE TEENAGE BOYS: Kidnapped and coerced by terrorist leaders. Often beaten to ensure compliance.
SUCCESSFUL SUICIDE? Sometimes

MULTIPLE UNIDENTIFIED ATTACKERS: Threatened with harm against families if they did not carry out suicide attacks.
SUCCESSFUL SUICIDE? Sometimes

APPENDIX B

LIST OF DIFFERENT TYPES OF SUICIDE ATTACKERS IN THE UNITED STATES, 1990–2010

There were a total of 81 suicide attacks in the United States during this time period.

Year	Name	Type[a]	Location
1990	James E. Pough	RS	Jacksonville, FL
1991	Thomas McIlvane	WP	Royal Oak, MI
1991	Gang Lu	SS	Iowa City, IA
1991	George Jo Hennard	RS	Killeen, TX
1993	Paul Calden	WP	Tampa, FL
1993	Mir Aimal Kasi	ST	Langley, VA
1993	Gian Luigi Ferri	RS	San Francisco, CA
1993	Alan Winterbourne	RS	Oxnard, CA
1993	Larry Jasion	WP	Dearborn, MI
1994	Tuan Nguyen	WP	Santa Fe Springs, CA
1995	James Simpson	WP	Corpus Christi, TX
1995	Toby Sincino	SS	Blackville, SC
1996	Douglas Bradley	SS	Palo Alto, CA
1996	Clifton McCree	WP	Fort Lauderdale, FL
1996	Kenneth Tornes	WP	Jackson, MS
1997	Arturo R. Torres	WP	Orange, CA
1997	Anthony Deculit	WP	Milwaukee, WI
1997	Arthur Hastings Wise	WP	Aiken, SC
1997	Daniel S. Marsden	WP	Santa Fe Springs, CA
1997	Ali Hassan Abu Kamal	ST	New York, NY
1997	Michael Carneal	SS	West Paducah, KY
1997	Evan Ramsey	SS	Bethel, AK

(continues)

Year	Name	Type[a]	Location
1998	Matthew Beck	WP	Hartford, CT
1998	Joseph Neale	ST	Riverside, CA
1998	Kip Kinkel	SS	Springfield, OR
1999	Mark Barton	WP	Atlanta, GA
1999	Eric Harris	SS	Littleton, CO
1999	Thomas Solomon	SS	Conyers, GA
1999	Sergei Babarin	RS	Salt Lake City, UT
1999	Joseph Brooks, Jr.	RS	Southfield, MI
2001	Robert Wissman	WP	Goshen, IN
2001	William D. Baker	WP	Melrose Park, IL
2001	Mohamed Atta	ST	New York, NY
2001	Ziad Jarrah	ST	Washington, DC[b]
2001	Marwan al Shehhi	ST	New York, NY
2001	Hani Hanjour	ST	Washington, DC
2002	Hesham Mohamed Hadayet	ST	Los Angeles, CA
2002	Robert Flores	SS	Tucson, AZ
2003	William Lockley	WP	South Bend, IN
2003	Jonathon Russell	WP	Jefferson City, MO
2003	Ron Thomas	WP	San Antonio, TX
2003	Ricky Shadle	WP	Andover, OH
2003	Salvador Tapia	WP	Chicago, IL
2003	Doug Williams	WP	Meridian, MS
2004	Elijah Brown	WP	Kansas City, KS
2004	James A. Webb	WP	Seminole, FL
2004	Justin Cudar	RS	St. Petersburg, FL
2005	Myles Meyers	WP	Toledo, OH
2005	Jeff Weise	SS	Red Lake, MN
2005	Joe Cobb	WP	Glen Burnie, MD
2005	Victor M. Piazza	WP	New Windsor, NY
2006	Jennifer San Marco	WP	Santa Barbara, CA
2006	Herbert Chalmers Jr.	WP	St . Louis, MO
2006	Christopher A. Williams	SS	Essex, VT
2006	Charles Carl Roberts	RS	Nickel Mines, PA
2006	Kyle Aaron Huff	RS	Seattle, WA
2007	Jose Mendez	WP	Signall Hill, CA
2007	Asa Coon	SS	Cleveland, OH
2007	Matthew Murray	SS	Colorado Springs, CO
2007	Seung-Hui Cho	SS	Blacksburg, VA
2007	Robert Hawkins	RS	Omaha, NE
2007	Tyler Peterson	RS	Crandon, WI
2007	Jason Hamilton	RS	Moscow, ID
2007	Vincent Dortch	RS	Philadelphia, PA
2008	Wesley N. Higdon	WP	Henderson, KY
2008	Jim David Adkisson	ST	Knoxville, TN
2008	Charles Lee Thornton	ST	Kirkwood, MO
2008	Latina Williams	SS	Baton Rouge, LA
2008	Steven Phillip Kazmierczak	SS	DeKalb, IL

(continues)

Year	Name	Type[a]	Location
2008	Alburn Edward Blake	RS	West Palm Beach, FL
2009	Nidal Hasan	ST	Fort Hood, TX
2009	Odane Greg Maye	SS	Hampton, VA
2009	George Sodini	RS	Bridgeville, PA
2009	Jiverly Wong	RS	Binghamton, NY
2009	Erik Salvador Ayala	RS	Portland, OR
2009	Mario Ramirez	WP	Long Beach, CA
2010	Abdo Ibssa	RS	Knoxville, TN
2010	Akouch Kashoual	WP	Crete, NE
2010	Omar S. Thorton	WP	Hartford, CT
2010	Timothy Hendron	WP	St. Louis, MO
2010	Nathaniel Brown	WP	Columbus, OH
2010	Joseph Stack	ST	Austin, TX

a. Types = ST: suicide terrorist; RS: rampage shooter; SS: school shooter; WP: workplace shooter

b. Hijacked United Airlines Flight 93 never reached its target, crashing near Shanksville, Pennsylvania.

Note: Cases were excluded if they involved fewer than two victims or were primarily domestic in nature (targeting family members or significant others).

THE FOUR TYPES OF SUICIDE TERRORISTS

BEHAVIORAL EXPECTATIONS AND SECURITY COUNTERMEASURES[1]

	Conventional Suicide Terrorists	Coerced Suicide Terrorists	Escapist Suicide Terrorists	Indirect Suicide Terrorists
Description of type	Suicidal in the most typical sense.	Suicidal because they fear the consequences of not carrying out attacks.	Suicidal because they fear being captured or killed by the enemy.	Suicidal at an unconscious level.
Warning signs	For years, months, weeks, or days, there may be previous suicide attempts, suicidal thoughts, depression, hopelessness,	For weeks or days, there may be psychological distress manifesting itself as crying, distractedness, irritability, or other erratic	For years, months, weeks, or days, there may be candid discussion of death as an exit strategy. Once the enemy draws near,	For years, months, weeks, or days, there may be risk taking and self-destructive behavior, including substance abuse,

(continues)

	Conventional Suicide Terrorists	Coerced Suicide Terrorists	Escapist Suicide Terrorists	Indirect Suicide Terrorists
	PTSD, guilt, shame, rage, social marginalization, or low self-worth. Precipitating crises may include substance abuse, work or school problems, romantic problems, health problems, and/or the death of a loved one.	emotions.	signs of desperation and final preparations may appear.	gambling, high-risk recreation, deviant sexual behavior, erratic driving, self-mutilation, and other criminality.
Level of training and combat experience	Minimal: They may have undergone the basic training necessary to avoid premature exposure and perform self-detonation. However, in many cases, the suicide attack is their first combat experience.	Minimal: They may have undergone the basic training necessary to avoid premature exposure and perform self-detonation. However, in many cases, the suicide attack is their first combat experience.	Moderate: They should be expected to have the same level of training and combat experience as non-suicide terrorist operatives.	Moderate/High: They may have more training and combat experience than most terrorists, given their attraction to risk taking and the thrill they get from wielding firearms and explosives.
Attack style	Since they genuinely want to die, they are unlikely to launch elaborate attacks with significant potential for survival. Most	Since they are not fully trusted by dispatchers, they are more likely to be armed with explosive belts or vests than escape-	Since they are usually besieged by security forces and genuinely want to escape capture, they are likely to detonate all	Since their suicidal desire is unconscious, they are willing to risk death, injury, capture, or any other result. They may go

commonly, they will attack with explosive belts, vests, or vehicle bombs.	tempting vehicles. Some individuals, who are more victims than suicide terrorists, may be fitted with remote detonation devices.	remaining explosives within reach. However, some may grab explosives and run toward security forces.	on shooting sprees with automatic weapons, engage in hostage taking, or attempt to blow up heavily guarded, high-value targets.
Strategies for on-site negotiation of surrender and arrest Somewhat likely to surrender. They may be uncertain about killing themselves, like other suicidal individuals. Officers should employ the strategies used by suicide hotlines, including emphasizing options to those who feel trapped and providing hope to those who feel hopeless.	Most likely to surrender. They may view police or soldiers as a potential rescue from their coerced situation. Officers should offer empathy, since these individuals often feel like they are victims of the terrorists who pressured them.	Not likely to surrender. They are usually dead-set against surrender. However, sometimes these individuals have exaggerated ideas of the punishment they would receive upon arrest, so officers who correct these misconceptions may get them to surrender. At the same time, officers should be particularly careful not to let these individuals get too close, since they may fake interest in surrendering in order to increase casualties upon detonation of their explosives.	Least likely to surrender. They pride themselves on being fearless and may find the idea of a fatal confrontation with authorities incredibly alluring. Short of physically incapacitating these individuals, there may be little that officers can do to take them alive.

(continues)

	Conventional Suicide Terrorists	Coerced Suicide Terrorists	Escapist Suicide Terrorists	Indirect Suicide Terrorists
Strategies for interrogation	Moderately likely to cooperate. Interrogators should identify the individual's specific suicidal motive, and then offer empathy and provide hope for a brighter future. If the suicidal motive is the death of a loved one at the hands of the interrogator's own security forces, the individual's rage may be exploited to provoke discussion and disclosure.	Most likely to cooperate. Interrogators should be able to redirect these individuals' despair, frustration, or anger about their current predicament toward the terrorists who coerced them. If this approach fails, interrogators who take a hard-line approach should expect success, given that these individuals have already proven to be susceptible to coercive pressure.	Least likely to cooperate. Interrogators are likely to encounter significant resistance to cooperation. Offers of better prison treatment or reduced sentences may successfully facilitate discussion, but these individuals are a risk to rejoin their terrorist organizations if actually released. These individuals may be particularly apt to provide false information.	Somewhat likely to cooperate. Interrogators should take a soft approach and employ basic reverse psychology, putting minimal pressure on these individuals to cooperate and framing the choice to speak freely as a dangerous risk. For example: "I understand if you're too frightened to speak up—I'm sure your leaders don't allow you to say a word." Given their self-destructive urges, these individuals should eventually start speaking on their own. However, these individuals may be particularly apt to provide false information.

Note: It is possible for an individual suicide terrorist to be a combination of types.

NOTES

CHAPTER 1: THE MYTH OF MARTYRDOM

1. The research findings presented in this book have been vetted by a number of peer-reviewed scholarly journals. Portions of this book were previously published as parts of the following articles, although the ideas have been heavily edited for inclusion, and in most cases, extended: Adam Lankford, "A Comparative Analysis of Suicide Terrorists and Rampage, Workplace, and School Shooters in the United States from 1990–2010," *Homicide Studies* (2012); Adam Lankford, "A Psychological Autopsy of 9/11 Ringleader Mohamed Atta," *Journal of Police and Criminal Psychology* 27 (2012), 150-159; Adam Lankford, "A Suicide-Based Typology of Suicide Terrorists: Conventional, Coerced, Escapist, and Indirect," *Security Journal* (2012); Adam Lankford, "Could Suicide Terrorists Actually Be Suicidal?" *Studies in Conflict & Terrorism* 34 (2011): 337–66; Adam Lankford, "Do Suicide Terrorists Exhibit Clinically Suicidal Risk Factors? A Review of Initial Evidence and Call for Future Research," *Aggression and Violent Behavior* 15 (2010): 334–40; Adam Lankford, "Human Time Bombs: Before The 9/11 Pilots Were Suicide Terrorists, They Were Just Suicidal," *Foreign Policy,* September 9, 2011, accessed November 11, 2011, http://www.foreignpolicy.com/articles/2011/09/09/human_time_bombs; Adam Lankford, "Martyr Complex: How Will Bin Laden's Supporters Interpret His Death?" *Foreign Policy,* May 2, 2011, accessed August 14, 2012, http://www.foreignpolicy.com/articles/2011/05/02/hes_dead_but_how_much_does_osamas_death_matter?page=0,3; Adam Lankford, "On Sacrificial Heroism," *Critical Review of International Social and Political Philosophy* (2012); Adam Lankford, "Requirements and Facilitators for Suicide Terrorism: An Explanatory Framework for Prediction and Prevention," *Perspectives on Terrorism* 5, 6 (2011): 70–80; Adam Lankford, "Suicide Terrorism as a Socially Approved Form of Suicide," *Crisis* 31 (2010): 287–89; Adam Lankford and Nayab Hakim, "From Columbine to Palestine: A Comparative Analysis of Rampage Shooters in the United States and Volunteer Suicide Bombers in the Middle East," *Aggression and Violent Behavior* 16 (2011): 98–107.
2. Associated Press, "Donkey Bomb Kills Three Children in Afghanistan," *Herald Sun,* April 19, 2010, accessed June 4, 2011, http://www.heraldsun.com.au/news/world/donkey-bomb-kills-three-children-in-afghanistan/story-e6frf7lf-1225855722687; "Colombian 'Donkey Bombs' Kill Drug Crop Eradicators," *Reuters,* September 11, 2009, accessed June 6, 2011,

http://www.reuters.com/article/2009/09/12/idUSN11469928; Michael Evans, "Donkey 'Suicide' Bombing Is Latest Tactic Against Patrols," *Sunday Times,* April 30, 2009, accessed June 4, 2011, http://www.timesonline .co.uk/tol/news/uk/article6194874.ece; Rob Quinn, "Israeli Jets Strike Gaza After Donkey Bomb Fizzles," *Newser,* May 26, 2010, accessed June 4, 2011, http://www.newser.com/story/90056/israelis-hit-gaza-after-donkey -bomb-fizzles.html; Laura J. Winter and Richard Sisk, "Donkey Bombs New Iraqi Weapon," *New York Daily News,* November 22, 2003, accessed June 4, 2011, http://www.nydailynews.com/archives/news/2003/11/22/2003-11 -22_donkey_bombs_new_iraqi_weapon.html.

3. Daniel Byman and Christine Fair, "The Case for Calling Them Nitwits," *Atlantic,* July/August 2010, accessed June 7, 2011, http://www.theatlantic .com/magazine/archive/2010/07/the-case-for-calling-them-nitwits/8130/.

4. Tom A. Peter, "U.S. Begins Hunting Iraq's Bombmakers, Not Just Bombs," *Christian Science Monitor,* September 8, 2008, accessed June 7, 2011, http://www.csmonitor.com/World/Middle-East/2008/0908/p04s01-wome .html.

5. National Commission on Terrorist Attacks Upon the United States, "The 9/11 Commission Report," August 21, 2004, accessed May 4, 2011, http:// govinfo.library.unt.edu/911/report/index.htm.

6. Ibid.

7. Sir Ken Robinson, "2005 National Forum of Education Policy: Chairman's Breakfast," *Education Commission of the States,* July 14, 2005, accessed June 7, 2011, http://www.ecs.org/html/projectsPartners/chair2005/docs/Sir _Ken_Robinson_Speech.pdf, 4.

8. As we mature, we generally learn that cognitive shortcuts improve our ability to function with optimal efficiency, as opposed to actually analyzing all the possibilities we face, which would slow us down. The problem is that these shortcuts sometimes lead us to overlook critical vulnerabilities—and opportunities.

9. Robinson, "2005 National Forum of Education Policy," 4.

10. Christopher Browning, *Ordinary Men: Reserve Police Battalion 101 and the Final Solution in Poland* (New York: HarperCollins Publishers, Inc., 1998); Jerry Burger, "Replicating Milgram," *APS Observer,* December 2007, accessed April 22, 2011, http://www.psychologicalscience.org /observer/getArticle.cfm?id=2264; Robert Johnson, "Institutions and the Promotion of Violence," in *Violent Transactions: The Limits of Personality,* eds. Anne Campbell and John J. Gibbs, 181–204 (Oxford: Basil Blackwell, 1986); Fred E. Katz, *Confronting Evil: Two Journeys* (New York: State University of New York Press, 2004); Stanley Milgram, "Behavioral Study of Obedience," *Journal of Abnormal & Social Psychology* 67 (1963): 371–78; Ervin Staub, *The Roots of Evil: The Origins of Genocide and Other Group Violence* (Cambridge: Cambridge University Press, 1989); James Waller, *Becoming Evil: How Ordinary People Commit Genocide and Mass Killing* (New York: Oxford University Press, 2002); Philip Zimbardo, "Pathology of Imprisonment," *Society* 9 (6) (1972): 4–8.

11. Caleb Carr, *The Lessons of Terror* (New York: Random House, 2002); Bruce Hoffman, *Inside Terrorism* (New York: Columbia University Press, 2006); Adam Lankford, *Human Killing Machines: Systematic Indoctrination in Iran, Nazi Germany, Al Qaeda and Abu Ghraib* (Lanham, MD:

Lexington Books, 2009); Marc Sageman, *Understanding Terror Networks* (Philadelphia: University of Pennsylvania Press, 2004); Paul L. Williams, *Al Qaeda: Brotherhood of Terror* (Upper Saddle River, NJ: Alpha Books and Pearson Education, Inc., 2002).

12. Carolyn Weaver, "New Video Shows 9/11 Hijackers Mohammed Atta, Ziad Jarrah at Al-Qaida meeting," *Voice of America News,* October 4, 2006, accessed May 27, 2011, http://www.militaryinfo.com/news_story .cfm?textnewsid=2149.

13. Robert A. Pape, *Dying to Win: The Strategic Logic of Suicide Terrorism* (New York: Random House, 2005), 211.

14. Scott Atran, "Genesis of Suicide Terrorism," *Science* 299 (2003): 1536.

15. Riaz Hassan, "What Motivates the Suicide Bombers," *Yale Global,* September 3, 2009, accessed May 28, 2011, http://yaleglobal.yale.edu/content /what-motivates-suicide-bombers-0.

16. Robert Brym, "Six Lessons of Suicide Bombers," *Contexts* 6 (2007): 40.

17. Ellen Townsend, "Suicide Terrorists: Are They Suicidal?" *Suicide & Life-Threatening Behavior* 37 (2007): 47.

18. "Head of Psychiatry at Cairo's 'Ein Shams University, Prof. Adel Sadeq, on the Psychological Make-up of a Suicide Bomber," *MEMRI,* April 25, 2002, accessed March 9, 2011, http://www.memritv.org/clip_transcript/en/927.htm.

19. Larry H. Pastor, "Countering the Psychological Consequences of Suicide Terrorism," *Psychiatric Annals* 34 (2004): 704.

20. Pape, *Dying to Win,* 218.

21. Mohammed M. Hafez, *Manufacturing Human Bombs: The Making of Palestinian Suicide Bombers* (Washington, DC: U.S. Institute of Peace, 2006), 6.

22. The presidential candidate is congressional representative Ron Paul. His statements about suicide terrorism will be discussed in later chapters.

23. John P. Bradley, Leo F. Daniels, and Thomas C. Jones, *The International Dictionary of Thoughts* (Chicago: J. G. Ferguson Publishing Company, 1969), 699.

24. Ariel Merari, *Driven to Death: Psychological and Social Aspects of Suicide Terrorism* (Oxford: Oxford University Press, 2010), 137.

25. *American Heritage Dictionary,* "Sacrifice" (Houghton Mifflin Company, 2004), accessed November 15, 2009, http://dictionary.reference.com /browse/sacrifice.

26. Paul Kix, "The Truth About Suicide Bombers," *Boston Globe,* December 5, 2010, accessed June 7, 2011, http://www.boston.com/bostonglobe/ideas /articles/2010/12/05/the_truth_about_suicide_bombers/?page=full.

27. Ibid.

28. Ronald W. Maris, Alan L. Berman, and Morton M. Silverman, *Comprehensive Textbook of Suicidology* (New York: Guilford, 2000).

29. Ibid., 31.

30. Kix, "The Truth About Suicide Bombers."

31. David Lester and Ariel Merari are among the few scholars whose published work has suggested that a significant percentage of suicide terrorists are suicidal. Their contributions will be discussed in the pages to come.

32. "Support for Suicide Bombing," *Pew Research Center,* 2007–2010, accessed July 11, 2011, http://pewglobal.org/database/?indicator=19.

33. Richard Wike, "Little Support for Terrorism Among Muslim Americans," *Pew Research Center,* December 17, 2009, accessed February

12, 2011, http://pewresearch.org/pubs/1445/little-support-for-terrorism-among-muslim-americans.

34. These figures are calculated by multiplying the percentage of Pew Research Center–surveyed Muslims who stated that suicide terrorism attacks are "often" or "sometimes" justified by the total Muslim population in the respective countries where surveys were conducted. Naturally, there may be some *non-Muslims* who believe that suicide terrorism attacks are "often" or "sometimes" justified as well, but at the present time, no data exist to accurately quantify this segment of the global population. In addition, the number of countries where surveys were conducted is a very small minority, so again, the actual total number worldwide would be expected to be much higher.

35. Office of the Director of National Intelligence, "2009 Report on Terrorism," *National Counterterrorism Center,* April 30, 2010, accessed June 21, 2011, http://www.nctc.gov/witsbanner/docs/2009_report_on_terrorism.pdf.

36. Robert Fein and Bryan Vossekuil, "Assassination in the United States: An Operational Study of Recent Assassins, Attackers, and Near-Lethal Approachers," *Journal of Forensic Sciences* 44 (1999): 321–33.

37. Ibid.

38. Joseph Stack, "Raw Data: Joseph Stack Suicide Manifesto," *Fox News,* February 18, 2010, accessed June 16, 2011, http://www.foxnews.com/us/2010/02/18/raw-data-joseph-stack-suicide-manifesto/. The word "ensure" was misspelled by Stack but has been corrected here for clarity's sake.

39. Katie Nelson, "Joe Stack's Daughter, Samantha Bell Calls Deadly Austin Attack on IRS 'Wrong,' But Labels Dad Hero," *New York Daily News,* February 22, 2010, accessed January 4, 2011, http://www.nydailynews.com/news/national/2010/02/22/2010-02-22_joe_stacks_daughter_samantha_bell_calls_deadly_austin_attack_on_irs_wrong_but_la.html.

40. Stack, "Raw Data."

41. Peggy O'Hare and R. G. Ratcliffe, "Suicide Flier Described as 'Offbeat,' 'Brilliant,'" *Houston Chronicle,* February 19, 2010, accessed December 4, 2011, http://www.chron.com/default/article/Suicide-flier-described-as-offbeat-brilliant-1716342.php.

42. As will be discussed in Chapter 2 in more depth, we have to be careful when we trust the words of any source, including a suicide terrorist. However, it would seem unlikely for a suicide terrorist on his or her way to the grave to make false claims about struggling with mental health problems. Given their social contexts and ulterior motives, suicide terrorists appear far more likely to lie to conceal their psychological problems than lie to invent them.

43. Edwin Shneidman, "Clues to Suicide, Reconsidered," *Suicide and Life-Threatening Behavior* 24 (1994): 395.

44. Merari, *Driven to Death,* 131.

45. Pape, *Dying to Win,* 220.

46. "Global Terrorism Database," *National Consortium for the Study of Terrorism and Responses to Terrorism,* 2012. Accessed May 14, 2012, http://www.start.umd.edu/gtd/.

47. Within the United States, a number of suicide attacks have been avoided due to mere luck. For instance, the December 25, 2009, attempted suicide bombing of Northwest Airlines Flight 253 would have likely killed nearly

three hundred people had the terrorist's explosives not failed to properly detonate.

CHAPTER 2: LIES, DAMN LIES, AND PREVIOUS RESEARCH ON SUICIDE TERRORISM

1. Robert Baer, *The Cult of the Suicide Bomber 2* [DVD] (London: Many Rivers Films, 2008).
2. Ibid.
3. Ibid.
4. Ibid.
5. Ibid.
6. Ibid.
7. Ibid.
8. Ibid.
9. Mahmoud Al-Zahar, "Palestinian Foreign Minister Mahmoud Al-Zahar Defends 'Martyrdom-Seeking Operations,'" *MEMRI*, April 6, 2006, accessed January 9, 2010, http://www.memritv.org/Transcript.asp?P1=1107.
10. Lankford, *Human Killing Machines*.
11. Baer, *The Cult of the Suicide Bomber 2*.
12. Robert Baer, *The Cult of the Suicide Bomber* [DVD] (London: Many Rivers Films, 2005).
13. Glen Evans and Norman L. Farberow, *The Encyclopedia of Suicide* (New York: Facts on File, 1988).
14. Baer, *The Cult of the Suicide Bomber*; Kix, "The Truth About Suicide Bombers."
15. Jerrold M. Post, Farhana Ali, Schuyler Henderson, Stephen Shanfield, Jeff Victoroff, and Stevan Weine, "The Psychology of Suicide Terrorism," *Psychiatry* 72 (1) (2009): 13–31.
16. Baer, *The Cult of the Suicide Bomber 2*; Judith Miller, "The Bomb Under the Abaya: Women Who Became Suicide Bombers," *Policy Review*, June 2007, accessed June 8, 2011, http://www.judithmiller.com/754/the-bomb-under-the-abaya.
17. Baer, *The Cult of the Suicide Bomber 2*.
18. Wafa al-Biss ultimately received a twelve-year prison sentence for her attempted attack.
19. Baer, *The Cult of the Suicide Bomber 2*; Miller, "The Bomb Under The Abaya."
20. Miller, "The Bomb Under The Abaya."
21. Post et al., "The Psychology of Suicide Terrorism."
22. Abu M. Al-San'ani, "An Al Qaeda Released Video of Attacks in Afghanistan," *MEMRI*, May 4, 2006, accessed December 9, 2010, http://www.memritv.org/clip/en/1131.htm.
23. Stephen Holmes, "Al Qaeda, September 11, 2001," in *Making Sense of Suicide Missions*, ed. Diego Gambetta, 131–72 (Oxford: Oxford University Press, 2005).
24. Townsend, "Suicide Terrorists," 47.
25. Townsend, "Suicide Terrorists."
26. Kix, "The Truth About Suicide Bombers."
27. Hassan, "What Motivates the Suicide Bombers"; Pape, *Dying to Win*, 218; Townsend, "Suicide Terrorists," 47.

28. Karen Crouse, "Bear Coach Smith Reflects on His Roots," *New York Times,* January 23, 2007, accessed June 8, 2011, http://www.nytimes .com/2007/01/23/sports/football/23bears.html?ref=sports.

29. Ben Montgomery and Howard Altman, "Friends Stunned by Suicide of Dungy's Son," *MSNBC,* December 23, 2005, accessed June 2, 2011, http:// nbcsports.msnbc.com/id/10588639//.

30. Ibid.

31. "Dungy's Son, 18, Found Dead in Tampa Suburb," *ESPN,* December 23, 2005, accessed June 2, 2011, http://sports.espn.go.com/nfl/news/story?id =2268593.

32. David Lester, Bijou Yang, and Mark Lindsay, "Suicide Bombers: Are Psychological Profiles Possible?" *Studies in Conflict & Terrorism* 27 (2004): 289.

33. Pape, *Dying to Win,* 202–03.

34. Ibid., 210–11. Italics added.

35. For instance, see Robert Brym, *Sociology as a Life or Death Issue* (Belmont, CA: Wadsworth, 2009), 38, who writes, "A study of all 462 suicide bombers who attacked targets worldwide between 1980 and 2003 found not a single case of depression, psychosis, past suicide attempts, or other such disorders and only one case of probable mental retardation." An exception is the critique of Pape's work by Scott Ashworth, Joshua D. Clinton, Adam Meirowitz, and Kristopher W. Ramsay, "Design, Inference, and the Strategic Logic of Suicide Terrorism," *American Political Science Review* 102 (2008): 270–73.

36. Philip Weiss, "Mr. Zbig: Brzezinski Brings Wisdom—and Controversy— to Barack Obama's Campaign," *American Conservative,* May 5, 2008, accessed February 17, 2012, http://www.theamericanconservative.com /article/2008/may/05/00013/.

37. "CDC: One in 20 Americans Depressed," *CBS News,* February 11, 2009, accessed May 28, 2011, http://www.cbsnews.com/stories/2008/09/04 /health/webmd/main4414655.shtml.

38. "Powerball: Prizes and Odds," May 28, 2011, accessed May 28, 2011, http://www.powerball.com/powerball/pb_prizes.asp.

39. Elsi Vassdal Ellis, "Letters to Mohamed Atta," March 11, 2002, accessed June 8, 2011, http://faculty.wwu.edu/vassdae/book_arts/atta/letter_open .html; Patricia Pearson, "Apocalyptic Cult Methods Explain Bin Laden," *USA Today,* November 5, 2001, accessed June 8, 2011, http://www.usa today.com/news/comment/2001-11-05-ncguest1.htm; "Tabloids Belittle Bin Laden, Hijackers," *Miami Herald,* October 9, 2001.

40. Personal communication to Adam Lankford, November 16, 2010.

41. Lankford, *Human Killing Machines.*

42. Hoffman, *Inside Terrorism.*

43. Lankford, *Human Killing Machines.*

44. Bryan Caplan, "Terrorism: The Relevance of the Rational Choice Model," *Public Choice* 128 (2006): 91–107; Charles K. Rowley, "Terrorist Attacks on Western Civilization," *Public Choice* 128 (2006): 1–6.

45. Emile Durkheim, *Le Suicide: Étude de Sociologie* (Paris: Alcan, 1897); Maurice L. Farber, *Theory of Suicide* (New York: Funk and Wagnalls, 1968); David Lester, *Making Sense Of Suicide: An In-Depth Look at Why People Kill Themselves* (Philadelphia: The Charles Press, 1997); Ronald W. Maris, *Pathways to Suicide: A Survey of Self-Destructive Behaviors* (Baltimore: Johns Hopkins University Press, 1981); Edwin S. Shneidman, "An

Overview: Personality, Motivation, and Behavior Theories," in Leon D. Hankoff and Bernice Einsidler, eds., *Suicide: Theory and Clinical Aspects*, 143–63 (Littleton, MA: PSG Publishing, 1979).

46. Ibid.

47. Post et al., "The Psychology of Suicide Terrorism."

48. Ami Pedahzur, *Suicide Terrorism* (Cambridge: Polity, 2005). In other words, most of these individuals have never carried out a single terrorist attack before attempting their suicide attack.

49. There are some suicide terrorists who are not volunteers: they are kidnapped or coerced. They will be discussed in Chapter 7.

50. National Commission on Terrorist Attacks Upon the United States, "The 9/11 Commission Report," 99.

51. Merari, *Driven to Death.*

52. Ibid.

53. Ibid., 119.

54. Merari, *Driven to Death.*

55. Ibid., 152–53.

56. Ibid., 152.

57. "Admission Against Interest Law and Legal Definition," *U.S. Legal,* 2011, accessed December 17, 2011, http://definitions.uslegal.com/a/admission-against-interest/.

58. For example, Ahmed al-Shayea recalls that when he and twelve other men joined Al Qaeda in Iraq, they were taken before a leader and given the chance to volunteer for suicide attacks. Their response was typical for non-suicidal individuals: "Then he asked us a question: 'Those who want to carry out martyrdom attacks, raise your hands,'" said al-Shayea. "No one did." See Associated Press, "Truck Bomber Turns Against Jihad in Iraq," *MSNBC,* July 29, 2007, accessed December 17, 2011, http://www.msnbc.msn.com/id/20018405/ns/world_news-mideast_n_africa/t/truck-bomber-turns-against-jihad-iraq/. A much fuller description of this encounter appears in Ken Ballen, *Terrorists in Love: The Real Lives of Islamic Radicals* (New York: Simon & Schuster, 2011).

59. Merari, *Driven to Death.*

60. Brym, "Six Lessons About Suicide Bombers," 40.

61. "Jerrold M. Post, Full-time Faculty, Elliot School of International Affairs," George Washington University, 2011, accessed February 17, 2012, http://elliott.gwu.edu/faculty/post.cfm.

62. Weaver, "New Video Shows 9/11 Hijackers Mohammed Atta, Ziad Jarrah at Al-Qaida meeting."

63. To be fair, at least at first, I bought into this same perspective as well. And despite his claims here, Post appears to be open-minded regarding new evidence about the psychological abnormality of suicide terrorists. By contrast, Brym remains committed to the fallacy that suicide terrorists are normal, stable, and nonsuicidal—and many others do the same.

64. Adam Lankford, "Do Suicide Terrorists Exhibit Clinically Suicidal Risk Factors? A Review of Initial Evidence and Call for Future Research," *Aggression and Violent Behavior* 15 (2010): 334–40; Assaf Moghadam, *The Globalization of Martyrdom: Al Qaeda, Salafi Jihad, and the Diffusion of Suicide Attacks* (Baltimore: Johns Hopkins University Press, 2008).

65. Adam Lankford, "Could Suicide Terrorists Actually Be Suicidal?" *Studies in Conflict & Terrorism* 34 (2011): 337–66; Damien McElroy,

"Baghdad Market Bombers 'Mentally Impaired,'" *Telegraph*, February 2, 2008, accessed June 8, 2011, http://www.telegraph.co.uk/news/world news/1577373/Baghdad-market-bombers-mentally-impaired.html.

66. Post et al., "The Psychology of Suicide Terrorism."

67. Lankford, "Could Suicide Terrorists Actually Be Suicidal?"; Merari, *Driven to Death*.

68. Hassan, "What Motivates the Suicide Bombers."

69. Pape, *Dying to Win*.

70. Brym, "Six Lessons About Suicide Bombers"; "Head of Psychiatry at Cairo's 'Ein Shams University, Prof. Adel Sadeq, on the Psychological Make-up of a Suicide Bomber"; Townsend, "Suicide Terrorists."

71. Townsend, "Suicide Terrorists."

72. Pape, *Dying to Win*.

73. Brym, "Six Lessons About Suicide Bombers."

74. Hassan, "What Motivates the Suicide Bombers"; Robert Pape and James Feldman, *Cutting the Fuse: The Explosion of Global Suicide Terrorism and How to Stop It* (Chicago: University of Chicago Press, 2010).

75. Pape, *Dying to Win*; Weaver, "New Video Shows 9/11 Hijackers Mohammed Atta, Ziad Jarrah at Al-Qaida meeting."

76. Lankford, "Do Suicide Terrorists Exhibit Clinically Suicidal Risk Factors?"; Lankford, "Could Suicide Terrorists Actually Be Suicidal?"

CHAPTER 3: WHY SUICIDE TERRORISTS ARE SUICIDAL

1. N. R. Kleinfield, "From Teacher to Gunman: U.S. Visit Ends in Fatal Rage," *New York Times*, February 25, 1997, accessed June 13, 2011, http://www.nytimes.com/1997/02/25/nyregion/from-teacher-to-gunman-us-visit-ends-in-fatal-rage.html.

2. Tom Hays, "N.Y. Killer Carried Political Note," *Associated Press*, February 25, 1997.

3. Matthew Purdy, "The Gunman Premeditated the Attack, Officials Say," *New York Times*, February 25, 1997, accessed June 13, 2011, http://www.nytimes.com/1997/02/25/nyregion/the-gunman-premeditated-the-attack-officials-say.html.

4. Ibid.

5. Ali Hassan Abu Kamal, "Charter of Honour," *Investigative Project on Terrorism*, February 23, 1997, accessed June 13, 2011, http://www.investigativeproject.org/case/334.

6. Ibid.

7. Notably, the people who had done him wrong were his own countrymen—not people from the West or Israel.

8. Kleinfield, "From Teacher to Gunman." Some of these accounts were disputed a decade later by Abu Kamal's daughter, who claimed that her father was purely politically motivated. The veracity of her statements could not be confirmed.

9. Baer, *The Cult of The Suicide Bomber 2*.

10. Charles Lave and James March, *Introduction to Models in the Social Sciences* (New York: Harper and Row, 1975).

11. Merari, *Driven to Death*.

12. Ibid.

13. This is a pseudonym assigned by Merari, not the individual's real name.

14. Merari, *Driven to Death,* 116–17.
15. Ibid., 117.
16. Merari, *Driven to Death.*
17. This is a pseudonym assigned by Merari, not the individual's real name.
18. Merari, *Driven to Death,* 131.
19. Ibid.
20. Baer, *The Cult of the Suicide Bomber;* Merari, *Driven to Death.*
21. Robert Brym and Bader Araj, "Are Suicide Bombers Suicidal?" *Studies in Conflict & Terrorism* 35 (2012): 432–43.
22. Ibid.
23. Maris, Berman, and Silverman, *Comprehensive Textbook of Suicidology.*
24. Merari, *Driven to Death,* 132.
25. An alternative explanation, that prison *made* these individuals suicidal, seems unlikely. After all, the other groups of non-suicide terrorists were also in prison under the same conditions, and they did not exhibit suicidal tendencies.
26. Merari, *Driven to Death,* 114–15. This is a pseudonym assigned by Merari, not the individual's real name.
27. Ibid., 115–16. This is a pseudonym assigned by Merari, not the individual's real name.
28. "The Most Influential US Liberals," *Daily Telegraph,* October 31, 2007, accessed June 20, 2011, http://www.telegraph.co.uk/news/world news/1435442/The-most-influential-US-liberals-1-20.html.
29. Aliyah Shahid, "Oprah Winfrey to Piers Morgan: I Contemplated Suicide as Pregnant Teen, Drank Detergent," *New York Daily News,* January 18, 2011, accessed June 20, 2011, http://articles.nydailynews.com/2011-01-18 /gossip/27088007_1_stedman-graham-pregnancy-detergent.
30. Ibid. The word "was" has been changed to "is" in the text. The exact quote was actually: "Before the baby was born, I'm going to have to kill myself."
31. Ibid.
32. Ibid.
33. Pedahzur, *Suicide Terrorism;* "Blackmailing Young Women into Suicide Terrorism," *Israeli Ministry of Foreign Affairs,* February 12, 2002, accessed May 27, 2012, http://www.mfa.gov.il/MFA/Government/Communiques /2003/Blackmailing+Young+Women+into+Suicide+Terrorism+-.htm.
34. B. Abu Ruqaiyah, "The Islamic Legitimacy of the 'Martyrdom Operations,'" *International Institute for Counterterrorism,* 1997, accessed September 27, 2009, http://www.ict.org.il/Articles/tabid/66/Articlsid/726 /currentpage/33/Default.aspx.
35. Adam Lankford, "Suicide Terrorism as a Socially Approved Form of Suicide," *Crisis* 31 (2010): 287–89.
36. Ibid.
37. Pedahzur, *Suicide Terrorism,* 140.
38. Ibid.
39. Duncan Gardham and Richard Savill, "Exeter Terror Bomber Nicky Reilly Was Known as 'Big Friendly Giant,'" *Telegraph,* October 15, 2008, accessed June 20, 2011, http://www.telegraph.co.uk/news/uknews/3201863/Exeter-terror-bomber-Nicky-Reilly-was-known-as-Big-Friendly-Giant.html.
40. Craig Smith, "Raised as Catholic in Belgium, She Died as a Muslim Bomber," *New York Times,* December 6, 2005, accessed June 21, 2011, http://www .nytimes.com/2005/12/06/international/europe/06brussels.html.

41. "Bomber Nicky Reilly's Suicide Note," *This Is Exeter,* November 21, 2008, accessed December 4, 2011, http://www.thisisexeter.co.uk/Bomber-Nicky -Reilly-s-suicide-note/story-11795579-detail/story.html.

42. "Nail Bomber Blames 'War on Islam,'" *BBC,* November 21, 2008, accessed June 20, 2011, http://news.bbc.co.uk/go/pr/fr/-/2/hi/uk_news/7741766.stm.

43. Gardham and Savill, "Exeter Terror Bomber Nicky Reilly Was Known as 'Big Friendly Giant.'"

44. Adam Fresco, "Nicky Reilly, Muslim Convert, Jailed for 18 Years for Exeter Bomb Attack," *Times Online,* January 31, 2009, accessed June 20, 2011, http://www.timesonline.co.uk/tol/news/uk/crime/article5619151.ece.

45. Gardham and Savill, "Exeter Terror Bomber Nicky Reilly Was Known as 'Big Friendly Giant.'"

46. Ibid.

47. Ibid.

48. Fresco, "Nicky Reilly, Muslim Convert, Jailed for 18 Years for Exeter Bomb Attack."

49. Ibid.

50. Smith, "Raised as Catholic in Belgium, She Died as a Muslim Bomber."

51. Nicola Smith, "Making of Muriel the Suicide Bomber," *Times Online,* December 4, 2005, accessed June 9, 2011, http://www.timesonline.co.uk/tol /news/article745407.ece.

52. Ibid.

53. Ibid.

54. Ibid. Italics added.

55. Smith, "Raised as Catholic in Belgium, She Died as a Muslim Bomber"; Smith, "Making of Muriel the Suicide Bomber."

56. Smith, "Making of Muriel the Suicide Bomber."

57. Lester et al., "Suicide Bombers," 290.

58. Ibid., 292.

59. Atran, "Genesis of Suicide Terrorism," 1536. Italics added.

60. Pape, *Dying to Win,* 210–11.

61. All efforts have been made to reduce the chances of redundancy. However, since some of these individuals are not identified by name, it is possible that a few cases appear on this list more than once.

62. Christine Fair, *Suicide Attacks in Afghanistan: 2001–2007* (United Nations Assistance Mission in Afghanistan, 2007).

63. Mia Bloom, *Bombshell: The Many Faces of Women Terrorists* (Toronto: Penguin, 2011); Bloom, *Dying to Kill;* Lankford, "Do Suicide Terrorists Exhibit Clinically Suicidal Risk Factors?"; Pedahzur, *Suicide Terrorism.*

64. Pedahzur, *Suicide Terrorism.*

65. Ibid.

66. "The Mother of Two Who Became a Suicide Bomber," *Sunday Tribune,* September 17, 2006, accessed August 21, 2009, http://www.tribune.ie/archive /article/2006/sep/17/the-mother-of-two-who-became-a-suicide-bomber/.

67. Pedahzur, *Suicide Terrorism.*

68. Merari, *Driven to Death.* This is a pseudonym assigned by Merari, not the individual's real name.

69. Lester et al., "Suicide Bombers," 290.

70. Hafez, *Manufacturing Human Bombs,* 49.

71. Pape, *Dying to Win;* Pearson, "Apocalyptic Cult Methods Explain bin Laden."

72. Pedahzur, *Suicide Terrorism.*
73. Ibid.
74. Anat Berko, *The Path to Paradise: The Inner World of Suicide Bomb-ers and Their Dispatchers* (London: Praeger, 2007), 1; Pedahzur, *Suicide Terrorism.*

CHAPTER 4: THE TRUTH ABOUT 9/11

1. Neta C. Crawford, Catherine Lutz, and Andrea Mazzarino, "Costs of War," *Eisenhower Study Group,* June 2011, accessed June 29, 2011, http://costsofwar.org/.
2. Pape, *Dying to Win,* 220.
3. Ibid., 224.
4. Joel Achenbach, "You Never Imagine a Hijacker Next Door," *Washington Post,* September 16, 2001, accessed May 4, 2011, http://www.washington post.com/ac2/wp-dyn?pagename=article&node=&contentId=A38026 -2001Sep15; Weaver, "New Video Shows 9/11 Hijackers Mohamed Atta, Ziad Jarrah at Al-Qaida Meeting."
5. Weaver, "New Video Shows 9/11 Hijackers Mohamed Atta, Ziad Jarrah at Al-Qaida Meeting."
6. Ibid.
7. Terry McDermott, *Perfect Soldiers: The 9/11 Hijackers—Who They Were, Why They Did It* (New York: HarperCollins, 2005), 68.
8. National Commission on Terrorist Attacks Upon the United States, "The 9/11 Commission Report."
9. Ibid.
10. Ibid.
11. Ibid., 250.
12. Jonathan Cavanagh, A. J. Carson, M. Sharpe, and S. M. Lawrie, "Psycho-logical Autopsy Studies of Suicide: A Systematic Review," *Psychological Medicine* 33 (2003): 395.
13. Ibid.
14. Although this same assertion could potentially be made about almost any complex human being, the critical point here is that the gap between these different identities appears to have been much more sizable in Atta's case.
15. John Crewdson, "From Kind Teacher to Murderous Zealot," *Chicago Tribune,* September 12, 2004, available at http://articles.chicagotribune .com/2004-09-12/news/0409120328_1_hijackers-world-trade-center -americans; Unni Wikan, "'My Son—a Terrorist?' (He was such a gentle boy)," *Anthropological Quarterly* 75 (2001): 117–28.
16. "The 19 Plotters and Their Day of Terror," *St. Petersburg Times,* Sep-tember 11, 2002, accessed June 24, 2011, http://www.sptimes.com/2002 /09/01/911/plotters.shtml.
17. One could argue that a psychological autopsy would be better conducted by going back today and interviewing all associates of Mohamed Atta, with the express purpose of uncovering signs of suicidality. However, given the many years that have passed since 9/11, any statements these witnesses would make today would arguably be less valid and reliable than the interviews they granted right after 9/11, when their memories of Atta were still fresh.
18. Stephen S. Ilardi, *The Depression Cure: The 6-Step Program to Beat De-pression without Drugs* (Cambridge, MA: De Capo Press, 2009); Ronald

W. Maris, Alan L. Berman, and Morton M. Silverman, *Comprehensive Textbook of Suicidology* (New York: Guilford, 2000); National Institute of Mental Health, "Signs and Symptoms of Depression," March 31, 2009, accessed May 4, 2011, http://www.nimh.nih.gov/health/topics/depression /men-and-depression/signs-and-symptoms-of-depression/index.shtml.

19. Terry McDermott, *Perfect Soldiers,* 13.

20. Ibid., 13–14.

21. Andrew Buncombe, "Childhood Clues to What Makes a Killer," *Independent,* October 12, 2001, accessed May 4, 2011, http://www.independent .co.uk/news/world/middle-east/childhood-clues-to-what-makes-a-killer -748415.html.

22. McDermott, *Perfect Soldiers,* 19.

23. Maris, Berman, and Silverman, *Comprehensive Textbook of Suicidology,* xvi–xvii.

24. Buncombe, "Childhood Clues to What Makes a Killer"; Crewdson, "From Kind Teacher to Murderous Zealot"; Elena Lappin, "Atta in Hamburg," *Prospect,* September 20, 2002, accessed May 4, 2011, http://www.prospect magazine.co.uk/2002/09/attainhamburg/; McDermott, *Perfect Soldiers.*

25. McDermott, *Perfect Soldiers.*

26. Ibid.

27. Yellow Ribbon Suicide Prevention Program, "Warning Signs & Risk Factors of Suicide," 2009, accessed May 4, 2011, http://www.yellowribbon .org/WarningSigns.html.

28. McDermott, *Perfect Soldiers,* 27.

29. Ibid.

30. Ibid., 32.

31. Lappin, "Atta in Hamburg."

32. McDermott, *Perfect Soldiers.*

33. Ibid., 47.

34. Ibid., 23.

35. Maris, Berman, and Silverman, *Comprehensive Textbook of Suicidology,* 252–53.

36. John Cloud, "Atta's Odyssey," *Time,* September 30, 2001, accessed May 4, 2011, http://www.time.com/time/magazine/article/0,9171,1101011008 -176917,00.html.

37. McDermott, *Perfect Soldiers,* 60.

38. Ibid.

39. Crewdson, "From Kind Teacher to Murderous Zealot."

40. McDermott, *Perfect Soldiers.*

41. American Foundation for Suicide Prevention, "Risk Factors for Suicide," 2010, accessed May 4, 2011, http://www.afsp.org/index.cfm?page_id =05147440-E24E-E376-BDF4BF8BA6444E76; Ilardi, *The Depression Cure;* National Institute of Mental Health, "Signs and Symptoms of Depression."

42. Lankford, "Could Suicide Terrorists Actually Be Suicidal?"; J. Reid Meloy, "Indirect Personality Assessment of the Violent True Believer," *Journal of Personality Assessment* 82 (2004): 138–46; Merari, *Driven to Death.*

43. National Institute of Mental Health, "Signs and Symptoms of Depression."

44. Crewdson, "From Kind Teacher to Murderous Zealot."

45. Ibid.

46. Ibid.

47. Ibid.
48. Cloud, "Atta's Odyssey."
49. Crewdson, "From Kind Teacher to Murderous Zealot." Maglad states that Atta "was convinced that there was *not enough time in one's life* to have fun." It is not clear whether we can reliably attribute these words—or this general meaning—to Atta himself. Perhaps this is how Atta spoke, or perhaps this is simply Maglad's expression. If Atta actually expressed that there was "not enough time in one's life," that phrasing itself could be evidence of his suicidal thoughts and plan to end his life prematurely.
50. McDermott, *Perfect Soldiers*, 61. There is some dispute about whether this statement was made by Atta or fellow 9/11 hijacker Marwan al-Shehhi. McDermott attributes it to Atta.
51. Ibid., 61.
52. American Foundation for Suicide Prevention, "Risk Factors for Suicide"; National Institute of Mental Health, "Signs and Symptoms of Depression."
53. Wikan, "'My Son—a Terrorist?'"
54. McDermott, *Perfect Soldiers*.
55. Ibid.
56. Ibid.
57. Crewdson, "From Kind Teacher to Murderous Zealot."
58. Ibid.; McDermott, *Perfect Soldiers*, 67.
59. McDermott, *Perfect Soldiers*, 26.
60. National Institute of Mental Health, "Signs and Symptoms of Depression."
61. E. Salander Renberg, "Self-Reported Life-Weariness, Death-Wishes, Suicidal Ideation, Suicidal Plans and Suicide Attempts in General Population Surveys in the North of Sweden 1986 and 1996," *Social Psychiatry and Psychiatric Epidemiology* 36 (2001): 429–36.
62. McDermott, *Perfect Soldiers*, 84. Italics added.
63. Durkheim, *Le Suicide*; Farber, *Theory of Suicide*; Maris, *Pathways to Suicide*; Shneidman, "An Overview."
64. McDermott, *Perfect Soldiers*.
65. Ibid., 26.
66. Lankford, "Do Suicide Terrorists Exhibit Clinically Suicidal Risk Factors?"
67. Lankford, "Suicide Terrorism as a Socially Approved Form of Suicide"; "Support for Suicide Bombing," *Pew Research Center*, 2002, accessed July 11, 2011, http://pewglobal.org/database/?indicator=19.
68. McDermott, *Perfect Soldiers*, 26.
69. Mohamed Atta, "Mohamed Atta's Last Will & Testament," *PBS*, April 11, 1996, accessed May 4, 2011, http://www.pbs.org/wgbh/pages/frontline/shows/network/personal/attawill.html.
70. Ibid.
71. Ibid.
72. Ibid.
73. Ibid.
74. Ibid.
75. McDermott, *Perfect Soldiers*, 22.
76. Ibid., 26.
77. McDermott, *Perfect Soldiers*.
78. Ibid., 61.
79. American Foundation for Suicide Prevention, "Risk Factors for Suicide"; Lester, *Making Sense of Suicide*; Maris, Berman, and Silverman,

Comprehensive Textbook of Suicidology; National Institute of Mental Health, "Suicide in the U.S."

80. American Foundation for Suicide Prevention, "Risk Factors for Suicide"; Farber, *Theory of Suicide;* Lester, *Making Sense of Suicide;* National Institute of Mental Health, "Signs and Symptoms of Depression."

81. Mohamed Atta, "Mohamed Atta's Last Will & Testament."

82. Barry Rubin and Judith C. Rubin, *Anti-American Terrorism and the Middle East* (Oxford: Oxford University Press, 2002), 233–36.

83. National Commission on Terrorist Attacks Upon the United States, "The 9/11 Commission Report."

84. Evan Thomas, "Cracking the Terror Code," *Newsweek,* October 15, 2001, accessed May 4, 2011, http://www.newsweek.com/id/75613.

85. McDermott, *Perfect Soldiers.*

86. Lappin, "Atta in Hamburg"; Amany Radwan, "Portrait of the Terrorist as a Young Man," *Time,* October 6, 2001, accessed May 4, 2011, http://www .time.com/time/nation/article/0,8599,178383,00.html.

87. Michael J. Bader, *Arousal: The Secret Logic of Sexual Fantasies* (New York: St. Martin's Press, 2002).

88. Bader, *Arousal,* 33.

89. McDermott, *Perfect Soldiers.*

90. Radwan, "Portrait of the Terrorist as a Young Man."

91. Crewdson, "From Kind Teacher to Murderous Zealot."

92. McDermott, *Perfect Soldiers,* 20.

93. McDermott, *Perfect Soldiers.*

94. Bader, *Arousal.*

95. Lappin, "Atta in Hamburg."

96. Buncombe, "Childhood Clues to What Makes a Killer."

97. Ibid.

98. Lappin, "Atta in Hamburg."

99. Crewdson, "From Kind Teacher to Murderous Zealot."

100. Atta, "Mohamed Atta's Last Will & Testament."

101. McDermott, *Perfect Soldiers.*

102. Bader, *Arousal.*

103. American Foundation for Suicide Prevention, "Risk Factors for Suicide"; National Institute of Mental Health, "Signs and Symptoms of Depression."

104. Maris, Berman, and Silverman, *Comprehensive Textbook of Suicidology.*

105. Cloud, "Atta's Odyssey."

106. Crewdson, "From Kind Teacher to Murderous Zealot."

107. McDermott, *Perfect Soldiers,* 29.

108. Ibid., 32.

109. Lappin, "Atta in Hamburg."

110. Cloud, "Atta's Odyssey."

111. Ibid.

112. Ibid.

113. Rubin and Rubin, *Anti-American Terrorism and the Middle East,* 233.

114. McDermott, *Perfect Soldiers.*

115. Crewdson, "From Kind Teacher to Murderous Zealot."

116. McDermott, *Perfect Soldiers,* 279.

117. Crewdson, "From Kind Teacher to Murderous Zealot."

118. Michael Slackman, "Bin Laden Kin Wait and Worry," *Los Angeles Times,* November 13, 2001, accessed May 4, 2011, http://articles.latimes.com /2001/nov/13/news/mn-3564.

119. McDermott, *Perfect Soldiers.*

120. Crewdson, "From Kind Teacher to Murderous Zealot."

121. Ibid.

122. Ibid.

123. McDermott, *Perfect Soldiers.*

124. Ibid., 83.

125. Ibid., 29.

126. Achenbach, "You Never Imagine a Hijacker Next Door"; Pape, *Dying to Win;* Weaver, "New Video Shows 9/11 Hijackers Mohamed Atta, Ziad Jarrah at Al-Qaida Meeting."

127. National Commission on Terrorist Attacks Upon the United States, "The 9/11 Commission Report."

128. Sonya Fatah, "Why the Disabled Do Taliban's Deadly Work: With So Few Rehabilitation Services Available, Suicide Attacks Can Offer Easy Escape," *Globe and Mail,* May 7, 2007, accessed November 19, 2010, http://www .theglobeandmail.com/servlet/story/LAC.20070507.SUICIDE07/TPStory /Front.

129. Ibid.

130. McDermott, *Perfect Soldiers;* National Commission on Terrorist Attacks Upon the United States, "The 9/11 Commission Report."

131. Ibid.

132. McDermott, *Perfect Soldiers,* 215.

133. Ibid., 205.

134. Ibid., 206.

135. National Commission on Terrorist Attacks Upon the United States, "The 9/11 Commission Report."

136. McDermott, *Perfect Soldiers,* 206.

137. Ibid., 51–52; National Commission on Terrorist Attacks Upon the United States, "The 9/11 Commission Report."

138. McDermott, *Perfect Soldiers.*

139. Jim Popkin, "An Intimate Look at One 9/11 Hijacker." *NBC News,* 2008, accessed May 4, 2011, http://current.com/1iuhu4c#27858161.

140. National Commission on Terrorist Attacks Upon the United States, "The 9/11 Commission Report."

141. Maris, Berman, and Silverman, *Comprehensive Textbook of Suicidology.*

142. Charles M. Sennott, "Before Oath to Jihad, Drifting and Boredom," *Boston Globe,* March 3, 2002, accessed November 8, 2011, http://www.boston .com/news/packages/underattack/news/driving_a_wedge/part1_side.shtml.

143. Ibid.

144. Maris, Berman, and Silverman, *Comprehensive Textbook of Suicidology.*

CHAPTER 5: WHAT REAL HEROES ARE MADE OF

1. "The Birth of Jesus Christ," *The Holy Bible,* Matthew 1.21, accessed August 11, 2011, http://niv.scripturetext.com/matthew/1.htm.

2. "Saint Joan of Arc," *Encyclopedia Britannica,* 2011, accessed August 11, 2011, http://www.britannica.com/EBchecked/topic/304220/Saint-Joan-of-Arc.

3. Dumas Malone, Hirst Milhollen, and Milton Kaplan, *The Story of the Declaration of Independence* (Oxford: Oxford University Press, 1975), 91.

4. Charles Dickens, *A Tale of Two Cities* (Oxford: Oxford University Press, 1859), 358.

5. Jill Lawless, "Harry Potter Wizard Series to Be Sold as E-books," *Bloomberg BusinessWeek,* June 23, 2011, accessed October 6, 2011, http://www.businessweek.com/ap/financialnews/D9O1M59G0.htm.

6. Derek Murphy, *Jesus Potter Harry Christ: The Fascinating Parallels between Two of the World's Most Popular Literary Characters* (Portland, OR: HB Press, 2011).

7. J. K. Rowling, *Harry Potter and the Deathly Hallows* (New York: Scholastic, 2007), 554.

8. "History," *Congressional Medal of Honor Society,* 2011, accessed August 12, 2011, http://www.cmohs.org/medal-history.php; italics added.

9. This is meant to be a basic visual representation of the relationship between risk and heroism, as perceived by many terrorists and terrorist sympathizers, according to Merari, *Driven to Death,* and others.

10. Post et al., "The Psychology of Suicide Terrorism."

11. This claim also appears in Christopher Coker, *The Warrior Ethos: Military Culture and the War on Terror* (London: Routledge, 2007); Paul W. Kahn, *Sacred Violence: Torture, Terror, and Sovereignty* (Ann Arbor: University of Michigan Press, 2008); Gary D. Lynne, "On the Economics of Subselves: Toward a Metaeconomics," in Morris Altman, ed., 99–124, *Handbook of Contemporary Behavioral Economics: Foundations and Developments* (Armonk, NY: M.E. Sharpe Publishers, 2006); Michael J. McMains and Wayman C. Mullins, *Managing Critical Incidents and Hostage Situations in Law Enforcement and Corrections* (Cincinnati, OH: Anderson, 2010).

12. "What Nidal Hasan Said About Suicide Bombers," *Times Online,* November 6, 2009, accessed September 25, 2011, http://www.timesonline.co.uk/tol/news/world/us_and_americas/article6905976.ece; in his actual post, Hasan misspelled "It's," "amongst," "too," "intentionally," and "paralleled," but that has been corrected for clarity's sake.

13. "Memorable quotes for: *In the Line of Fire,*" *Internet Movie Database,* 1993, accessed October 1, 2011, http://www.imdb.com/title/tt0107206/quotes.

14. Ibid.

15. Ellen Crean, "He Took a Bullet for Reagan," *CBS News,* December 5, 2007, accessed September 25, 2011, http://www.cbsnews.com/stories/2004/06/11/earlyshow/main622527.shtml.

16. Crean, "He Took a Bullet for Reagan"; Kane Farabaugh, "Victims Recall Reagan Assassination Attempt 30 Years Later," *Voice of America News,* March 30, 2011, accessed October 1, 2011, http://www.voanews.com/english/news/usa/Victims-Recall-Reagan-Assassination-Attempt-30-Years-Later-118953314.html; William Welch, "Library Tells Story of Assassination Attempt on Reagan," *USA Today,* March 30, 2011, accessed October 1, 2011, http://www.usatoday.com/news/washington/2011-03-30-reagan-library-assassination_N.htm.

17. Ann S. Tyson and Josh White, "With Iraq War Come Layers of Loss," *Washington Post,* January 2, 2007, accessed September 25, 2011, http://www.washingtonpost.com/wp-dyn/content/article/2007/01/01/AR2007010100759.html.

18. "Specialist Ross A. McGinnis," *U.S. Army,* May 24, 2011, accessed September 25, 2011, http://www.army.mil/medalofhonor/mcginnis/.

19. "Sergeant First Class Leroy A. Petry," *U.S. Army,* July 12, 2011, accessed September 25, 2011, http://www.army.mil/medalofhonor/petry/.

20. Ibid.

21. Thomas Harding, "Royal Marine Who Jumped on Grenade Awarded George Cross," *Telegraph,* July 22, 2008, accessed September 25, 2011, http://www.telegraph.co.uk/news/uknews/2445513/Royal-Marine-who-jumped-on-grenade-awarded-George-Cross.html.

22. "Military Honours and Awards," *The British Monarchy,* 2011, accessed October 1, 2011, http://www.royal.gov.uk/MonarchUK/Honours/Military HonoursandAwards/MilitaryHonoursandAwards.aspx.

23. Maris, Berman, and Silverman, *Comprehensive Textbook of Suicidology.*

24. Ibid., 31.

25. Recall, for instance, suicide bomber Wafa al-Biss from Chapter 2, who had been thinking about a suicide attack for years.

26. See Chapter 4.

27. Crean, "He Took a Bullet for Reagan."

28. Maris, Berman, and Silverman, *Comprehensive Textbook of Suicidology.*

29. "Sergeant First Class Leroy A. Petry."

30. Harding, "Royal Marine Who Jumped on Grenade Awarded George Cross."

31. Tyson and White, "With Iraq War Come Layers of Loss."

32. Ibid.

33. Harding, "Royal Marine Who Jumped on Grenade Awarded George Cross."

34. Strobe Talbot, *The Age of Terror* (New York, Basic Books, 2002).

35. Alessandro Lanteri, Chiara Chelini, Salvatore Rizzello, "An Experimental Investigation of Emotions and Reasoning in the Trolley Problem," *Journal of Business Ethics* 83 (2008): 789–804.

36. Ibid., 795. The word "train" has been substituted for "trolley."

37. Lanteri, Chelini, Rizzello, "An Experimental Investigation of Emotions and Reasoning in the Trolley Problem."

38. Ibid., 795. The word "train" has been substituted for "trolley."

39. Lanteri, Chelini, Rizzello, "An Experimental Investigation of Emotions and Reasoning in the Trolley Problem."

40. Michael R. Waldmann and Jörn H. Dieterich, "Throwing a Bomb on a Person Versus Throwing a Person on a Bomb: Intervention Myopia in Moral Intuitions," *Psychological Science* 18 (2007): 247–53.

41. Ibid., 250.

42. Osama bin Laden, "Letter to the American People," *Guardian,* November 24, 2002, accessed March 12, 2011, http://www.guardian.co.uk /world/2002/nov/24/theobserver.

43. Previous research has shown that these claims are not accurate, and that terrorism is actually counterproductive to the cause of those organizations that sponsor it. See Max Abrahms, "The Political Effectiveness of Terrorism Revisited," *Comparative Political Studies* 45 (2012): 366–93; Max Abrahms, "Why Terrorism Does Not Work," *International Security* 31 (2006): 42–78.

44. "How Many People Died as a Result of the Atomic Bombings?" *Radiation Effects Research Foundation,* 2007, accessed October 6, 2011, http://www .rerf.or.jp/general/qa_e/qa1.html.

45. "Miramar to Dedicate Range to Famous Sniper," *Marine Corps Times,* March 27, 2007, accessed October 2, 2011, http://www.marinecorpstimes.com/news/2007/03/marine_hatchcock_rangededication_070327/.

CHAPTER 6: MURDER-SUICIDE: THE NATURAL COMPARISON

1. Abraham Lincoln, "You Can Have Anything You Want," *Famous Quotes,* 2011, accessed July 3, 2011, http://www.1-famous-quotes.com/quote/21284.
2. "Chris Crocker," *TMZ,* 2011, accessed July 3, 2011, http://www.tmz.com/person/chris-crocker/.
3. "University of Florida Student Tasered at Kerry Forum," *YouTube,* September 17, 2007, accessed July 3, 2011, http://www.youtube.com/watch?v=6bVa6jn4rpE.
4. Lankford, *Human Killing Machines.*
5. John Douglas, *Inside the Mind of BTK: The True Story Behind the Thirty-Year Hunt for the Notorious Wichita Serial Killer* (San Francisco: Jossey-Bass, 2007); David Schmid, *Natural Born Celebrities: Serial Killers in American Culture* (Chicago: University of Chicago Press, 2005); "Serial Killer Convicted of Murder," *BBC News,* March 16, 2006, accessed December 16, 2009, http://news.bbc.co.uk/2/hi/uk_news/england/southern_counties/4813234.stm.
6. Israel W. Charny, *Fighting Suicide Bombing: A Worldwide Campaign for Life* (Westport, CT: Praeger Security International, 2007); Jessica Stern, *Terror in the Name of God: Why Religious Militants Kill* (New York: Ecco, 2003).
7. Arie W. Kruglankski, Xiaoyan Chen, Mark Dechesne, Shira Fishman, and Edward Orehek, "Fully Committed: Suicide Bombers' Motivation and the Quest for Personal Significance," *Political Psychology* 30 (2009): 331.
8. Hafez, *Manufacturing Human Bombs,* 34; Pastor, "Countering the Psychological Consequences of Suicide Terrorism," 704; Post et al., "The Psychology of Suicide Terrorism," 21.
9. Hoffman, *Inside Terrorism.*
10. Shaul Shay, *The Shahids: Islam and Suicide Attacks* (New Brunswick, NJ: Transaction Publishers, 2004).
11. Pedahzur, *Suicide Terrorism.*
12. Ralph Larkin, "The Columbine Legacy: Rampage Shootings as Political Acts," *American Behavioral Scientist* 52 (2009): 1309–26.
13. Ibid., 1322.
14. Katherine Newman, "School Rampage Shootings," *Contexts* 6 (2007): 29.
15. Lankford and Hakim, "From Columbine to Palestine."
16. "Mall Shooter's Suicide Note: I Just Snapped," *USA Today,* December 7, 2007, accessed July 3, 2011, http://www.usatoday.com/news/nation/2007-12-07-mallshooter-suicidenote_N.htm; in the actual note, Hawkins misspelled "piece."
17. Nancy Gibbs and Timothy Roche, "The Columbine Tapes," *Time,* December 20, 1999, accessed July 4, 2011, http://www.time.com/time/magazine/article/0,9171,992873,00.html.
18. Ibid.
19. Ibid.
20. Benedict Carey, "For Rampage Killers, Familiar Descriptions, 'Troubled' and 'Loner,' but No Profile," *New York Times,* April 18, 2007, accessed

July 4, 2011, http://query.nytimes.com/gst/fullpage.html?res=9406E2DB1E
3FF93BA25757C0A9619C8B63.

21. There have been several exceptions. A comparative study has been con-
    ducted by Adam Lankford and Nayab Hakim, "From Columbine to Pal-
    estine: A Comparative Analysis of Rampage Shooters in the United States
    and Volunteer Suicide Bombers in the Middle East," *Aggression and Vio-
    lent Behavior* 16 (2011): 98–107. In addition, brief comparisons have been
    made by Cullen, *Columbine;* Joseph Lieberman, *The Shooting Game: The
    Making of School Shooters* (Santa Ana, CA: Seven Locks, 2006); Aftab
    Omer and Jürgen W. Kremer, "Between Columbine and the Twin Towers,"
    ReVision, 26 (2003): 37–40.

22. Carey, "For Rampage Killers, Familiar Descriptions, 'Troubled' and
    'Loner,' but No Profile."

23. Susan D. James, "Psychology of Virginia Tech, Columbine Killers Still Baf-
    fles Experts," *ABC News,* April 16, 2009, accessed July 4, 2011, http://
    abcnews.go.com/Health/story?id=7345607&page=1; Larkin, "The Col-
    umbine Legacy."

24. Larkin, "The Columbine Legacy."

25. "Police Questioned Health Club Gunman, Let Him Go Week Before Shoot-
    ing," *Fox News,* August 10, 2009, accessed July 4, 2011, http://www
    .foxnews.com/story/0,2933,538732,00.html.

26. "Former Student Dead After Storming German School," *CTV News,*
    November 20, 2006, accessed July 4, 2011, http://www.ctv.ca/CTVNews
    /CanadaAM/20061120/german_shooting_061120/.

27. Cullen, *Columbine.*

28. "Columbine Killer Envisioned Crashing Plane in NYC," *CNN,* Decem-
    ber 6, 2001, accessed July 4, 2011, http://archives.cnn.com/2001/US/12/05
    /columbine.diary/.

29. Joseph I. Lieberman and Susan M. Collins, *A Ticking Time Bomb: Coun-
    terterrorism Lessons from the U.S. Government's Failure to Prevent the
    Fort Hood Attack* (Washington, DC: U.S. Senate Committee on Homeland
    Security and Government Affairs, 2011).

30. Wike, "Little Support for Terrorism Among Muslim Americans." See
    Chapter 1 for an explanation of this figure.

31. George Sodini, "George Sodini's Blog: Full Text by Alleged Gym Shooter,"
    ABC News, 2009, accessed July 5, 2011, http://abcnews.go.com/US/
    story?id=8258001&page=1.

32. Maria Newman and Michael Brick, "Neighbor Says Hasan Gave Belong-
    ings Away Before Attack," *New York Times,* November 6, 2009, accessed
    July 5, 2011, http://www.nytimes.com/2009/11/07/us/07suspect.html;
    "Profile: Major Nidal Malik Hasan," *BBC News,* November 12, 2009,
    accessed July 5, 2011, http://news.bbc.co.uk/2/hi/8345944.stm.

33. Nancy Gibbs, "The Fort Hood Killer: Terrified . . . or Terrorist?" *Time,*
    November 11, 2009, accessed July 5, 2011, http://www.time.com/time/
    magazine/article/0,9171,1938698,00.html.

34. Sodini, "George Sodini's Blog."

35. "Profile: Major Nidal Malik Hasan."

36. James Dao, "Suspect Was 'Mortified' About Deployment," *New York
    Times,* November 5, 2009, accessed July 5, 2011, http://www.nytimes.
    com/2009/11/06/us/06suspect.html.

37. Sodini, "George Sodini's Blog."

38. Lieberman and Collins, *A Ticking Time Bomb.*

39. Sodini, "George Sodini's Blog."
40. Sodini, "George Sodini's Blog."
41. "Who Is Nidal Hasan?" *The Week,* November 6, 2009, accessed July 6, 2011, http://theweek.com/article/index/102580/who-is-nidal-hasan.
42. Sodini, "George Sodini's Blog."
43. Dao, "Suspect Was 'Mortified' About Deployment"; "Profile: Major Nidal Malik Hasan."
44. Sodini, "George Sodini's Blog."
45. Sodini, "George Sodini's Blog."
46. "Military Doctors Worried Hasan Was 'Psychotic,' Capable of Killing Fellow Soldiers," *Fox News,* November 12, 2009, accessed July 5, 2011, http://www.foxnews.com/us/2009/11/12/military-doctors-worried-hasan-psychotic-capable-killing-fellow-soldiers; "The Troubled Journey of Major Hasan," *Time,* 2009, accessed July 5, 2011, http://www.time.com/time/photogallery/0,29307,1938816_1988826,00.html.
47. "What Nidal Hasan Said About Suicide Bombers."
48. Sodini, "George Sodini's Blog"; "What Nidal Hasan Said About Suicide Bombers."
49. Lankford, "Could Suicide Terrorists Actually Be Suicidal?"
50. "Gunman in Health Club Shooting a 48-year-old Loner," *CTV News,* August 5, 2009, accessed July 5, 2011, http://www.ctv.ca/CTVNews/World/20090805/health_club_090805/; "Fort Hood Gunman had Nearly 200 Rounds of Ammo," *USA Today,* October 20, 2010, accessed July 5, 2011, http://www.usatoday.com/news/nation/2010–10–20-fort-hood-trial_N.htm.
51. Charles Bishop's suicide terrorism attack on January 5, 2002, did not yield the minimum qualifying requirement of two victims, so it was not included in the subsequent statistical analysis described here.
52. Data were collected from government reports, existing databases, media reports, and previous scholarship: sources that are commonly relied upon when studying these types of attackers.
53. Peter F. Langman, "Rampage School Shooters: A Typology," *Aggression and Violent Behavior* 14 (2009): 79–86; Larkin, "The Columbine Legacy"; Katherine S. Newman, Cybelle Fox, Wendy Roth, Jal Mehta, and David Harding, *Rampage: The Social Roots of School Shootings* (New York: Basic Books, 2004); Katherine S. Newman and Cybelle Fox, "Repeat Tragedy: Rampage Shootings in American High School and College Settings, 2002–2008," *American Behavioral Scientist* 52 (2009): 1286–1308; Mary E. O'Toole, "The School Shooter: A Threat Assessment Perspective," *Federal Bureau of Investigation,* 2000, accessed July 12, 2011, http://www.fbi.gov/stats-services/publications/school-shooter/; Karen L. Tonso, "Violent Masculinities as Tropes for School Shooters: The Montreal Massacre, the Columbine Attack, and Rethinking Schools," *American Behavioral Scientist* 52 (2009): 1266–85; Bryan Vossekuil, Robert A. Fein, Marissa Reddy, Randy Borum, and William Modzeleski, *The Final Report and Findings of the Safe School Initiative: Implications for the Prevention of School Attacks in the United States* (Washington, DC: United States Secret Service and United States Department of Education, 2002).
54. "Terrorism: Definitions," *Federal Bureau of Investigation,* 2009, accessed March 12, 2011, http://denver.fbi.gov/nfip.htm.

55. Hoffman, *Inside Terrorism.*

56. Although the September 11, 2001, attacks were planned in coordination and shared the same basic political objectives, they are listed as four separate strikes, which is how they appear in the "Global Terrorism Database," *National Consortium for the Study of Terrorism and Responses to Terrorism,* 2010, accessed February 24, 2011, http://www.start.umd.edu /gtd/.

57. Interested readers are welcome to contact the author for a more detailed description of the methods and findings.

58. Lankford, "Do Suicide Terrorists Exhibit Clinically Suicidal Risk Factors?"; Lankford, "Could Suicide Terrorists Actually Be Suicidal?"; Lester, Yang, and Lindsay, "Suicide Bombers"; Merari, *Driven to Death.*

59. Durkheim, *Le Suicide;* Farber, *Theory of Suicide;* Lester, *Making Sense of Suicide;* Karl Menninger, *Man Against Himself* (New York: Harcourt, Brace & World, 1938); Maris, Berman, and Silverman, *Comprehensive Textbook of Suicidology.*

60. Mark Ames, *Going Postal: From Reagan's Workplaces to Clinton's Columbine and Beyond* (Brooklyn, NY: Soft Skull, 2005); Stanley Duncan, "Death in the Office: Workplace Homicides," *FBI Law Enforcement Bulletin,* 2005; James A. Fox and Jack Levin, "Firing Back: The Growing Threat of Workplace Homicide," *Annals of the American Academy of Political and Social Science* 536 (1994): 16–30; Michael Kelleher, *Profiling the Lethal Employee: Case Studies of Workplace Violence* (Westport, CT: Praeger, 1997); Langman, "Rampage School Shooters"; Lankford and Hakim, "From Columbine to Palestine"; Larkin, "The Columbine Legacy"; Lieberman, *The Shooting Game;* Newman et al., *Rampage;* Newman and Fox, "Repeat Tragedy"; O'Toole, "The School Shooter"; Eugene Rugala, *Workplace Violence: Issues in Response* (Quantico, VA: National Center for the Analysis of Violent Crime, Federal Bureau of Investigation, 2003); Stephen Thompson and Ken Kyle, "Understanding Mass School Shootings: Links between Personhood and Power in the Competitive School Environment," *Journal of Primary Prevention* 26 (2005): 419–38; Tonso, "Violent Masculinities as Tropes for School Shooters"; Vossekuil et al., *The Final Report and Findings of the Safe School Initiative;* R. Craig Windham, Lisa M. Hooper, and Patricia E. Hudson, "Selected Spiritual, Religious and Family Factors in Prevention of School Violence," *Counseling and Values* 49 (2005): 208–16; Workplace Violence Prevention Operations Committee, "Violence Prevention: Maintaining a Safe Workplace," *University of California, Davis,* 2007, accessed January 14, 2010, http://www.hr.ucdavis.edu/supervisor/Er/Violence /Brochure.

61. Carey, "For Rampage Killers, Familiar Descriptions, 'Troubled' and 'Loner,' but No Profile."

62. Cullen, *Columbine.*

63. Ibid., 175–76.

64. Ibid., 175.

65. Ibid., 186–87.

66. Ibid., 186–87.

67. Ibid., 174.

68. Cullen, *Columbine.*

69. Ibid., 239. Italics added.

70. Cullen, *Columbine.*

71. Lauren Slater, "The Trouble with Self-Esteem," *New York Times*, February 3, 2002, accessed July 7, 2011, http://www.nytimes.com/2002/02/03/magazine/the-trouble-with-self-esteem.html.

72. Cullen, *Columbine*, 216.

73. Ibid., 276.

74. Cullen, *Columbine.*

75. Ibid., 216.

CHAPTER 7: THE FOUR TYPES OF SUICIDE TERRORISTS

1. "Race and the Peoples Temple," *PBS*, 2010, accessed July 13, 2011, http://www.pbs.org/wgbh/americanexperience/features/general-article/jonestown-race/.

2. "Cult of Death," *Time*, December 4, 1978, accessed July 14, 2011, http://www.time.com/time/covers/0,16641,19781204,00.html; "The Cult of Death," *Newsweek*, December 4, 1978.

3. "Death Tape," *Federal Bureau of Investigation*, December 13, 1978, accessed July 13, 2011, http://jonestown.sdsu.edu/AboutJonestown/Tapes/Tapes/DeathTape/Q042fbi.html.

4. Ibid.

5. Mary McCormick Maaga, *Hearing the Voices of Jonestown* (Syracuse: Syracuse University Press, 1998); Fielding McGehee, *Jonestown Institute*, personal interview with author, July 19, 2011; Tim Reiterman and John Jacobs, *Raven: The Untold Story of the Rev. Jim Jones and His People* (New York: Dutton, 1982).

6. Dianne E. Scheid, "The Plain Ugly Truth," *Jonestown Institute*, November 16, 2008, accessed July 13, 2011, http://jonestown.sdsu.edu/AboutJonestown/PersonalReflections/v8/Scheid.htm.

7. "Letters to Dad," *Jonestown Institute*, April 12, 2011, accessed July 17, 2011, http://jonestown.sdsu.edu/AboutJonestown/PrimarySources/letterstodad.html.

8. Ibid.

9. Andrea Sachs, "Q&A: A Jonestown Survivor Remembers," *Time*, November 18, 2008, accessed July 13, 2011, http://www.time.com/time/arts/article/0,8599,1859903-2,00.html.

10. "Death Tape."

11. Ibid.

12. McGehee, *Jonestown Institute.*

13. Ibid.

14. McGehee, *Jonestown Institute*; Reiterman and Jacobs, *Raven.*

15. McGehee, *Jonestown Institute*; Scheid, "The Plain Ugly Truth."

16. "Who Survived the Jonestown Tragedy?" *Jonestown Institute*, February 15, 2011, accessed July 13, 2011, http://jonestown.sdsu.edu/AboutJonestown/WhoDied/whosurvived_list.htm.

17. Maris, Berman, and Silverman, *Comprehensive Textbook of Suicidology.*

18. Ibid.

19. American Foundation for Suicide Prevention, "Risk Factors for Suicide"; Durkheim, *Le Suicide*; Farber, *Theory of Suicide*; Lester, *Making Sense of Suicide*; Maris, Berman, and Silverman, *Comprehensive Textbook of Suicidology*; National Institute of Mental Health, "Suicide in the U.S."; Yellow

Ribbon Suicide Prevention Program, "Warning Signs & Risk Factors of Suicide."

20. "Duress," *West's Encyclopedia of American Law, Edition 2,* 2008, accessed July 17, 2011, http://legal-dictionary.thefreedictionary.com/duress.

21. "Death Tape."

22. Christian Goeschel, *Suicide in Nazi Germany* (Oxford: Oxford University Press, 2009).

23. Emiko Ohnuki-Tierney, *Kamikaze, Cherry Blossoms, and Nationalisms: The Militarization of Aesthetics in Japanese History* (Chicago: University Of Chicago Press, 2006), 166.

24. Ibid., 166.

25. Ibid., 166.

26. Ibid., 168.

27. Yasuo Kuwahara and Gordon T. Allred, *Kamikaze: A Japanese Pilot's Own Spectacular Story of the Famous Suicide Squadrons* (New York: Ballantine, 1957), 29, 64.

28. Ibid.

29. Moghadam, *The Globalization of Martyrdom.*

30. Berman and Laitin, "Hard Targets"; Bloom, *Bombshell.*

31. Fair, *Suicide Attacks in Afghanistan.*

32. Stan Grant, "Kidnapped Boys 'Brainwashed' to Die as Suicide Bombers," *CNN,* August 4, 2009, accessed July 26, 2011, http://edition.cnn.com /2009/WORLD/asiapcf/08/03/pakistan.boys/index.html.

33. Ibid.

34. Fair, *Suicide Attacks in Afghanistan.* This is a pseudonym assigned by Fair, not the individual's real name.

35. Merari, *Driven to Death.* This is a pseudonym assigned by Merari, not the individual's real name.

36. Berko, *The Path to Paradise,* 5–6. This is a pseudonym assigned by Berko, not the individual's real name.

37. Ibid., 7.

38. Bloom, *Dying to Kill;* Charny, *Fighting Suicide Bombing;* Hoffman, *Inside Terrorism;* Pedahzur, *Suicide Terrorism.*

39. Fair, *Suicide Attacks in Afghanistan.*

40. Merari, *Driven to Death,* 122. This is a pseudonym assigned by Merari, not the individual's real name.

41. Merari, *Driven to Death.*

42. Mohammed al-Qaisi, "Iraq Accuses Al-Qaeda of Using Mentally Ill Man to Kill 33 Civilians in Samarra," *Al-Shofra,* February 14, 2011, accessed November 12, 2011, http://al-shorfa.com/cocoon/meii/xhtml/en_GB/features /meii/features/main/2011/02/14/feature-02; Ken Ballen, *Terrorists In Love: The Real Lives of Islamic Radicals* (New York: Simon & Schuster, 2011); Bruce Hoffman, "The Logic of Suicide Terrorism," *Atlantic,* July 2003, accessed November 12, 2011, http://www.theatlantic.com/magazine /archive/2003/06/the-logic-of-suicide-terrorism/2739/; Kevin Toolis, "How I Came Face To Face With Taliban Teen Killers," *Daily Mail,* December 19, 2008, accessed November 12, 2011, http://www.dailymail.co.uk/debate /article-1098840/KEVIN-TOOLIS-How-I-came-face-face-Taliban-teen -killers.html.

43. Ballen, *Terrorists in Love;* Alissa J. Rubin, "Afghan Girl Tricked Into Carrying Bomb, Officials Say," *New York Times,* June 26, 2011,

accessed November 23, 2011, http://www.nytimes.com/2011/06/27/world
/asia/27afghanistan.html; McElroy, "Baghdad Market Bombers 'Mentally
Impaired.'"

44. John C. McManus, *Grunts: Inside the American Infantry Combat Experience, World War II Through Iraq* (New York: Penguin, 2010); Caryle
Murphy, "Prime Minister Struggles For Consensus: More Bombings Rock
Baghdad," *Sun Sentinel,* May 3, 2005, accessed November 21, 2011,
http://articles.sun-sentinel.com/2005-05-03/news/0505020469_1_sunni
-arabs-baath-party-jafari.

45. Lester, *Making Sense of Suicide;* Maris, Berman, and Silverman, *Comprehensive Textbook of Suicidology.*

46. David Lester, *Suicide and the Holocaust* (Hauppauge, NY: Nova Science
Publishers, 2006).

47. Goeschel, *Suicide in Nazi Germany.*

48. Ibid., 150.

49. Ibid., 150.

50. Walter C. Langer, *The Mind of Adolf Hitler: The Secret Wartime Report*
(New York: New American Library, 1973).

51. Goeschel, *Suicide in Nazi Germany,* 150.

52. Ibid.

53. Goeschel, *Suicide in Nazi Germany.*

54. Victoria Clark, "Charming and Chilling: Osama bin Laden's Bodyguard,"
Times Online, March 5, 2010, accessed July 26, 2011, http://www
.timesonline.co.uk/tol/news/world/middle_east/article7050537.ece; "Former Osama bin Laden Bodyguard in Al-Arabiya TV Interview: I Love Him
More Than I Love My Own Father," *MEMRI,* June 6, 2007, accessed July
26, 2011, http://www.memri.org/report/en/0/0/0/0/0/0/2644.htm.

55. "Former Osama bin Laden Bodyguard in Al-Arabiya TV Interview."

56. Ibid.

57. "Bin Laden Killing Caps Decade-Long Manhunt," *CNN,* May 2, 2011,
accessed July 26, 2011, http://www.cnn.com/2011/WORLD/asiapcf/05/02
/bin.laden.dead/index.html.

58. Peter Finn, "WikiLeaks Discloses New Details on Whereabouts of Al-Qaeda
Leaders on 9/11," *Washington Post,* April 24, 2011, accessed July 26, 2011,
http://www.washingtonpost.com/world/wikileaks-discloses-new-details
-on-whereabouts-of-al-qaeda-leaders-on-911/2011/04/24/AFvvzIeE_story
.html.

59. Matthew Alexander and John Bruning, *How to Break a Terrorist: The U.S.
Interrogators Who Used Brains, Not Brutality, to Take Down the Deadli-
est Man in Iraq* (New York: Free Press, 2008); Peter Bergen, *Manhunt:
The Ten-Year Search for Bin Laden—from 9/11 to Abbottabad* (New York:
Crown, 2012).

60. "200403110007," *National Consortium for the Study of Terrorism and
Responses to Terrorism,* 2010, accessed July 24, 2011, http://www.start
.umd.edu/gtd/.

61. Baer, *The Cult of The Suicide Bomber 2.*

62. "200403110007."

63. "Train Suspects Among Madrid Suicide Bombers," *Telegraph,* April 4,
2004, accessed July 31, 2011, http://www.telegraph.co.uk/news/1458502
/Train-suspects-among-Madrid-suicide-bombers.html.

64. Alonso and Reinares, "Maghreb Immigrants Becoming Suicide Terrorists," 194.
65. Ibid.
66. Ibid.
67. Ibid., 190.
68. Alonso and Reinares, "Maghreb Immigrants Becoming Suicide Terrorists."
69. "Suspected Madrid Bombing Ringleader Killed," *CNN*, April 4, 2004, accessed July 3, 2012, http://articles.cnn.com/2004-04-04/world/spain .bombings_1_train-bombings-sarhane-ben-abdelmajid-fakhet-bomb-plot ?_s=PM:WORLD.
70. Maris, Berman, and Silverman, *Comprehensive Textbook of Suicidology.*
71. Ibid.
72. Norman L. Farberow, *The Many Faces of Suicide* (New York: McGraw-Hill, 1980).
73. Russell Adams, Martin Giffen, and Frances Garfield, "Risk Taking Among Suicide Attempters, *Journal of Abnormal Psychology* 82 (1973): 262–67; Jeffrey Hutchinson, Jeffery Green, and Shana Hansen, "Evaluating Active Duty Risk-Taking: Military Home, Education, Activity, Drugs, Sex, Suicide, and Safety Method," *Military Medicine* 173 (2008): 1164–67; Maris, Berman, and Silverman, *Comprehensive Textbook of Suicidology;* Peter Miller, "Dancing With Death: The Gray Area Between Suicide Related Behavior, Indifference and Risk Behaviors of Heroin Users," *Contemporary Drug Problems* 33 (2006): 427–50; U.S. Army, "Army Health Promotion, Risk Reduction and Suicide Prevention Report," July 28, 2010, accessed July 26, 2011, http://www.army.mil/-news/2010/07/28/42934-army-health -promotion-risk-reduction-and-suicide-prevention-report/index.html.
74. Casey Grove, "Ex-Soldier Sentenced for Role in Russian Roulette Case," *Chicago Tribune,* May 3, 2012, accessed May 29, 2012, http://www .chicagotribune.com/news/sns-mct-ex-soldier-sentenced-for-role-in-russian -roulette-20120503,0,2317617.story; "Woman Gets 18 Months in Russian Roulette Killing," *Richmond Times-Dispatch,* May 24, 2012, accessed May 29, 2012, http://www2.timesdispatch.com/news/2012/may/24 /tdmet02-crime-and-police-news-for-thursday-may-24-ar-1938440/.
75. Maris, Berman, and Silverman, *Comprehensive Textbook of Suicidology,* 451.
76. Maris, Berman, and Silverman, *Comprehensive Textbook of Suicidology.*
77. "Australia: Alleged Terrorist Plot Foiled," *CNN,* August 3, 2009, accessed July 26, 2011, http://articles.cnn.com/2009-08-03/world/australia.terror .raids_1_australian-federal-police-suspects-terrorist?_s=PM:WORLD.
78. Clark County Prosecuting Attorney, "Mir Aimal Kasi"; Department of Defense, *Fort Hood Army Internal Review Team: Final Report,* 2010, accessed June 3, 2011, http://usarmy.vo.llnwd.net/e1/rv5_downloads/misc /FtHoodAIRTwebversion.pdf; Feldman, "Federal Investigators."
79. Tom Gjelten, "Mumbai Attacks Suggest Terrorists Are Evolving," *National Public Radio,* December 2, 2008, accessed July 26, 2011, http://www.npr .org/templates/story/story.php?storyId=97682012.
80. Bruce Crumley, "Were the Mumbai Terrorists Fueled by Coke?" *Time,* December 3, 2008, accessed July 26, 2011, http://www.time.com/time/world /article/0,8599,1864049,00.html.
81. Speckhard and Ahkmedova, "The Making of a Martyr."

82. John Kohan, "Assault at High Noon," *Time,* June 26, 1995, accessed July 28, 2011, http://www.time.com/time/printout/0,8816,983088,00.html.

83. Associated Press, "Chechen Terror Leader Shamil Basayev Killed in Russia," *Fox News,* July 10, 2006, accessed July 26, 2011, http://www.fox news.com/story/0,2933,202753,00.html.

84. Malcolm Gladwell, "Dangerous Minds: Criminal Profiling Made Easy," *New Yorker,* November 12, 2006, accessed August 2, 2011, http://www .newyorker.com/reporting/2007/11/12/071112fa_fact_gladwell.

CHAPTER 8: MISSION IMPOSSIBLE? HOW TO STOP SUICIDE TERRORISM

1. Associated Press, "Musharraf: Pakistan Isn't Hunting Bin Laden," *MSNBC,* January 22, 2008, accessed November 23, 2011, http://www .msnbc.msn.com/id/22791422/; Joan Walsh, "How the Iraq War Saved Bin Laden's Life," *Salon,* May 10, 2011, accessed November 23, 2011, http:// www.salon.com/2011/05/10/iraq_war_saved_bin_laden/.

2. "General Plays Down Value of Capturing Bin Laden," *Washington Post,* February 24, 2007, accessed November 23, 2011, http://www .washingtonpost.com/wp-dyn/content/article/2007/02/23/AR2007022 301799.html.

3. Lankford, *Human Killing Machines,* 160.

4. Beyond simple logic, the best evidence that access to enemy targets is a critical requirement for suicide terrorism comes from Israel, where a fence was built to prevent suicide terrorists from entering the country's cities. Of course, even fences cannot deny all access, but the result of this countermeasure was a dramatic decrease in attacks. From 2001 to 2003, there were eighty-two suicide attacks on Israeli soil. After the initial portions of the fence were finished in late 2003, there were just sixteen suicide attacks over the next three years. After the fence's path was finalized in 2006, there were just three suicide attacks over the next three-year span. See "Global Terrorism Database" and "Israel's Security Fence," *Ministry of Defense,* January 31, 2007, accessed November 12, 2011, http://www.seamzone .mod.gov.il/pages/eng/purpose.htm.

5. Kix, "The Truth About Suicide Bombers."

6. Peter Allen, "'He Should Have Shot Himself': Father of Anders Breivik Says He Wishes His Son Had Committed Suicide," *Daily Mail,* July 26, 2011, accessed November 24, 2011, http://www.dailymail.co.uk/news /article-2018604/Norway-massacre-Anders-Behring-Breivik-shot-says -father.html#ixzz1efbpwoQG; Nick Carbone, "Bullying and Plastic Surgery: Childhood Friend Speaks Out on Anders Behring Breivik's Life," *Time,* July 26, 2011, accessed November 24, 2011, http://newsfeed.time .com/2011/07/26/bullying-and-plastic-surgery-childhood-friend-speaks -out-on-anders-breiviks-life/#ixzz1efdZtJCy; Robert Mendick, "Norway Massacre: The Real Anders Behring Breivik," *Telegraph,* July 31, 2001, accessed November 24, 2011, http://www.telegraph.co.uk/news/worldnews /europe/norway/8672801/Norway-massacre-the-real-Anders-Behring -Breivik.html.

7. Mendick, "Norway Massacre."

8. Anders Behring Breivik, *2083: A European Declaration of Independence* (Unpublished: 2011), 733, 1220.

9. Ibid., 1025, 1160.

10. Ibid., 1146.
11. David S. Holmes, "Projection as a Defense Mechanism," *Psychological Bulletin* 85 (1978): 677–88.
12. Breivik, *2083*, 1401.
13. Robert Graysmith, *Unabomber: A Desire to Kill* (Washington, DC: Regnery, 1997), 358.
14. Breivik, *2083*, 1366, 1373.
15. Ibid., 1346–48.
16. Allen, "'He Should Have Shot Himself.'"
17. Breivik, *2083*, 1346–48.
18. Charlie Savage, "As Acts of War or Despair, Suicides Rattle a Prison," *New York Times*, April 24, 2011, accessed November 25, 2011, http://www.nytimes.com/2011/04/25/world/guantanamo-files-suicide-as-act-of-war-or-despair.html.
19. Ibid.
20. Breivik, *2083*, 1472.
21. John Stevens, "Massacre Gunman Posted YouTube Video Calling Followers to 'Embrace Martyrdom' Six Hours Before Attacks," *Daily Mail*, July 25, 2011, accessed November 20, 2011, http://www.dailymail.co.uk/news/article-2018148/Anders-Behring-Breivik-posted-YouTube-video-6-hours-Norway-attacks.html.
22. Reid J. Esptein, "Norway Shooter: Ammo Clips Were from U.S.," *Politico*, July 28, 2011, accessed November 25, 2011, http://www.politico.com/news/stories/0711/60154.html.
23. Mark Townsend, "Survivors of Norway Shootings Return to Island of Utøya," *Guardian*, August 20, 2011, accessed November 13, 2011, http://www.guardian.co.uk/world/2011/aug/21/utoya-anders-behring-breivik-norway.
24. Breivik, *2083*.
25. Jarle Brenna, Gordon Andersen, and Morten Hopperstad, "Breivik Er Overrasket Over At Han Lyktes," *VG Nett*, July 26, 2011, accessed November 12, 2011, http://www.vg.no/nyheter/innenriks/oslobomben/artikkel.php?artid=10080811.
26. "Mass Killer Anders Breivik's Chilling Phone Call to Cops—Audio," *Mirror*, November 24, 2011, accessed November 25, 2011, http://www.mirror.co.uk/news/top-stories/2011/11/24/mass-killer-anders-breivik-s-chilling-phone-call-to-cops-audio-115875-23586085/.
27. Helen Pidd and James Meikle, "Anders Behring Breivik: 'It Was A Normal Arrest,'" *Guardian*, July 27, 2011, accessed November 25, 2011, http://www.guardian.co.uk/world/2011/jul/27/anders-behring-breivik-arrest-norway.
28. Raf Sanchez, "Norway Killer Placed on Suicide Watch," *Telegraph*, July 26, 2011, accessed November 25, 2011, http://www.telegraph.co.uk/news/worldnews/europe/norway/8663320/Norway-killer-placed-on-suicide-watch.html.
29. Maris et al., *Comprehensive Textbook of Suicidology*.
30. Newman et al., *Rampage*.
31. Peter Walker and Matthew Taylor, "Far Right on Rise in Europe, Says Report," *Guardian*, November 6, 2011, accessed November 13, 2011, http://www.guardian.co.uk/world/2011/nov/06/far-right-rise-europe-report.
32. "Global Terrorism Database."
33. Thomas Hegghammer and Dominic Tierney, "Why Does Al-Qaeda Have a Problem with Norway?" *Atlantic*, July 13, 2010, accessed November

25, 2011, http://www.theatlantic.com/international/archive/2010/07/why
-does-al-qaeda-have-a-problem-with-norway/59649/.

34. "Three Held in Norway 'Al-Qaeda Bomb Plot,'" *BBC*, July 8, 2010, accessed November 25, 2011, http://www.bbc.co.uk/news/10554523.

35. Ron Paul, "Foreign Occupation Leads to More Terror," *Texas Straight
Talk*, September 12, 2011, accessed November 13, 2011, http://paul.house
.gov/index.php?option=com_content&task=view&id=1909&Itemid=69.

36. "A Dossier of Civilian Casualties 2003-2005," *Iraq Body Count*, July 19,
2005, accessed December 13, 2011, http://reports.iraqbodycount.org/a
_dossier_of_civilian_casualties_2003-2005.pdf.

37. Ibid.

38. Lankford, "Could Suicide Terrorists Actually Be Suicidal?"

39. "A Dossier of Civilian Casualties 2003-2005."

40. Ibid.

41. Paul, "Foreign Occupation Leads to More Terror."

42. Drone missile strikes should also be expected to increase suicidal intent,
homicidal intent, and social approval of suicide terrorism among local inhabitants. For instance, U.S. drones have reportedly killed as many as 2,250
people in Pakistan over the past three years. Right or wrong, those attacks
have profound psychological consequences beyond simply fueling ideology. See Karen DeYoung, "Secrecy Defines Obama's Drone War," *Washington Post,* December 19, 2011, accessed December 20, 2011, http://www
.washingtonpost.com/world/national-security/secrecy-defines-obamas
-drone-war/2011/10/28/gIQAPKNR5O_story.html.

43. Moghadam, *The Globalization of Martyrdom.*

44. Madelyn Hsiao-Rei Hicks, Hamit Dardagan, Peter M. Bagnall, Michael
Spagat, and John A. Sloboda, "Casualties in Civilians and Coalition Soldiers from Suicide Bombings in Iraq, 2003-10: A Descriptive Study," *Lancet* 378 (2011): 906–14.

45. Lara Jakes, "Officials: 29 Dead in Suicide Bomb in Iraq Mosque," *Guardian,* August 28, 2011, accessed December 3, 2011, http://www.guardian
.co.uk/world/feedarticle/9819546.

46. Ernesto Londoño, "Dozens Dead in Rare Attacks on Shiite Targets in Afghanistan," *Washington Post,* December 6, 2011, accessed December 10,
2011, http://www.washingtonpost.com/world/rare-attack-in-kabul-targets
-shiite-mosque/2011/12/06/gIQAVnEkYO_story.html.

47. Julian Borger, "Prepare for Attack, Cheney Tells US," *Guardian*, May 19,
2002, accessed December 3, 2011, http://www.guardian.co.uk/world/2002
/may/20/usa.dickcheney.

48. "2001 'Worst Year for Terrorism'" *BBC*, May 21, 2002, accessed December 3, 2011, http://news.bbc.co.uk/2/hi/americas/1999514.stm.

49. Philip Shenon, "Security Chief Says Nation Must Expect Suicide Attacks,"
New York Times, March 14, 2003, accessed December 3, 2011, http://
www.nytimes.com/2003/03/14/national/14RIDG.html.

50. See Chapter 6.

51. Lymari Morales, "One in Three Americans 'Extremely Patriotic,'" *Gallup,* July 2, 2010, accessed December 3, 2011, http://www.gallup.com
/poll/141110/one-three-americans-extremely-patriotic.aspx; Wike, "Little
Support for Terrorism Among Muslim Americans."

52. Wike, "Little Support for Terrorism among Muslim Americans"; This
figure is calculated by multiplying the percentage of Pew Research

Center–surveyed Muslims who stated that suicide terrorism attacks are "often" or "sometimes" justified by the total Muslim population in the country. Naturally, there may be some *non-Muslims* who believe that suicide terrorism attacks are "often" or "sometimes" justified as well, but unfortunately, no data exist to quantify this segment of the population.

53. This calculation assumes that the mental health of Americans who state that suicide terrorism attacks are "often" or "sometimes" justified is, on average, no better or worse than the mental health of other Americans. Of course, that assumption could be wrong.

54. Hoffman, "The Logic of Suicide Terrorism"; Pedahzur, *Suicide Terrorism.*

55. Baer, *Cult of Suicide Bombing 2*; Cullen, *Columbine.*

56. Walid Phares, *Future Jihad: Terrorist Strategies against the West* (New York: Palgrave Macmillan, 2005).

57. Dave Grossman, *On Killing: The Psychological Cost of Learning to Kill in War and Society* (Boston: Little, Brown and Company, 1995).

58. Tom Gorman, "6 Wounded in Shootout at Riverside City Hall," *Los Angeles Times,* October 7, 1998, accessed November 12, 2011, http://articles .latimes.com/1998/oct/07/news/mn-30170; Joseph I. Lieberman and Susan M. Collins, *A Ticking Time Bomb: Counterterrorism Lessons from the U.S. Government's Failure to Prevent the Fort Hood Attack* (Washington, DC: U.S. Senate Committee on Homeland Security and Government Affairs, 2011).

59. Scott Eliason, "Murder-Suicide: A Review of the Recent Literature," *Journal of the American Academy of Psychiatry and Law* 37 (2009): 371–76.

60. "Support for Suicide Bombing"; Wike, "Little Support for Terrorism among Muslim Americans."

61. U.S. Homeland Security Director Janet Napolitano has been working with the European Union and other international bodies to prevent these potential attackers' access to America, but much more needs to be done. See Associated Press, "Napolitano: Lone Wolf Terror Threat Growing," *CBS News,* December 2, 2011, accessed December 13, 2011, http:// www.cbsnews.com/8301-201_162-57336080/napolitano-lone-wolf-terror -threat-growing/.

62. "Suicide," *Centers for Disease Control and Prevention,* 2010, accessed December 3, 2011, http://www.cdc.gov/violenceprevention/pdf/Suicide_Data Sheet-a.pdf.

63. Phares, *Future Jihad.*

64. American Foundation for Suicide Prevention, "Risk Factors for Suicide"; Durkheim, *Le Suicide*; Eliason, "Murder-Suicide"; Farber, *Theory of Suicide*; Maris, Berman, and Silverman, *Comprehensive Textbook of Suicidology.*

65. David Kaczynski, "Missing Parts," in *Brothers: 26 Stories of Love and Rivalry,* eds. Andrew Blauner and Frank McCourt, 15–30 (New York: Wiley, 2010), 15.

66. Ibid., 17.

67. Ibid.

68. Vincent Gragnani, "Unabomber's Brother Addresses Staten Island Audience," *Staten Island Live,* May 13, 2011, accessed December 12, 2011, http://www.silive.com/news/index.ssf/2011/05/unabombers_brother _addresses_s.html.

69. Ibid.

70. Ibid.
71. Leonard Greene, "Sex Torment Drove Him Nuts," *New York Post*, December 31, 2009, accessed December 13, 2011, http://www.nypost.com/p/news/national/sex_torment_jiHq0SZCZ0zevbRKdpjEKM.
72. Xan Rice, "Bombing Suspect Was Pious Pupil Who Shunned High Life of the Rich," *Guardian*, December 31, 2009, accessed December 13, 2011, http://www.guardian.co.uk/world/2009/dec/31/bombing-suspect-abdul mutallab-nigeria-home.
73. Andrew Gregory, "Syringe Bomber Umar Abdulmutallab Chilling Text Messages to Dad," *Daily Mirror*, January 1, 2010, accessed December 13, 2011, http://www.mirror.co.uk/news/top-stories/2010/01/01/forget-me-i-m -never-coming-back-115875-21934727/.
74. Ibid.
75. Ibid.
76. Ibid.
77. Additional evidence comes from the case of Anders Behring Breivik, whose sister warned his mother about him two years before his attack. If she had known to contact the authorities instead, his attack might have been prevented. See Richard Orange, "Anders Behring Breivik's Sister Warned Mother about His Behaviour Two Years Ago," *Telegraph*, December 4, 2011, accessed December 13, 2011, http://www.telegraph.co.uk/news /worldnews/europe/norway/8934136/Anders-Behring-Breiviks-sister -warned-mother-about-his-behaviour-two-years-ago.html.
78. For instance, as the mother of suicide terrorist Hanadi Jaradat explained after her daughter's attack, if she had known what Hanadi was about to do, "I would not have let her go. I would have tied her up. I would have locked her in her room, and stayed with her for an entire year." "Al-Jazeera Special on Female Suicide Bomber Hanadi Jaradat," *MEMRI*, August 22, 2005, accessed May 31, 2012, http://www.memri.org/report/en/0/0/0/0/0/0/1449 .htm.
79. Lankford, "Could Suicide Terrorists Actually Be Suicidal?"
80. "If You See Something, Say Something," *Department of Homeland Security*, 2011, accessed December 13, 2011, http://www.dhs.gov/files/reportin-cidents/see-something-say-something.shtm.
81. Maria Glod, "Arlington Man Charged with Terror Threat," *Washington Post*, December 15, 2010, accessed December 11, 2011, http://www .washingtonpost.com/wp-dyn/content/article/2010/12/14/AR201012140 7020.html.
82. It is not only suicide terrorists who have posted their plans online, but also a series of rampage, workplace, and school shooters who were also suicidal.
83. Guadagno et al., "Social Influence in the Online Recruitment of Terrorists and Terrorist Sympathizers."
84. Arthur C. Clarke, *Profiles of the Future: An Inquiry into the Limits of the Possible* (New York: Harper & Row, 1973).
85. Matthew K. Nock, Jennifer M. Park, Christine T. Finn, Tara L. Deliberto, Halina J. Dour, and Mahzarin R. Banaji, "Measuring the Suicidal Mind: Implicit Cognition Predicts Suicidal Behavior," *Psychological Science* 21 (2010): 511–17.
86. Ibid.
87. Ibid.

88. "Background," *Project Implicit,* 1999, accessed December 12, 2011, https://implicit.harvard.edu/implicit/demo/background/index.jsp.

89. As mentioned in Chapter 1, portions of this book were previously published as parts of the following articles, although the ideas have been heavily edited for inclusion, and in most cases, extended: Lankford, "A Psychological Autopsy of 9/11 Ringleader Mohamed Atta"; Lankford, "A Suicide-Based Typology of Suicide Terrorists"; Lankford, "Could Suicide Terrorists Actually Be Suicidal?"; Lankford, "Do Suicide Terrorists Exhibit Clinically Suicidal Risk Factors?"; Lankford, "Human Time Bombs"; Lankford, "On Sacrificial Heroism"; Lankford, "Requirements and Facilitators for Suicide Terrorism"; Lankford, "Suicide Terrorism as a Socially Approved Form of Suicide"; Lankford and Hakim, "From Columbine to Palestine."

90. Baer, *The Cult of the Suicide Bomber 2; Charny, Fighting Suicide Bombing;* Kruglanksi et al., "Fully Committed"; Pedahzur, *Suicide Terrorism.*

91. Breivik, *2083,* 1346–48; Times Online, "What Nidal Hasan Said About Suicide Bombers."

92. Post et al., "The Psychology of Suicide Terrorism," 15.

93. Hoffman, *Inside Terrorism.*

94. Harold Bloom, *Leo Tolstoy* (New York: Chelsea House Publishing, 1986); "People with Mental Illnesses Enrich Our Lives," *National Alliance on Mental Illness,* 2011, accessed December 13, 2011, http://www.nami.org/Template.cfm?Section=Helpline1&template=/ContentManagement/ContentDisplay.cfm&ContentID=4858; Natalie M. Rosinsky, *Sir Isaac Newton: Brilliant Mathematician and Scientist* (Minneapolis, MN: Compass Point Books, 2008); Maynard Solomon, *Beethoven Essays* (Cambridge, MA: Harvard University Press, 1990); Alix Strauss, *Death Becomes Them: Unearthing the Suicides of the Brilliant, the Famous, and the Notorious* (New York: HarperCollins, 2009).

95. Marianne Garvey, "George Clooney Shocker: 'I Contemplated Suicide,'" *E! Online,* November 11, 2011, accessed December 13, 2011, http://www.eonline.com/news/george_clooney_shocker_i_contemplated/274631; Chris Rojek, *Frank Sinatra* (Cambridge: Polity Press, 2004); "Sammy Davis Jr.'s Wedding Night Suicide Attempt," *Contact Music,* June 10, 2003, accessed December 13, 2011, http://www.contactmusic.com/news-article/sammy-davis-jr.s-wedding-night-suicide-attempt; Strauss, *Death Becomes Them.*

APPENDIX A

1. "Afghan Officer Kills Nine At Base," *MSN News,* April 28, 2011, accessed June 11, 2011, http://news.uk.msn.com/world/articles.aspx?cp-documentid=157196750; Rogelio Alonso and Fernando Reinares, "Maghreb Immigrants Becoming Suicide Terrorists: A Case Study on Religious Radicalization Processes in Spain," in *Root Causes of Suicide Terrorism: The Globalization of Martyrdom,* ed. Ami Pedahzur, 179–98 (New York: Routledge, 2006); Baer, *The Cult of The Suicide Bomber 2;* Berko, *The Path to Paradise;* Anat Berko and Edna Erez, "'Ordinary People' and 'Death Work': Palestinian Suicide Bombers as Victimizers and Victims," *Violence and Victims* 20 (2005): 603–23; Anat Berko and Edna Erez, "Martyrs or Murderers? Victims or Victimizers? The Voices of Would-Be

Palestinian Female Suicide Bombers," in *Female Terrorism and Militancy: Agency, Utility and Organization*, ed. Cindy D. Ness, 146–66 (London: Routledge, 2008); Eli Berman and David Laitin, "Hard Targets: Evidence on the Tactical Use of Suicide Attacks," *National Bureau of Economic Research Working Papers*, 2005, accessed July 26, 2011, http://www.nber .org/papers/w11740; "Blackmailing Young Women into Suicide Terrorism"; Bloom, *Bombshell*; Bloom, *Dying to Kill*; Brym and Araj, "Are Suicide Bombers Suicidal?"; Dave Cullen, *Columbine* (New York: Twelve, 2009); Fair, *Suicide Attacks in Afghanistan*; Christine Fair and Frederic Grare, "Suicide Attacks in Afghanistan," *Carnegie Endowment for International Peace*, October 19, 2007, accessed July 27, 2011, http://www.carnegie endowment.org/events/?fa=eventDetail&id=1067; Sonya Fatah, "Why the Disabled Do Taliban's Deadly Work: With So Few Rehabilitation Services Available, Suicide Attacks Can Offer Easy Escape," *Globe and Mail*, May 7, 2001, accessed September 27, 2010, http://www.theglobeandmail.com /servlet/story/LAC.20070507.SUICIDE07/TPStory/Front; Leonard Greene, "Sex Torment Drove Him Nuts," *New York Post*, December 31, 2009, accessed October 25, 2011, http://www.nypost.com/p/news/national/sex _torment_jiHq0SZCZ0zevbRKdpjEKM; Helle Lho Hansen and Andreas Karker, "Lors' Mor: Han Ville Dø I København," *B.T.*, September 28, 2010, accessed June 16, 2011, http://www.bt.dk/krimi/lors-mor-han-ville -doe-i-koebenhavn; "'I'm Off to Kill Someone': Knifeman Planned to Kill Train Passenger to Commit 'Suicide by Cop,'" *Daily Mail*, March 1, 2011, accessed July 1, 2011, http://www.dailymail.co.uk/news/article-1361836 /Im-kill-Knifeman-planned-kill-train-passenger-commit-suicide-cop.html; "Iraq's 'Female Bomber Recruiter,'" *BBC News*, February 4, 2009, accessed July 27, 2011, http://news.bbc.co.uk/2/hi/7869570.stm; "Jurors Sequestered In CIA Shooting Case," *CNN*, November 12, 1997, accessed July 27, 2011, http://cgi.cnn.com/US/9711/12/cia.shooting.trial/index. html; Lankford, "Do Suicide Terrorists Exhibit Clinically Suicidal Risk Factors?"; David Leppard and Abul Taher, "MI5 Fears Jihadis Will Use Mentally Ill as Suicide Bombers," *Times Online*, May 25, 2008, accessed June 4, 2011, http://www.timesonline.co.uk/tol/news/uk/article3999058. ece; Lester et al., "Suicide Bombers"; McElroy, "Baghdad Market Bombers 'Mentally Impaired'"; Merari, *Driven to Death*; "Militant Held Over Iraq Suicide Bombings," *CNN*, February 20, 2010, accessed July 27, 2011, http://www.cnn.com/2010/WORLD/meast/02/20/iraq.bomber.arrest/in-dex.html; Soraya Nelson, "Disabled Often Carry Out Afghan Suicide Missions," *National Public Radio*, October 15, 2007, accessed July 27, 2011, http://www.npr.org/templates/story/story.php?storyId=15276485;   Larry Neumeister and Tom Hays, "2 NY Collaborators Give Firsthand Look at Al-Qaida," *Yahoo News*, May 6, 2012, accessed May 7, 2012, http://news .yahoo.com/2-ny-cooperators-firsthand-look-al-qaida-211626418.html; Pape, *Dying to Win*; Pedahzur, *Suicide Terrorism*; "Police: Tampa Flyer Voiced Support For Bin Laden," *CNN*, January 6, 2002, accessed July 27, 2011, http://articles.cnn.com/2002-01-06/us/tampa.crash_1_plane-charles -j-bishop-crash?_s=PM:US; "Qian Mingqi Blew Himself Up to Demand Justice and Call Attention to His Plight," *Asia News*, May 28, 2011, accessed December 27, 2011, http://www.asianews.it/news-en/Qian-Mingqi -blew-himself-up-to-demand-justice-and-call-attention-to-his-plight -21688.html; Ravi Somaiya, "Swedish Bombing Suspect's Drift to

Extremism," *New York Times,* December 13, 2010, accessed July 27, 2011, http://www.nytimes.com/2010/12/14/world/europe/14suspect.html?hp=&; Anne Speckhard and Khapta Ahkmedova, "The Making of a Martyr: Chechen Suicide Terrorism," *Studies in Conflict and Terrorism* 29 (2006): 429–92; Kevin Toolis, "Face to Face with the Women Suicide Bombers," *Daily Mail,* February 7, 2009, accessed February 8, 2009, http://www.daily mail.co.uk/femail/article-1138298/Face-face-women-suicide-bombers .html; Nick Walsh, "Man Opens Fire on Americans in Kabul; 9 Dead," *CNN,* April 28, 2011, accessed June 11, 2011, http://www.cnn.com/2011 /WORLD/asiapcf/04/27/afghanistan.violence/index.html; Carrie Weimar, "Teen Pilot's Family Drops Drug Lawsuit: The 15-Year-Old Killed Himself By Crashing A Plane Into A High-Rise," *St. Petersburg Times,* June 28, 2007, accessed July 18, 2011, http://www.sptimes.com/2007/06/28/news _pf/Hillsborough/Teen_pilot_s_family_d.shtml; Michael Wilson, "From Smiling Coffee Vendor to Terror Suspect," *New York Times,* September 25, 2009, accessed May 26, 2012, http://www.nytimes.com/2009/09/26 /nyregion/26profile.htm. Additional evidence for this table is discussed in more depth throughout the text and cited accordingly.

APPENDIX C

1. Lankford, "A Suicide-Based Typology of Suicide Terrorists."

BIBLIOGRAPHY

"2001 'Worst Year for Terrorism.'" *BBC,* May 21, 2002. Accessed December 3, 2011, http://news.bbc.co.uk/2/hi/americas/1999514.stm.

"200403110007." *National Consortium for the Study of Terrorism and Responses to Terrorism,* 2010. Accessed July 24, 2011, http://www.start.umd.edu/gtd/.

"A Dossier of Civilian Casualties 2003-2005." *Iraq Body Count,* July 19, 2005. Accessed December 13, 2011, http://reports.iraqbodycount.org/a_dossier_of_civilian_casualties_2003-2005.pdf.

Abrahms, Max. "The Political Effectiveness of Terrorism Revisited." *Comparative Political Studies* 45 (2012): 366–93.

Abrahms, Max. "Why Terrorism Does Not Work." *International Security* 31 (2006): 42–78.

Abu Kamal, Ali Hassan. "Charter of Honour." *Investigative Project on Terrorism,* February 23, 1997. Accessed June 13, 2011, http://www.investigativeproject.org/case/334.

Abu Ruqaiyah, B. "The Islamic Legitimacy of the 'Martyrdom Operations.'" *The International Institute for Counterterrorism,* 1997. Accessed September 27, 2009, http://www.ict.org.il/Articles/tabid/66/Articlsid/726/currentpage/33/Default.aspx.

Achenbach, Joel. "You Never Imagine a Hijacker Next Door." *Washington Post,* September 16, 2001. Accessed May 4, 2011. http://www.washingtonpost.com/ac2/wp-dyn?pagename=article&node=&contentId=A38026-2001Sep15

Adams, Russell, Martin Giffen, and Frances Garfield. "Risk Taking Among Suicide Attempters." *Journal of Abnormal Psychology* 82 (1973): 262–67.

Adkisson, Jim. "To Whom It May Concern." *Knoxville News Sentinel,* February 10, 2009. Accessed March 14, 2011, http://web.knoxnews.com/pdf/021009church-manifesto.pdf.

"Admission Against Interest Law and Legal Definition." *U.S. Legal,* 2011. Accessed December 17, 2011, http://definitions.uslegal.com/a/admission-against-interest/.

"Afghan Officer Kills Nine at Base." *MSN News,* April 28, 2011. Accessed June 11, 2011, http://news.uk.msn.com/world/articles.aspx?cp-documentid=157196750.

"Al-Jazeera Special on Female Suicide Bomber Hanadi Jaradat." *MEMRI,* August 22, 2005. Accessed May 31, 2012, http://www.memri.org/report/en/0/0/0/0/0/0/1449.htm.

Al-San'ani, Abu M. "An Al Qaeda Released Video of Attacks in Afghanistan." *MEMRI,* May 4, 2006. Accessed December 9, 2010, http://www.memritv .org/clip/en/1131.htm.

Al-Qaisi, Mohammed. "Iraq Accuses Al-Qaeda of Using Mentally Ill Man to Kill 33 Civilians in Samarra." *Al-Shofra,* February 14, 2011. Accessed November 12, 2011, http://al-shorfa.com/cocoon/meii/xhtml/en_GB/features/meii /features/main/2011/02/14/feature-02.

Al-Zahar, Mahmoud. "Palestinian Foreign Minister Mahmoud Al-Zahar Defends 'Martyrdom-Seeking Operations.'" *MEMRI,* April 6, 2006. Accessed January 9, 2010, http://www.memritv.org/Transcript.asp?P1=1107.

Alexander, Matthew, and John Bruning. *How to Break a Terrorist: The U.S. Interrogators Who Used Brains, Not Brutality, to Take Down the Deadliest Man in Iraq.* New York: Free Press, 2008.

Allen, Peter. "'He Should Have Shot Himself': Father of Anders Breivik Says He Wishes His Son Had Committed Suicide." *Daily Mail,* July 26, 2011. Accessed November 24, 2011, http://www.dailymail.co.uk/news/article -2018604/Norway-massacre-Anders-Behring-Breivik-shot-says-father .html#ixzz1efbpwoQG.

Alonso, Rogelio, and Fernando Reinares. "Maghreb Immigrants Becoming Suicide Terrorists: A Case Study on Religious Radicalization Processes in Spain." In *Root Causes of Suicide Terrorism: The Globalization of Martyrdom,* ed. Ami Pedahzur, 179–98. New York: Routledge, 2006.

American Foundation for Suicide Prevention. "Risk Factors for Suicide." 2010. Accessed May 4, 2011, http://www.afsp.org/index.cfm?page_id=0514 7440-E24E-E376-BDF4BF8BA6444E76.

American Heritage Dictionary. "Sacrifice." *Houghton Mifflin Company,* 2004. Accessed November 15, 2009, http://dictionary.reference.com/browse /sacrifice.

Ames, Mark. *Going Postal: From Reagan's Workplaces to Clinton's Columbine and Beyond.* Brooklyn, NY: Soft Skull, 2005.

Arballo, Jose. "City Hall Shooter Recalled as 'Very Intelligent Man.'" *The Press-Enterprise,* October 5, 2008. Accessed February 22, 2011, http://www .pe.com/reports/2008/cityhall/stories/PE_News_Local_S_neale05.2eb926 .htm.

Ashworth, Scott, Joshua D. Clinton, Adam Meirowitz, and Kristopher W. Ramsay. "Design, Inference, and the Strategic Logic of Suicide Terrorism." *American Political Science Review* 102 (2008): 270–73.

Associated Press. "Chechen Terror Leader Shamil Basayev Killed in Russia." *Fox News,* July 10, 2006. Accessed July 26, 2011, http://www.foxnews .com/story/0,2933,202753,00.html.

Associated Press. "Donkey Bomb Kills Three Children in Afghanistan." *Herald Sun,* April 19, 2010. Accessed June 4, 2011, http://www.heraldsun .com.au/news/world/donkey-Bomb-Kills-three-children-in-afghanistan /story-e6frf7lf-1225855722687.

Associated Press. "Musharraf: Pakistan Isn't Hunting Bin Laden." *MSNBC,* January 22, 2008. Accessed November 23, 2011, http://www.msnbc.msn .com/id/22791422/.

Associated Press. "Napolitano: Lone Wolf Terror Threat Growing." *CBS News,* December 2, 2011. Accessed December 13, 2011, http://www.cbs news.com/8301-201_162-57336080/napolitano-lone-wolf-terror-threat -growing/.

Associated Press. "Truck Bomber Turns Against Jihad in Iraq." *MSNBC*, July 29, 2007. Accessed December 17, 2011, http://www.msnbc.msn.com/id/2001 8405/ns/world_news-mideast_n_africa/t/truck-bomber-turns-against -jihad-iraq/.

Atran, Scott. "Genesis of Suicide Terrorism." *Science* 299 (2003): 1534–39.

Atta, Mohamed. "Mohamed Atta's Last Will & Testament." *PBS*, April 11, 1996. Accessed May 4, 2011. http://www.pbs.org/wgbh/pages/frontline /shows/network/personal/attawill.html.

"Australia: Alleged Terrorist Plot Foiled." *CNN*, August 3, 2009. Accessed July 26, 2011, http://articles.cnn.com/2009-08-03/world/australia.terror .raids_1_australian-federal-police-suspects-terrorist?_s=PM:WORLD.

"Background." *Project Implicit*, 1999. Accessed December 12, 2011, https:// implicit.harvard.edu/implicit/demo/background/index.jsp.

Bader, Michael J. *Arousal: The Secret Logic of Sexual Fantasies.* New York: St. Martin's Press, 2002.

Ballen, Ken. *Terrorists in Love: The Real Lives of Islamic Radicals.* New York: Simon & Schuster, 2011.

Baer, Robert. *The Cult of the Suicide Bomber.* [DVD]. London: Many Rivers Films, 2005.

Baer, Robert. *The Cult of the Suicide Bomber 2.* [DVD]. London: Many Rivers Films, 2008.

Bergen, Peter. *Manhunt: The Ten-Year Search for Bin Laden—from 9/11 to Abbottabad.* New York: Crown, 2012.

Berko, Anat. *The Path to Paradise: The Inner World of Suicide Bombers and Their Dispatchers.* London: Praeger, 2007.

Berko, Anat, and Edna Erez. "'Ordinary People' and 'Death Work': Palestinian Suicide Bombers as Victimizers and Victims." *Violence and Victims* 20 (2005): 603–23.

Berko, Anat, and Edna Erez. "Martyrs or Murderers? Victims or Victimizers? The Voices of Would-Be Palestinian Female Suicide Bombers." In *Female Terrorism and Militancy: Agency, Utility and Organization*, ed. Cindy D. Ness, 146–66. London: Routledge, 2008.

Berman, Eli, and David Laitin. "Hard Targets: Evidence on the Tactical Use of Suicide Attacks." *National Bureau of Economic Research Working Papers*, 2005. Accessed July 26, 2011, http://www.nber.org/papers/w11740.

"Bin Laden Killing Caps Decade-Long Manhunt." *CNN*, May 2, 2011. Accessed July 26, 2011, http://www.cnn.com/2011/WORLD/asiapcf/05/02 /bin.laden.dead/index.html.

Bin Laden, Osama. "Letter to the American People." *Guardian*, November 24, 2002. Accessed March 12, 2011, http://www.guardian.co.uk/world/2002 /nov/24/theobserver.

"Blackmailing Young Women into Suicide Terrorism." *Israeli Ministry of Foreign Affairs*, February 12, 2002. Accessed May 27, 2012, http://www.mfa .gov.il/MFA/Government/Communiques/2003/Blackmailing+Young +Women+into+Suicide+Terrorism+-.htm.

Bloom, Harold. *Leo Tolstoy.* New York: Chelsea House Publishing, 1986.

Bloom, Mia. *Bombshell: The Many Faces of Women Terrorists.* Toronto: Penguin, 2011.

Bloom, Mia. *Dying to Kill: The Allure of Suicide Terror.* New York: Columbia University Press, 2005.

"Bomber Nicky Reilly's Suicide Note." *This Is Exeter,* November 21, 2008. Accessed December 4, 2011, http://www.thisisexeter.co.uk/Bomber-Nicky -Reilly-s-suicide-note/story-11795579-detail/story.html.

Borger, Julian. "Prepare for Attack, Cheney Tells US." *Guardian,* May 19, 2002. Accessed December 3, 2011, http://www.guardian.co.uk/world/2002/may /20/usa.dickcheney.

Bradley, John P., Leo F. Daniels, and Thomas C. Jones. *The International Dictionary of Thoughts.* Chicago: J. G. Ferguson Publishing Company, 1969.

Breivik, Anders Behring. *2083: A European Declaration of Independence.* Unpublished: 2011.

Brenna, Jarle, Gordon Andersen, and Morten Hopperstad. "Breivik Er Overrasket Over At Han Lyktes." *VG Nett,* July 26, 2011. Accessed November 12, 2011, http://www.vg.no/nyheter/innenriks/oslobomben/artikkel .php?artid=10080811.

Browning, Christopher. *Ordinary Men: Reserve Police Battalion 101 and the Final Solution in Poland.* New York: HarperCollins Publishers, Inc., 1998.

Brym, Robert. "Six Lessons of Suicide Bombers." *Contexts* 6 (2007): 40–45.

Brym, Robert. *Sociology as a Life or Death Issue.* Belmont, CA: Wadsworth, 2009.

Brym, Robert, and Bader Araj. "Are Suicide Bombers Suicidal?" *Studies in Conflict & Terrorism* 35 (2012): 432–43.

Buncombe, Andrew. "Childhood Clues to What Makes a Killer." *Independent,* October 12, 2001. Accessed May 4, 2011, http://www.independent.co.uk /news/world/middle-east/childhood-clues-to-what-makes-a-Killer-748415 .html.

Burger, Jerry. "Replicating Milgram." *APS Observer,* December 2007. Accessed April 22, 2011, http://www.psychologicalscience.org/observer/getArticle .cfm?id=2264.

Byman, Daniel, and Christine Fair. "The Case for Calling Them Nitwits.'" *Atlantic,* July/August 2010. Accessed June 7, 2011, http://www.theatlantic .com/magazine/archive/2010/07/the-case-for-calling-them-nitwits/8130/.

Caplan, Bryan. "Terrorism: The Relevance of the Rational Choice Model." *Public Choice* 128 (2006): 91–107.

Carbone, Nick. "Bullying and Plastic Surgery: Childhood Friend Speaks Out on Anders Behring Breivik's Life." *Time,* July 26, 2011. Accessed November 24, 2011, http://newsfeed.time.com/2011/07/26/bullying-and-plastic -surgery-childhood-friend-speaks-out-on-anders-breiviks-life/#ixzz1efdZt JCy.

Carey, Benedict. "For Rampage Killers, Familiar Descriptions, 'Troubled' and 'Loner,' but No Profile." *New York Times,* April 18 2007. Accessed July 4, 2011, http://query.nytimes.com/gst/fullpage.html?res=9406E2DB1E3FF93 BA25757C0A9619C8B63.

Carr, Caleb. *The Lessons of Terror.* New York: Random House, 2002.

Cavanagh, Jonathan, A. J. Carson, M. Sharpe, and S. M. Lawrie. "Psychological Autopsy Studies of Suicide: A Systematic Review." *Psychological Medicine* 33 (2003): 395–405.

"CDC: One in 20 Americans Depressed." *CBS News,* February 11, 2009. Accessed May 28, 2011, http://www.cbsnews.com/stories/2008/09/04/health /webmd/main4414655.shtml.

Charny, Israel W. *Fighting Suicide Bombing: A Worldwide Campaign For Life.* Westport, CT: Praeger Security International, 2007.

"Chris Crocker." *TMZ*, 2011. Accessed July 3, 2011, http://www.tmz.com /person/chris-crocker/.

Clark, Victoria. "Charming and Chilling: Osama bin Laden's Bodyguard." *Times Online*, March 5, 2010. Accessed July 26, 2011, http://www.times online.co.uk/tol/news/world/middle_east/article7050537.ece.

Clarke, Arthur C. *Profiles of the Future: An Inquiry into the Limits of the Possible*. New York: Harper & Row, 1973.

Cloud, John. "Atta's Odyssey." *Time*, September 30, 2001. Accessed May 4, 2011. http://www.time.com/time/magazine/article/0,9171,1101011008-17 6917,00.html

Coker, Christopher. *The Warrior Ethos: Military Culture and the War on Terror.* London: Routledge, 2007.

"Colombian 'Donkey Bombs' Kill Drug Crop Eradicators." *Reuters*, September 11, 2009. Accessed June 6, 2011, http://www.reuters.com/article /2009/09/12/idUSN11469928.

"Columbine Killer Envisioned Crashing Plane in NYC." *CNN*, December 6, 2001. Accessed July 4, 2011, http://archives.cnn.com/2001/US/12/05 /columbine.diary/.

Crawford, Neta C., Catherine Lutz, and Andrea Mazzarino. "Costs of War." *Eisenhower Study Group*, June 2011. Accessed June 29, 2011, http://costs ofwar.org/.

Crean, Ellen. "He Took a Bullet for Reagan." *CBS News*, December 5, 2007. Accessed September 25, 2011, http://www.cbsnews.com/stories/2004/06/11 /earlyshow/main622527.shtml.

Crewdson, John. "From Kind Teacher to Murderous Zealot." *Chicago Tribune*, September 12, 2004. Accessed May 4, 2011, http://articles.chicago tribune.com/2004-09-12/news/0409120328_1_hijackers-world-trade -center-americans.

Crouse, Karen. "Bear Coach Smith Reflects on His Roots." *New York Times*, January 23, 2007. Accessed June 8, 2011, http://www.nytimes.com /2007/01/23/sports/football/23bears.html?ref=sports.

Crumley, Bruce. "Were the Mumbai Terrorists Fueled by Coke?" *Time*, December 3, 2008. Accessed July 26, 2011, http://www.time.com/time/world /article/0,8599,1864049,00.html.

Cullen, Dave. *Columbine*. New York: Twelve, 2009.

"Cult of Death." *Time*, December 4, 1978. Accessed July 14, 2011, http://www .time.com/time/covers/0,16641,19781204,00.html.

Dao, James. "Suspect Was 'Mortified' About Deployment." *New York Times*, November 5, 2009. Accessed July 5, 2011, http://www.nytimes .com/2009/11/06/us/06suspect.html.

Davies, Christie, and Mark Neal. "Durkheim's Altruistic and Fatalistic Suicide." In *Durkheim's Suicide: A Century of Research and Debate*, eds. William S. F. Pickering and Geoffrey Walford, 36–52. London: Routledge, 2000.

"Death Tape." *Federal Bureau of Investigation*, December 13, 1978. Accessed July 13, 2011, http://jonestown.sdsu.edu/AboutJonestown/Tapes/Tapes /DeathTape/Q042fbi.html.

Department of Defense. *Fort Hood Army Internal Review Team: Final Report,* 2010. Accessed June 3, 2011, http://usarmy.vo.llnwd.net/e1/rv5_down loads/misc/FtHoodAIRTwebversion.pdf.

DeYoung, Karen. "Secrecy Defines Obama's Drone War." *Washington Post,* December 19, 2011. Accessed December 20, 2011, http://www.washington

post.com/world/national-security/secrecy-defines-obamas-drone-war/2011
/10/28/gIQAPKNR5O_story.html.

Dickens, Charles. *A Tale of Two Cities*. Oxford: Oxford University Press, 1859.

Douglas, John. *Inside the Mind of BTK: The True Story Behind the Thirty-Year Hunt for the Notorious Wichita Serial Killer*. San Francisco: Jossey-Bass, 2007.

Duncan, Stanley. "Death in the Office: Workplace Homicides." *FBI Law Enforcement Bulletin*, 2005.

"Dungy's Son, 18, Found Dead in Tampa Suburb." *ESPN*, December 23, 2005. Accessed June 2, 2011, http://sports.espn.go.com/nfl/news/story?id=2268593.

"Duress." *West's Encyclopedia of American Law, Edition 2, 2008*. Accessed July 17, 2011, http://legal-dictionary.thefreedictionary.com/duress.

Durkheim, Emile. *Le Suicide: Étude de Sociologie*. Paris: Alcan, 1897.

Eliason, Scott. "Murder-Suicide: A Review of the Recent Literature." *Journal of the American Academy of Psychiatry and Law* 37 (2009): 371–76.

Ellis, Elsi Vassdal. "Letters to Mohamed Atta," March 11, 2002. Accessed June 8, 2011, http://faculty.wwu.edu/vassdae/book_arts/atta/letter_open.html.

Esptein, Reid J. "Norway Shooter: Ammo Clips Were From U.S." *Politico*, July 28, 2011. Accessed November 25, 2011, http://www.politico.com/news/stories/0711/60154.html.

Evans, Glen, and Norman L. Farberow. *The Encyclopedia of Suicide*. New York: Facts on File, 1988.

Evans, Michael. "Donkey 'Suicide' Bombing Is Latest Tactic Against Patrols." *Sunday Times*, April 30, 2009. Accessed June 4, 2011, http://www.times online.co.uk/tol/news/uk/article6194874.ece.

Fair, Christine. *Suicide Attacks in Afghanistan: 2001-2007*. United Nations Assistance Mission in Afghanistan, 2007.

Fair, Christine, and Frederic Grare. "Suicide Attacks in Afghanistan." *Carnegie Endowment for International Peace*, October 19, 2007. Accessed July 27, 2011, http://www.carnegieendowment.org/events/?fa=eventDetail&id=1067.

Farabaugh, Kane. "Victims Recall Reagan Assassination Attempt 30 Years Later." *Voice of America News*, March 30, 2011. Accessed October 1, 2011, http://www.voanews.com/english/news/usa/Victims-Recall-Reagan-Assassination-Attempt-30-Years-Later-118953314.html.

Farber, Maurice L. *Theory of Suicide*. New York: Funk and Wagnalls, 1968.

Farberow, Norman L. *The Many Faces of Suicide*. New York: McGraw-Hill, 1980.

Farrell, Stephen. "Murky Trail for 'Loner' in Attack on C.I.A." *New York Times*, January 7, 2010. Accessed May 26, 2012, http://www.nytimes.com/2010/01/08/world/middleeast/08jordan.html.

Fatah, Sonya. "Why the Disabled Do Taliban's Deadly Work: With So Few Rehabilitation Services Available, Suicide Attacks Can Offer Easy Escape." *Globe and Mail*, May 7, 2007. Accessed November 19, 2010, http://www.theglobeandmail.com/servlet/story/LAC.20070507.SUICIDE07/TPStory/Front.

Fein, Robert, and Bryan Vossekuil. "Assassination in the United States: An Operational Study of Recent Assassins, Attackers, and Near-Lethal Approachers." *Journal of Forensic Sciences* 44 (1999): 321–33.

Feldman, Charles. "Federal Investigators: L.A. Airport Shooting a Terrorist Act." *CNN*, September 5, 2002. Accessed March 11, 2011, http://archives.cnn.com/2002/US/09/04/lax.Shooting/index.html.

Finn, Peter. "WikiLeaks Discloses New Details on Whereabouts of Al-Qaeda Leaders on 9/11." *Washington Post,* April 24, 2011. Accessed July 26, 2011, http://www.washingtonpost.com/world/wikileaks-discloses-new-details-on -whereabouts-of-al-qaeda-leaders-on-911/2011/04/24/AFvvzIeE_story.html.

Finn, Peter, and Joby Warrick. "In Afghanistan Attack, CIA Fell Victim to Series of Miscalculations About Informant." *Washington Post,* January 16, 2010. Accessed May 25, 2012, http://www.washingtonpost.com/wp-dyn/content /article/2010/01/15/AR2010011504068_pf.html.

"Former Osama bin Laden Bodyguard in Al-Arabiya TV Interview: I Love Him More Than I Love My Own Father." *MEMRI,* June 6, 2007. Accessed July 26, 2011, http://www.memri.org/report/en/0/0/0/0/0/0/2644.htm.

"Former Student Dead After Storming German School." *CTV News,* November 20, 2006. Accessed July 4, 2011, http://www.ctv.ca/CTVNews /CanadaAM/20061120/german_Shooting_061120/.

"Fort Hood Gunman Had Nearly 200 Rounds of Ammo." *USA Today,* October 20, 2010. Accessed July 5, 2011, http://www.usatoday.com/news /nation/2010-10-20-fort-hood-trial_N.htm.

Fox, James A., and Jack Levin. "Firing Back: The Growing Threat of Workplace Homicide." *Annals of the American Academy of Political and Social Science* 536 (1994): 16–30.

Gambetta, Diego. *Making Sense of Suicide Missions.* Oxford: Oxford University Press, 2005.

Gardham, Duncan, and Richard Savill. "Exeter Terror Bomber Nicky Reilly Was Known as 'Big Friendly Giant.'" *Telegraph,* October 15, 2008. Accessed June 20, 2011, http://www.telegraph.co.uk/news/uknews/3201863/Exeter -terror-Bomber-Nicky-Reilly-was-known-as-Big-Friendly-Giant.html.

Garvey, Marianne. "George Clooney Shocker: 'I Contemplated Suicide.'" *E! Online,* November 11, 2011. Accessed December 13, 2011, http://www .eonline.com/news/george_clooney_shocker_i_contemplated/274631.

"General Plays Down Value of Capturing Bin Laden." *Washington Post,* February 24, 2007. Accessed November 23, 2011, http://www.washingtonpost .com/wp-dyn/content/article/2007/02/23/AR2007022301799.html.

Gibbs, Nancy. "The Fort Hood Killer: Terrified . . . or Terrorist?" *Time,* November 11, 2009. Accessed July 5, 2011, http://www.time.com/time/magazine /article/0,9171,1938698,00.html.

Gibbs, Nancy, and Timothy Roche. "The Columbine Tapes." *Time,* December 20, 1999. Accessed July 4, 2011, http://www.time.com/time/magazine /article/0,9171,992873,00.html.

Gjelten, Tom. "Mumbai Attacks Suggest Terrorists Are Evolving." *National Public Radio,* December 2, 2008. Accessed July 26, 2011, http://www.npr .org/templates/story/story.php?storyId=97682012.

Gladwell, Malcolm. "Dangerous Minds: Criminal Profiling Made Easy." *New Yorker,* November 12, 2006. Accessed August 2, 2011, http://www.new yorker.com/reporting/2007/11/12/071112fa_fact_gladwell.

"Global Terrorism Database." National Consortium for the Study of Terrorism and Responses to Terrorism, 2010. Accessed February 24, 2011, http:// www.start.umd.edu/gtd/.

Glod, Maria. "Arlington Man Charged with Terror Threat." *Washington Post,* December 15, 2010. Accessed December 11, 2011, http://www.washington post.com/wp-dyn/content/article/2010/12/14/AR2010121407020.html.

Goeschel, Christian. *Suicide in Nazi Germany.* Oxford: Oxford University Press, 2009.

Gorman, Tom. "6 Wounded in Shootout at Riverside City Hall." *Los Angeles Times,* October 7, 1998. Accessed November 12, 2011, http://articles.la times.com/1998/oct/07/news/mn-30170.

Gragnani, Vincent. "Unabomber's Brother Addresses Staten Island Audience." *Staten Island Live,* May 13, 2011. Accessed December 12, 2011, http:// www.silive.com/news/index.ssf/2011/05/unabombers_brother_addresses_s .html.

Grant, Stan. "Kidnapped Boys 'Brainwashed' to Die as Suicide Bombers." *CNN,* August 4, 2009. Accessed July 26, 2011, http://edition.cnn.com/2009 /WORLD/asiapcf/08/03/pakistan.boys/index.html.

Graysmith, Robert. *Unabomber: A Desire to Kill.* Washington, DC: Regnery, 1997.

Greene, Leonard. "Sex Torment Drove Him Nuts." *New York Post,* December 31, 2009. Accessed December 13, 2011, http://www.nypost.com/p/news /national/sex_torment_jiHq0SZCZ0zevbRKdpjEKM.

Gregory, Andrew. "Syringe Bomber Umar Abdulmutallab Chilling Text Messages to Dad." *Daily Mirror,* January 1, 2010. Accessed December 13, 2011, http://www.mirror.co.uk/news/top-stories/2010/01/01/forget-me-i-m -never-coming-back-115875-21934727/.

Grossman, Dave. *On Killing: The Psychological Cost of Learning to Kill in War and Society.* Boston: Little, Brown and Company, 1995.

Grove, Casey. "Ex-Soldier Sentenced for Role in Russian Roulette Case." *Chicago Tribune,* May 3, 2012. Accessed May 29, 2012, http://www .chicagotribune.com/news/sns-mct-ex-soldier-sentenced-for-role-in-russian -roulette-20120503,0,2317617.story.

Guadagno, Rosanna, Adam Lankford, Nicole Muscanell, Bradley Okdie, and Debra McCallum. "Social Influence in the Online Recruitment of Terrorists and Terrorist Sympathizers: Implications for Social Psychology Research." *International Review of Social Psychology* 23 (2010): 25–55.

"Gunman in Health Club Shooting a 48-year-old Loner." *CTV News,* August 5, 2009. Accessed July 5, 2011, http://www.ctv.ca/CTVNews /World/20090805/health_club_090805/.

Hafez, Mohammed M. *Manufacturing Human Bombs: The Making of Palestinian Suicide Bombers.* Washington, DC: U.S. Institute of Peace, 2006.

Hansen, Helle Lho, and Andreas Karker. "Lors' Mor: Han Ville Dø I København." *B.T.,* September 28, 2010. Accessed June 16, 2011, http://www .bt.dk/krimi/lors-mor-han-ville-doe-i-koebenhavn.

Harding, Thomas. "Royal Marine Who Jumped on Grenade Awarded George Cross." *Telegraph,* July 22, 2008. Accessed September 25, 2011, http:// www.telegraph.co.uk/news/uknews/2445513/Royal-Marine-who-jumped -on-grenade-awarded-George-Cross.html.

Hassan, Riaz. "What Motivates the Suicide Bombers." *Yale Global,* September 3, 2009. Accessed May 28, 2011, http://yaleglobal.yale.edu/content /what-motivates-Suicide-Bombers-0.

Hays, Tom. "N.Y. Killer Carried Political Note." *Associated Press,* February 25, 1997.

"Head of Psychiatry at Cairo's 'Ein Shams University, Prof. Adel Sadeq, on the Psychological Make-up of a Suicide Bomber." *MEMRI,* April 25 2002. Accessed March 9, 2011, http://www.memritv.org/clip_transcript/en/927.htm.

Hegghammer, Thomas, and Dominic Tierney. "Why Does Al-Qaeda Have a Problem with Norway?" *Atlantic,* July 13, 2010. Accessed November 25,

2011, http://www.theatlantic.com/international/archive/2010/07/why-does
-al-qaeda-have-a-problem-with-norway/59649/.

"History." *Congressional Medal of Honor Society,* 2011. Accessed August 12,
2011, http://www.cmohs.org/medal-history.php.

Hoffman, Bruce. *Inside Terrorism.* New York: Columbia University Press, 2006.

Hoffman, Bruce. "The Logic of Suicide Terrorism." *Atlantic,* July 2003. Accessed
November 12, 2011, http://www.theatlantic.com/magazine/archive/2003/06
/the-logic-of-suicide-terrorism/2739/.

Holmes, David S. "Projection as a Defense Mechanism." *Psychological Bulletin*
85 (1978): 677–88.

Holmes, Stephen. "Al Qaeda, September 11, 2001." In *Making Sense of Suicide Missions,* ed. Diego Gambetta, 131–72. Oxford: Oxford University Press, 2005.

"How Many People Died as a Result of the Atomic Bombings?" *Radiation Effects Research Foundation,* 2007. Accessed October 6, 2011, http://www
.rerf.or.jp/general/qa_e/qa1.html.

Hsiao-Rei Hicks, Madelyn, Hamit Dardagan, Peter M. Bagnall, Michael Spagat,
John A. Sloboda. "Casualties in Civilians and Coalition Soldiers from Suicide
Bombings in Iraq, 2003-10: A Descriptive Study." *Lancet* 378 (2011): 906–14.

Hutchinson, Jeffrey, Jeffery Green, and Shana Hansen. "Evaluating Active Duty
Risk-Taking: Military Home, Education, Activity, Drugs, Sex, Suicide, and
Safety Method." *Military Medicine* 173 (2008): 1164–67.

"'I'm Off to Kill Someone': Knifeman Planned to Kill Train Passenger to
Commit 'Suicide by Cop.'" *Daily Mail,* March 1, 2011. Accessed July 1,
2011, http://www.dailymail.co.uk/news/article-1361836/Im-kill-Knifeman
-planned-kill-train-passenger-commit-suicide-cop.html.

"If You See Something, Say Something." *Department of Homeland Security,*
2011. Accessed December 13, 2011, http://www.dhs.gov/files/report
incidents/see-something-say-something.shtm.

Ilardi, Stephen S. *The Depression Cure: The 6-Step Program to Beat Depression
without Drugs.* Cambridge, MA: De Capo Press, 2009.

"Iraq's 'Female Bomber Recruiter.'" *BBC News,* February 4, 2009. Accessed
July 27, 2011, http://news.bbc.co.uk/2/hi/7869570.stm.

"Israel's Security Fence." *Ministry of Defense,* January 31, 2007. Accessed November 12, 2011, http://www.seamzone.mod.gov.il/pages/eng/purpose.htm.

Israeli, Raphael. "Islamikaze and Their Significance." *Terrorism and Political
Violence* 9 (1997): 96–121.

Jakes, Lara. "Officials: 29 Dead in Suicide Bomb in Iraq Mosque." *Guardian,*
August 28, 2011. Accessed December 3, 2011, http://www.guardian.co.uk
/world/feedarticle/9819546.

James, Susan D. "Psychology of Virginia Tech, Columbine Killers Still Baffles
Experts." *ABC News,* April 16, 2009. Accessed July 4, 2011, http://abc
news.go.com/Health/story?id=7345607&page=1.

"Jerrold M. Post, Full-time Faculty, Elliot School of International Affairs."
George Washington University, 2011. Accessed February 17, 2012, http://
elliott.gwu.edu/faculty/post.cfm.

Johnson, Robert. "Institutions and the Promotion of Violence." In *Violent
Transactions: The Limits of Personality,* eds. Anne Campbell and John J.
Gibbs, 181–204. Oxford: Basil Blackwell, 1986.

"Jurors Sequestered in CIA Shooting Case." *CNN,* November 12, 1997. Accessed July 27, 2011, http://cgi.cnn.com/US/9711/12/cia.shooting.trial
/index.html.

Kaczynski, David. "Missing Parts." In *Brothers: 26 Stories of Love and Rivalry,* eds. Andrew Blauner and Frank McCourt, 15–30. New York: Wiley, 2010.

Kahn, Paul W. *Sacred Violence: Torture, Terror, and Sovereignty.* Ann Arbor: University of Michigan Press, 2008.

Katz, Fred E. *Confronting Evil: Two Journeys.* New York: State University of New York Press, 2004.

Kelleher, Michael. *Profiling the Lethal Employee: Case Studies of Workplace Violence.* Westport, CT: Praeger, 1997.

Kix, Paul. "The Truth About Suicide Bombers." *Boston Globe,* December 5, 2010. Accessed June 7, 2011, http://www.boston.com/bostonglobe/ideas /articles/2010/12/05/the_truth_about_Suicide_Bombers/?page=full.

Kleinfield, N. R. "From Teacher to Gunman: U.S. Visit Ends in Fatal Rage." *New York Times,* February 25, 1997. Accessed June 13, 2011, http://www .nytimes.com/1997/02/25/nyregion/from-teacher-to-gunman-us-visit-ends -in-fatal-rage.html.

Kohan, John. "Assault at High Noon." *Time,* June 26, 1995. Accessed July 28, 2011, http://www.time.com/time/printout/0,8816,983088,00.html.

Kruglanksi, Arie W., Xiaoyan Chen, Mark Dechesne, Shira Fishman, and Edward Orehek. "Fully Committed: Suicide Bombers' Motivation and the Quest for Personal Significance." *Political Psychology* 30 (2009): 331–57.

Kuwahara, Yasuo, and Gordon T. Allred. *Kamikaze: A Japanese Pilot's Own Spectacular Story of the Famous Suicide Squadrons.* New York: Ballantine, 1957.

Langer, Walter C. *The Mind of Adolf Hitler: The Secret Wartime Report.* New York: New American Library, 1973.

Langman, Peter F. "Rampage School Shooters: A Typology," *Aggression and Violent Behavior* 14 (2009): 79–86.

Lankford, Adam. "A Comparative Analysis of Suicide Terrorists and Rampage, Workplace, and School Shooters in the United States from 1990–2010." *Homicide Studies* (2012).

Lankford, Adam. "A Psychological Autopsy of 9/11 Ringleader Mohamed Atta." *Journal of Police and Criminal Psychology* 27 (2012), 150–159.

Lankford, Adam. "A Suicide-Based Typology of Suicide Terrorists: Conventional, Coerced, Escapist, and Indirect." *Security Journal* (2012).

Lankford, Adam. "Could Suicide Terrorists Be Suicidal?" *Studies in Conflict & Terrorism* 34 (2011): 337–66.

Lankford, Adam. "Do Suicide Terrorists Exhibit Clinically Suicidal Risk Factors? A Review of Initial Evidence and Call for Future Research." *Aggression and Violent Behavior* 15 (2010): 334–40.

Lankford, Adam. *Human Killing Machines: Systematic Indoctrination in Iran, Nazi Germany, Al Qaeda and Abu Ghraib.* Lanham, MD: Lexington Books, 2009.

Lankford, Adam. "Human Time Bombs: Before the 9/11 Pilots Were Suicide Terrorists, They Were Just Suicidal." *Foreign Policy,* September 9, 2011. Accessed November 11, 2011, http://www.foreignpolicy.com/articles /2011/09/09/human_time_bombs.

Lankford, Adam. "Martyr Complex: How Will Bin Laden's Supporters Interpret His Death?" *Foreign Policy,* May 2, 2011. Accessed August 14, 2012, http://www.foreignpolicy.com/articles/2011/05/02/hes_dead_but_how _much_does_osamas_death_matter?page=0,3.

Lankford, Adam. "On Sacrificial Heroism." *Critical Review of International Social and Political Philosophy* (2012).

Lankford, Adam. "Requirements and Facilitators for Suicide Terrorism: An Explanatory Framework for Prediction and Prevention." *Perspectives on Terrorism,* 5, 6 (2011): 70–80.

Lankford, Adam. "Suicide Terrorism as a Socially Approved Form of Suicide." *Crisis* 31 (2010): 287–89.

Lankford, Adam, and Nayab Hakim. "From Columbine to Palestine: A Comparative Analysis of Rampage Shooters in the United States and Volunteer Suicide Bombers in the Middle East." *Aggression and Violent Behavior* 16 (2011): 98–107.

Lanteri, Alessandro, Chiara Chelini, and Salvatore Rizzello. "An Experimental Investigation of Emotions and Reasoning in the Trolley Problem." *Journal of Business Ethics* 83 (2008): 789–804.

Lappin, Elena. "Atta in Hamburg." *Prospect,* September 20, 2002. Accessed May 4, 2011, http://www.prospectmagazine.co.uk/2002/09/attainhamburg/.

Larkin, Ralph. "The Columbine Legacy: Rampage Shootings as Political Acts." *American Behavioral Scientist* 52 (2009): 1309–26.

Lave, Charles, and James March. *Introduction to Models in the Social Sciences.* New York: Harper and Row, 1975.

Lawless, Jill. "Harry Potter Wizard Series to Be Sold as E-books." *Bloomberg BusinessWeek,* June 23, 2011. Accessed October 6, 2011, http://www.businessweek.com/ap/financialnews/D9O1M59G0.htm.

Leppard, David, and Abul Taher. "MI5 Fears Jihadis Will Use Mentally Ill as Suicide Bombers." *Times Online,* May 25, 2008. Accessed June 4, 2011, http://www.timesonline.co.uk/tol/news/uk/article3999058.ece.

Lester, David. *Making Sense of Suicide: An In-Depth Look at Why People Kill Themselves.* Philadelphia: The Charles Press, 1997.

Lester, David. *Suicide and the Holocaust.* Hauppauge, NY: Nova Science Publishers, 2006.

Lester, David, Bijou Yang, and Mark Lindsay. "Suicide Bombers: Are Psychological Profiles Possible?" *Studies in Conflict & Terrorism* 27 (2004): 283–95.

"Letters to Dad." *Jonestown Institute,* April 12, 2011. Accessed July 17, 2011, http://jonestown.sdsu.edu/AboutJonestown/PrimarySources/letterstodad.html.

Lieberman, Joseph. *The Shooting Game: The Making of School Shooters.* Santa Ana, CA: Seven Locks, 2006.

Lieberman, Joseph I., and Susan M. Collins. *A Ticking Time Bomb: Counterterrorism Lessons from the U.S. Government's Failure to Prevent the Fort Hood Attack.* Washington, DC: U.S. Senate Committee on Homeland Security and Government Affairs, 2011.

Lincoln, Abraham. "You Can Have Anything You Want." *Famous Quotes,* 2011. Accessed July 3, 2011, http://www.1-famous-quotes.com/quote/21284.

Londoño, Ernesto. "Dozens Dead in Rare Attacks on Shiite Targets in Afghanistan." *Washington Post,* December 6, 2011. Accessed December 10, 2011, http://www.washingtonpost.com/world/rare-attack-in-kabul-targets-shiite-mosque/2011/12/06/gIQAVnEkYO_story.html.

Lynne, Gary D. "On the Economics of Subselves: Toward a Metaeconomics." In Morris Altman, ed., 99–124, *Handbook of Contemporary Behavioral Economics: Foundations and Developments.* Armonk, NY: M.E. Sharpe Publishers, 2006.

Maaga, Mary M. *Hearing the Voices of Jonestown.* Syracuse: Syracuse University Press, 1998.

"Mall Shooter's Suicide Note: I just Snapped." *USA Today,* December 7, 2007. Accessed July 3, 2011, http://www.usatoday.com/news/nation/2007-12-07 -mallShooter-Suicidenote_N.htm.

Malone, Dumas, Hirst Milhollen, and Milton Kaplan. *The Story of the Declaration of Independence.* Oxford: Oxford University Press, 1975.

Maris, Ronald W. *Pathways to Suicide: A Survey of Self-Destructive Behaviors.* Baltimore: Johns Hopkins University Press, 1981.

Maris, Ronald W., Alan L. Berman, and Morton M. Silverman. *Comprehensive Textbook of Suicidology.* New York: Guilford, 2000.

"Mass Killer Anders Breivik's Chilling Phone Call to Cops—Audio." *Mirror,* November 24, 2011. Accessed November 25, 2011, http://www.mirror .co.uk/news/top-stories/2011/11/24/mass-killer-anders-breivik-s-chilling -phone-call-to-cops-audio-115875-23586085/.

McDermott, Terry. *Perfect Soldiers: The 9/11 Hijackers—Who They Were, Why They Did It.* New York: HarperCollins, 2005.

McElroy, Damien. "Baghdad Market Bombers 'Mentally Impaired.'" *Telegraph,* February 2, 2008. Accessed June 8, 2011, http://www.telegraph.co.uk/news /worldnews/1577373/Baghdad-market-Bombers-mentally-impaired.html.

McGehee, Fielding. *Jonestown Institute.* Personal interview with author, July 19, 2011.

McMains, Michael J., and Wayman C. Mullins. *Managing Critical Incidents and Hostage Situations in Law Enforcement and Corrections.* Cincinnati, OH: Anderson, 2010.

McManus, John C. *Grunts: Inside the American Infantry Combat Experience, World War II Through Iraq.* New York: Penguin, 2010.

Meloy, J. Reid. "Indirect Personality Assessment of the Violent True Believer." *Journal of Personality Assessment* 82 (2004): 138–46.

"Memorable Quotes for: In the Line of Fire." *Internet Movie Database,* 1993. Accessed October 1, 2011, http://www.imdb.com/title/tt0107206/quotes.

Mendick, Robert. "Norway Massacre: The Real Anders Behring Breivik." *Telegraph,* July 31, 2001. Accessed November 24, 2011, http://www.telegraph .co.uk/news/worldnews/europe/norway/8672801/Norway-massacre-the -real-Anders-Behring-Breivik.html.

Menninger, Karl. *Man Against Himself.* New York: Harcourt, Brace & World, 1938.

Merari, Ariel. *Driven to Death: Psychological and Social Aspects of Suicide Terrorism.* Oxford: Oxford University Press, 2010.

Milgram, Stanley. "Behavioral Study of Obedience." *Journal of Abnormal & Social Psychology* 67 (1963): 371–78.

"Militant Held Over Iraq Suicide Bombings." *CNN,* February 20, 2010. Accessed July 27, 2011, http://www.cnn.com/2010/WORLD/meast/02/20/iraq .bomber.arrest/index.html.

"Military Doctors Worried Hasan Was 'Psychotic,' Capable of Killing Fellow Soldiers." *Fox News,* November 12, 2009. Accessed July 5, 2011, http://www.foxnews.com/us/2009/11/12/military-doctors-worried -hasan-psychotic-capable-of-Killing-fellow-soldiers.

"Military Honours and Awards." *The British Monarchy,* 2011. Accessed October 1, 2011, http://www.royal.gov.uk/MonarchUK/Honours/Military HonoursandAwards/MilitaryHonoursandAwards.aspx.

Miller, Judith. "The Bomb Under the Abaya: Women Who Became Suicide Bombers." *Policy Review,* June 2007. Accessed June 8, 2011, http://www .judithmiller.com/754/the-Bomb-under-the-abaya.

Miller, Peter. "Dancing With Death: The Gray Area Between Suicide Related Behavior, Indifference and Risk Behaviors of Heroin Users." *Contemporary Drug Problems* 33 (2006): 427–50.

"Mir Aimal Kasi." *Clark County Prosecuting Attorney,* 2002. Accessed February 24, 2011, http://www.clarkprosecutor.org/html/death/US/kasi807.htm.

"Miramar to Dedicate Range to Famous Sniper." *Marine Corps Times,* March 27, 2007. Accessed October 2, 2011, http://www.marinecorpstimes.com /news/2007/03/marine_hatchcock_rangededication_070327/.

Moghadam, Assaf. *The Globalization of Martyrdom: Al Qaeda, Salafi Jihad, and the Diffusion of Suicide Attacks.* Baltimore: Johns Hopkins University Press, 2008.

Montgomery, Ben, and Howard Altman. "Friends Stunned by Suicide of Dungy's Son." *MSNBC,* December 23, 2005. Accessed June 2, 2011, http://nbc sports.msnbc.com/id/10588639//.

Morales, Lymari. "One in Three Americans 'Extremely Patriotic.'" *Gallup,* July 2, 2010. Accessed December 3, 2011, http://www.gallup.com/poll/141110 /one-three-americans-extremely-patriotic.aspx.

Murphy, Caryle. "Prime Minister Struggles for Consensus: More Bombings Rock Baghdad." *Sun Sentinel,* May 3, 2005. Accessed November 21, 2011, http://articles.sun-sentinel.com/2005-05-03/news/0505020469_1_sunni -arabs-baath-party-jafari.

Murphy, Derek. *Jesus Potter Harry Christ: The Fascinating Parallels Between Two of the World's Most Popular Literary Characters.* Portland, OR: HB Press, 2011.

"Nail Bomber Blames 'War on Islam.'" *BBC,* November 21, 2008. Accessed June 20, 2011, http://news.bbc.co.uk/go/pr/fr/-/2/hi/uk_news/7741766 .stm.

National Commission on Terrorist Attacks upon the United States. "The 9/11 Commission Report." August 21, 2004. Accessed May 4, 2011, http://gov info.library.unt.edu/911/report/index.htm.

National Institute of Mental Health. "Signs and Symptoms of Depression." March 31, 2009. Accessed May 4, 2011, http://www.nimh.nih.gov/health /topics/depression/men-and-depression/signs-and-symptoms-of-depression /index.shtml.

Nelson, Katie. "Joe Stack's Daughter, Samantha Bell Calls Deadly Austin Attack on IRS 'Wrong,' but Labels Dad Hero." *New York Daily News,* February 22, 2010. Accessed January 4, 2011, http://www.nydailynews.com/news /national/2010/02/22/2010-02-22_joe_stacks_daughter_samantha_bell _calls_Deadly_austin_attack_on_irs_wrong_but_la.html.

Nelson, Soraya. "Disabled Often Carry Out Afghan Suicide Missions." *National Public Radio,* October 15, 2007. Accessed July 27, 2011, http://www.npr .org/templates/story/story.php?storyId=15276485.

Neumeister, Larry, and Tom Hays. "2 NY Collaborators Give Firsthand Look at Al-Qaida." *Yahoo News,* May 6, 2012. Accessed May 7, 2012, http://news .yahoo.com/2-ny-cooperators-firsthand-look-al-qaida-211626418.html.

Newman, Katherine S. "School Rampage Shootings." *Contexts* 6 (2007): 28–29.

Newman, Katherine S., and Cybelle Fox. "Repeat Tragedy: Rampage Shootings in American High School and College Settings, 2002-2008." *American Behavioral Scientist* 52 (2009): 1286–1308.

Newman, Katherine S., Cybelle Fox, Wendy Roth, Jal Mehta, and David Harding. *Rampage: The Social Roots of School Shootings.* New York: Basic Books, 2004.

Newman, Maria, and Michael Brick. "Neighbor Says Hasan Gave Belongings Away Before Attack." *New York Times,* November 6, 2009. Accessed July 5, 2011, http://www.nytimes.com/2009/11/07/us/07suspect.html.

Nock, Matthew K., Jennifer M. Park, Christine T. Finn, Tara L. Deliberto, Halina J. Dour, and Mahzarin R. Banaji. "Measuring The Suicidal Mind: Implicit Cognition Predicts Suicidal Behavior." *Psychological Science* 21 (2010): 511–517.

Office of the Director of National Intelligence. "2009 Report on Terrorism." *National Counterterrorism Center,* April 30, 2010. Accessed June 21, 2011, http://www.nctc.gov/witsbanner/docs/2009_report_on_terrorism .pdf.

O'Hare, Peggy, and R. G. Ratcliffe. "Suicide Flier Described As 'Offbeat,' 'Brilliant.'" *Houston Chronicle,* February 19, 2010. Accessed December 4, 2011, http://www.chron.com/default/article/Suicide-flier-described-as-offbeat -brilliant-1716342.php.

Ohnuki-Tierney, Emiko. *Kamikaze, Cherry Blossoms, and Nationalisms: The Militarization of Aesthetics in Japanese History.* Chicago: University of Chicago Press, 2006.

Omer, Aftab, and Jürgen W. Kremer. "Between Columbine and the Twin Towers." *ReVision* 26 (2003): 37–40.

Orange, Richard. "Anders Behring Breivik's Sister Warned Mother About His Behaviour Two Years Ago." *Telegraph,* December 4, 2011. Accessed December 13, 2011, http://www.telegraph.co.uk/news/worldnews/europe /norway/8934136/Anders-Behring-Breiviks-sister-warned-mother-about -his-behaviour-two-years-ago.html.

O'Toole, Mary E. "The School Shooter: A Threat Assessment Perspective." *Federal Bureau of Investigation,* 2000. Accessed July 12, 2011, http://www.fbi .gov/stats-services/publications/school-shooter/.

Pape, Robert A. *Dying to Win: The Strategic Logic of Suicide Terrorism.* New York: Random House, 2005.

Pape, Robert A., and James Feldman. *Cutting the Fuse: The Explosion of Global Suicide Terrorism and How to Stop It.* Chicago: University of Chicago Press, 2010.

Pastor, Larry H. "Countering the Psychological Consequences of Suicide Terrorism." *Psychiatric Annals* 34 (2004): 701–07.

Paul, Ron. "Foreign Occupation Leads to More Terror." *Texas Straight Talk,* September 12, 2011. Accessed November 13, 2011, http://paul.house.gov /index.php?option=com_content&task=view&id=1909&Itemid=69.

Pearson, Patricia. "Apocalyptic Cult Methods Explain Bin Laden." *USA Today,* November 5, 2001. Accessed June 8, 2011, http://www.usatoday.com/news /comment/2001-11-05-ncguest1.htm.

Pedahzur, Ami. *Suicide Terrorism.* Cambridge: Polity, 2005.

"People with Mental Illnesses Enrich Our Lives." *National Alliance on Mental Illness,* 2011. Accessed December 13, 2011, http://www.nami.org/Template .cfm?Section=Helpline1&template=/ContentManagement/ContentDisplay .cfm&ContentID=4858.

Peter, Tom A. "U.S. Begins Hunting Iraq's Bombmakers, not just Bombs." *Christian Science Monitor,* September 8, 2008. Accessed June 7, 2011, http:// www.csmonitor.com/World/Middle-East/2008/0908/p04s01-wome.html.

Phares, Walid. *Future Jihad: Terrorist Strategies Against America.* New York: Palgrave Macmillan, 2005.

Pidd, Helen, and James Meikle. "Anders Behring Breivik: 'It Was a Normal Arrest.'" *Guardian,* July 27, 2011. Accessed November 25, 2011, http://www.guardian.co.uk/world/2011/jul/27/anders-behring-breivik-arrest-norway.

"Police Questioned Health Club Gunman, Let Him Go Week Before Shooting." *Fox News,* August 10, 2009. Accessed July 4, 2011, http://www.foxnews.com/story/0,2933,538732,00.html.

"Police: Tampa Flyer Voiced Support for Bin Laden." *CNN,* January 6, 2002. Accessed July 27, 2011, http://articles.cnn.com/2002-01-06/us/tampa.crash_1_plane-charles-j-bishop-crash?_s=PM:US.

Popkin, Jim. "An Intimate Look at One 9/11 Hijacker." *NBC News,* 2008. Accessed May 4, 2011, http://current.com/1iuhu4c#27858161.

Post, Jerrold M., Farhana Ali, Schuyler Henderson, Stephen Shanfield, Jeff Victoroff, and Stevan Weine. "The Psychology of Suicide Terrorism." *Psychiatry* 72 (1) (2009): 13–31.

"Powerball: Prizes and Odds." May 28, 2011. Accessed May 28, 2011, http://www.powerball.com/powerball/pb_prizes.asp.

"Profile: Major Nidal Malik Hasan." *BBC News,* November 12, 2009. Accessed July 5, 2011, http://news.bbc.co.uk/2/hi/8345944.stm.

Purdy, Matthew. "The Gunman Premeditated the Attack, Officials Say." *New York Times,* February 25, 1997. Accessed June 13, 2011, http://www.nytimes.com/1997/02/25/nyregion/the-gunman-premeditated-the-attack-officials-say.html.

"Qian Mingqi Blew Himself Up to Demand Justice and Call Attention to His Plight." *Asia News,* May 28, 2011. Accessed December 27, 2011, http://www.asianews.it/news-en/Qian-Mingqi-blew-himself-up-to-demand-justice-and-call-attention-to-his-plight-21688.html.

Quinn, Rob. "Israeli Jets Strike Gaza After Donkey Bomb Fizzles." *Newser,* May 26, 2010. Accessed June 4, 2011, http://www.newser.com/story/90056/israelis-hit-gaza-after-donkey-Bomb-fizzles.html.

"Race and the Peoples Temple." *PBS,* 2010. Accessed July 13, 2011, http://www.pbs.org/wgbh/americanexperience/features/general-article/jonestown-race/.

Radwan, Amany. "Portrait of the Terrorist as a Young Man." *Time,* October 6, 2001. Accessed May 4, 2011. http://www.time.com/time/nation/article/0,8599,178383,00.html.

Reiterman, Tim, and John Jacobs. *Raven: The Untold Story of the Rev. Jim Jones and His People.* New York: Dutton, 1982.

Renberg, E. Salander. "Self-Reported Life-Weariness, Death-Wishes, Suicidal Ideation, Suicidal Plans and Suicide Attempts in General Population Surveys in the North of Sweden 1986 and 1996." *Social Psychiatry and Psychiatric Epidemiology* 36 (2001): 429–36.

Rice, Xan. "Bombing Suspect Was Pious Pupil Who Shunned High Life of the Rich." *Guardian,* December 31, 2009. Accessed December 13, 2011, http://www.guardian.co.uk/world/2009/dec/31/bombing-suspect-abdulmutallab-nigeria-home.

Robinson, Sir Ken. "2005 National Forum of Education Policy: Chairman's Breakfast." *Education Commission of the States,* July 14, 2005. Accessed June 7, 2011, http://www.ecs.org/html/projectsPartners/chair2005/docs/Sir_Ken_Robinson_Speech.pdf.

Rojek, Chris. *Frank Sinatra.* Cambridge: Polity Press, 2004.

Rosinsky, Natalie M. *Sir Isaac Newton: Brilliant Mathematician and Scientist.* Minneapolis, MN: Compass Point Books, 2008.

Rowley, Charles K. "Terrorist Attacks on Western Civilization." *Public Choice* 128 (2006): 1–6.

Rowling, J. K. *Harry Potter and the Deathly Hallows.* New York: Scholastic, 2007.

Rubin, Alissa J. "Afghan Girl Tricked into Carrying Bomb, Officials Say." *New York Times,* June 26, 2011. Accessed November 23, 2011, http://www.ny times.com/2011/06/27/world/asia/27afghanistan.html.

Rubin, Barry, and Judith C. Rubin. *Anti-American Terrorism and the Middle East.* Oxford: Oxford University Press, 2002.

Rugala, Eugene. *Workplace Violence: Issues in Response.* Quantico, VA: National Center for the Analysis of Violent Crime, Federal Bureau of Investigation, 2003.

Sachs, Andrea. "Q&A: A Jonestown Survivor Remembers." *Time,* November 18, 2008. Accessed July 13, 2011, http://www.time.com/time/arts /article/0,8599,1859903-2,00.html.

Sageman, Marc. *Understanding Terror Networks.* Philadelphia: University of Pennsylvania Press, 2004.

"Saint Joan of Arc." *Encyclopedia Britannica,* 2011. Accessed August 11, 2011, http://www.britannica.com/EBchecked/topic/304220/Saint-Joan-of-Arc.

"Sammy Davis Jr.'s Wedding Night Suicide Attempt." *Contact Music,* June 10, 2003. Accessed December 13, 2011, http://www.contactmusic.com /news-article/sammy-davis-jr.s-wedding-night-suicide-attempt.

Sanchez, Raf. "Norway Killer Placed on Suicide Watch." *Telegraph,* July 26, 2011. Accessed November 25, 2011, http://www.telegraph.co.uk/news /worldnews/europe/norway/8663320/Norway-killer-placed-on-suicide -watch.html.

Savage, Charlie. "As Acts of War or Despair, Suicides Rattle a Prison." *New York Times,* April 24, 2011. Accessed November 25, 2011, http://www .nytimes.com/2011/04/25/world/guantanamo-files-suicide-as-act-of-war -or-despair.html.

Scheid, Dianne E. "The Plain Ugly Truth." *Jonestown Institute,* November 16, 2008. Accessed July 13, 2011, http://jonestown.sdsu.edu/AboutJonestown /PersonalReflections/v8/Scheid.htm.

Schmid, David. *Natural Born Celebrities: Serial Killers in American Culture.* Chicago: University of Chicago Press, 2005.

Sennott, Charles M. "Before Oath to Jihad, Drifting and Boredom." *Boston Globe,* March 3, 2002. Accessed November 8, 2011, http://www.boston .com/news/packages/underattack/news/driving_a_wedge/part1_side.shtml.

"Sergeant First Class Leroy A. Petry." *U.S. Army,* July 12, 2011. Accessed September 25, 2011, http://www.army.mil/medalofhonor/petry/.

"Serial Killer Convicted of Murder." *BBC News,* March 16, 2006. Accessed December 16, 2009, http://news.bbc.co.uk/2/hi/uk_news/england/southern _counties/4813234.stm.

Shahid, Aliyah. "Oprah Winfrey to Piers Morgan: I Contemplated Suicide as Pregnant Teen, Drank Detergent." *New York Daily News,* January 18, 2011. Accessed June 20, 2011, http://articles.nydailynews.com/2011-01-18 /gossip/27088007_1_stedman-graham-pregnancy-detergent.

Shay, Shaul. *The Shahids: Islam and Suicide Attacks.* New Brunswick, NJ: Transaction Publishers, 2004.

Shenon, Philip. "Security Chief Says Nation Must Expect Suicide Attacks." *New York Times,* March 14, 2003. Accessed December 3, 2011, http://www .nytimes.com/2003/03/14/national/14RIDG.html.

Shneidman, Edwin S. "An Overview: Personality, Motivation, and Behavior Theories." In *Suicide: Theory and Clinical Aspects,* eds. Leon D. Hankoff and Bernice Einsidler, 143–63. Littleton, MA: PSG Publishing, 1979.

Shneidman, Edwin S. "Clues to Suicide, Reconsidered." *Suicide and Life-Threatening Behavior* 24 (1994): 395–97.

"Six Dead in Missouri City Council Shooting." *CBS News,* February 8, 2008. Accessed March 14, 2011, http://www.cbsnews.com/stories/2008/02/07/national/main3805672.shtml.

Slackman, Michael. "Bin Laden Kin Wait and Worry." *Los Angeles Times,* November 13, 2001. Accessed May 4, 2011, http://articles.latimes.com/2001/nov/13/news/mn-3564.

Slater, Lauren. "The Trouble with Self-Esteem." *New York Times,* February 3, 2002. Accessed July 7, 2011, http://www.nytimes.com/2002/02/03/magazine/the-trouble-with-self-esteem.html.

Smith, Craig. "Raised as Catholic in Belgium, She Died as a Muslim Bomber." *New York Times,* December 6, 2005. Accessed June 21, 2011, http://www.nytimes.com/2005/12/06/international/europe/06brussels.html.

Smith, Nicola. "Making of Muriel the Suicide Bomber." *Times Online,* December 4, 2005. Accessed June 9, 2011, http://www.timesonline.co.uk/tol/news/article745407.ece.

Sodini, George. "George Sodini's Blog: Full Text by Alleged Gym Shooter." *ABC News,* 2009. Accessed July 5, 2011, http://abcnews.go.com/US/story?id=8258001&page=1.

Solomon, Maynard. *Beethoven Essays.* Cambridge, MA: Harvard University Press, 1990.

Somaiya, Ravi. "Swedish Bombing Suspect's Drift to Extremism." *New York Times,* December 13, 2010. Accessed July 27, 2011, http://www.nytimes.com/2010/12/14/world/europe/14suspect.html?hp=&.

"Specialist Ross A. McGinnis." *U.S. Army,* May 24, 2011. Accessed September 25, 2011, http://www.army.mil/medalofhonor/mcginnis/.

Speckhard, Anne, and Khapta Ahkmedova. "The Making of a Martyr: Chechen Suicide Terrorism." *Studies in Conflict and Terrorism* 29 (2006): 429–92.

Stack, Joseph. "Raw Data: Joseph Stack Suicide Manifesto." *Fox News,* February 18, 2010. Accessed June 16, 2011, http://www.foxnews.com/us/2010/02/18/raw-data-joseph-stack-Suicide-manifesto/.

Staub, Ervin. *The Roots of Evil: The Origins of Genocide and other Group Violence.* Cambridge: Cambridge University Press, 1989.

Stern, Jessica. *Terror in the Name of God: Why Religious Militants Kill.* New York: Ecco, 2003.

Stevens, John. "Massacre Gunman Posted YouTube Video Calling Followers to 'Embrace Martyrdom' Six Hours Before Attacks." *Daily Mail,* July 25, 2011. Accessed November 20, 2011, http://www.dailymail.co.uk/news/article-2018148/Anders-Behring-Breivik-posted-YouTube-video-6-hours-Norway-attacks.html.

Strauss, Alix. *Death Becomes Them: Unearthing the Suicides of the Brilliant, the Famous, and the Notorious.* New York: HarperCollins, 2009.

"Suicide." *Centers for Disease Control and Prevention,* 2010. Accessed December 3, 2011, http://www.cdc.gov/violenceprevention/pdf/Suicide_Data Sheet-a.pdf.

"Support for Suicide Bombing." *Pew Research Center,* 2002. Accessed July 11, 2011, http://pewglobal.org/database/?indicator=19.

"Support for Suicide Bombing." *Pew Research Center,* 2007–2010. Accessed July 11, 2011, http://pewglobal.org/database/?indicator=19.

"Suspected Madrid Bombing Ringleader Killed." *CNN,* April 4, 2004. Accessed July 3, 2012, http://articles.cnn.com/2004-04-04/world/spain.bombings_1_train-bombings-sarhane-ben-abdelmajid-fakhet-bomb-plot?_s=PM:WORLD.

"Tabloids Belittle Bin Laden, Hijackers." *Miami Herald,* October 9, 2001.

Talbot, Strobe. *The Age of Terror.* New York, Basic Books, 2002.

"Terrorism: Definitions." *Federal Bureau of Investigation,* 2009. Accessed March 12, 2011, http://denver.fbi.gov/nfip.htm.

"The 19 Plotters and Their Day of Terror." *St. Petersburg Times,* September 11, 2002. Accessed June 24, 2011, http://www.sptimes.com/2002/09/01/911/plotters.shtml.

"The Birth of Jesus Christ." *The Holy Bible,* Matthew 1.21. Accessed August 11, 2011, http://niv.scripturetext.com/matthew/1.htm.

"The Cult of Death." *Newsweek,* December 4, 1978.

"The Most Influential US Liberals." *Daily Telegraph,* October 31, 2007. Accessed June 20, 2011, http://www.telegraph.co.uk/news/worldnews/1435442/The-most-influential-US-liberals-1-20.html.

"The Mother of Two Who Became a Suicide Bomber." *Sunday Tribune,* September 17, 2006. Accessed August 21, 2009, http://www.tribune.ie/archive/article/2006/sep/17/the-mother-of-two-who-became-a-Suicide-Bomber/.

"The Troubled Journey of Major Hasan." *Time,* 2009. Accessed July 5, 2011, http://www.time.com/time/photogallery/0,29307,1938816_1988826,00.html.

Thomas, Evan. "Cracking the Terror Code." *Newsweek,* October 15, 2001. Accessed May 4, 2011. http://www.newsweek.com/id/75613.

Thompson, Stephen, and Ken Kyle. "Understanding Mass School Shootings: Links Between Personhood and Power in the Competitive School Environment." *Journal of Primary Prevention* 26 (2005): 419–38.

"Three Held in Norway 'Al-Qaeda Bomb Plot.'" *BBC,* July 8, 2010. Accessed November 25, 2011, http://www.bbc.co.uk/news/10554523.

Tonso, Karen L. "Violent Masculinities as Tropes for School Shooters: The Montreal Massacre, the Columbine Attack, and Rethinking Schools." *American Behavioral Scientist* 52 (2009): 1266–85.

Toolis, Kevin. "Face to Face with the Women Suicide Bombers." *Daily Mail,* February 7, 2009. Accessed February 8, 2009, http://www.dailymail.co.uk/femail/article-1138298/Face-face-women-suicide-bombers.html.

Toolis, Kevin. "How I Came Face To Face With Taliban Teen Killers." *Daily Mail,* December 19, 2008. Accessed November 12, 2011, http://www.dailymail.co.uk/debate/article-1098840/KEVIN-TOOLIS-How-I-came-face-face-Taliban-teen-killers.html.

Townsend, Ellen. "Suicide Terrorists: Are They Suicidal?" *Suicide & Life-Threatening Behavior* 37 (2007): 35–49.

Townsend, Mark. "Survivors of Norway Shootings Return to Island of Utøya." *Guardian,* August 20, 2011. Accessed November 13, 2011, http://www.guardian.co.uk/world/2011/aug/21/utoya-anders-behring-breivik-norway.

"Train Suspects Among Madrid Suicide Bombers." *Telegraph,* April 4, 2004. Accessed July 31, 2011, http://www.telegraph.co.uk/news/1458502/Train-suspects-among-Madrid-suicide-bombers.html.

Tyson, Ann S., and Josh White. "With Iraq War Come Layers of Loss." *Washington Post,* January 2, 2007. Accessed September 25, 2011, http://www.washingtonpost.com/wp-dyn/content/article/2007/01/01/AR2007010100759.html.

"University of Florida Student Tasered at Kerry Forum." *YouTube,* September 17, 2007. Accessed July 3, 2011, http://www.youtube.com/watch?v=6bVa6jn4rpE.

U.S. Army. "Army Health Promotion, Risk Reduction and Suicide Prevention Report." July 28, 2010. Accessed July 26, 2011, http://www.army.mil/-news/2010/07/28/42934-army-health-promotion-risk-reduction-and-suicide-prevention-report/index.html.

Waldmann, Michael R., and Jörn H. Dieterich. "Throwing a Bomb on a Person Versus Throwing a Person on a Bomb: Intervention Myopia in Moral Intuitions." *Psychological Science* 18 (2007): 247–53.

Walker, Peter, and Matthew Taylor. "Far Right on Rise in Europe, Says Report." *Guardian,* November 6, 2011. Accessed November 13, 2011, http://www.guardian.co.uk/world/2011/nov/06/far-right-rise-europe-report.

Waller, James. *Becoming Evil: How Ordinary People Commit Genocide and Mass Killing.* New York: Oxford University Press, 2002.

Walsh, Joan. "How The Iraq War Saved Bin Laden's Life." *Salon,* May 10, 2011. Accessed November 23, 2011, http://www.salon.com/2011/05/10/iraq_war_saved_bin_laden/.

Walsh, Nick. "Man Opens Fire on Americans in Kabul; 9 Dead." *CNN,* April 28, 2011. Accessed June 11, 2011, http://www.cnn.com/2011/WORLD/asiapcf/04/27/afghanistan.violence/index.html.

Weaver, Carolyn. "New Video Shows 9/11 Hijackers Mohamed Atta, Ziad Jarrah at Al-Qaida Meeting." *Voice of America News,* October 4, 2006.

Weimar, Carrie. "Teen Pilot's Family Drops Drug Lawsuit: The 15-Year-Old Killed Himself by Crashing A Plane into a High-Rise." *St. Petersburg Times,* June 28, 2007. Accessed July 18, 2011, http://www.sptimes.com/2007/06/28/news_pf/Hillsborough/Teen_pilot_s_family_d.shtml.

Weiss, Philip. "Mr. Zbig: Brzezinski Brings Wisdom—and Controversy—to Barack Obama's Campaign." *American Conservative,* May 5, 2008. Accessed February 17, 2012, http://www.theamericanconservative.com/article/2008/may/05/00013/.

Welch, William. "Library Tells Story of Assassination Attempt on Reagan." *USA Today,* March 30, 2011. Accessed October 1, 2011, http://www.usatoday.com/news/washington/2011-03-30-reagan-library-assassination_N.htm.

"What Nidal Hasan Said About Suicide Bombers." *Times Online,* November 6, 2009. Accessed July 5, 2011, http://www.timesonline.co.uk/tol/news/world/us_and_americas/article6905976.ece.

"Who Is Nidal Hasan?" *The Week,* November 6, 2009. Accessed July 6, 2011, http://theweek.com/article/index/102580/who-is-nidal-hasan.

"Who Survived the Jonestown Tragedy?" *Jonestown Institute,* February 15, 2011. Accessed July 13, 2011, http://jonestown.sdsu.edu/AboutJonestown/WhoDied/whosurvived_list.htm.

Wikan, Unni. "'My Son—a Terrorist?' (He was such a gentle boy)." *Anthropological Quarterly* 75 (2001): 117–28.

Wike, Richard. "Little Support for Terrorism Among Muslim Americans." *Pew Research Center,* December 17, 2009. Accessed February 12, 2011,

http://pewresearch.org/pubs/1445/little-support-for-terrorism-among
-muslim-americans.

Williams, Paul L. *Al Qaeda: Brotherhood of Terror.* Upper Saddle River, NJ:
Alpha Books and Pearson Education, Inc., 2002.

Wilson, Michael. "From Smiling Coffee Vendor to Terror Suspect." *New York
Times,* September 25, 2009. Accessed May 26, 2012, http://www.nytimes
.com/2009/09/26/nyregion/26profile.htm.

Windham, R. Craig, Lisa M. Hooper, and Patricia E. Hudson. "Selected Spiritual, Religious and Family Factors in Prevention of School Violence."
Counseling and Values 49 (2005): 208–16.

Winter, Laura J., and Richard Sisk. "Donkey Bombs New Iraqi Weapon." *New
York Daily News,* November 22, 2003. Accessed June 4, 2011, http://www
.nydailynews.com/archives/news/2003/11/22/2003-11-22_donkey_Bombs
_new_iraqi_weapon.html.

"Woman Gets 18 Months in Russian Roulette Killing." *Richmond Times-
Dispatch,* May 24, 2012. Accessed May 29, 2012, http://www2.times
dispatch.com/news/2012/may/24/tdmet02-crime-and-police-news-for
-thursday-may-24-ar-1938440/.

Workplace Violence Prevention Operations Committee. "Violence Prevention:
Maintaining a Safe Workplace." *University of California, Davis,* 2007. Ac-
cessed January 14, 2010, http://www.hr.ucdavis.edu/supervisor/Er/Violence
/Brochure.

Vossekuil, Bryan, Robert A. Fein, Marissa Reddy, Randy Borum, and William
Modzeleski. *The Final Report and Findings of the Safe School Initiative:
Implications for the Prevention of School Attacks in the United States.*
Washington, DC: United States Secret Service and United States Depart-
ment of Education, 2002.

Yellow Ribbon Suicide Prevention Program. "Warning Signs & Risk Factors
of Suicide." 2009. Accessed May 4, 2011. http://www.yellowribbon.org
/WarningSigns.html.

Zimbardo, Philip. "Pathology of Imprisonment." *Society* 9 (6) (1972): 4–8.

INDEX

9/11, truth about
  Atta and, 68–71
  hijackers, 85–88
  overview, 65–67
  putting puzzle pieces together,
    67–68
9/11 Commission, 2, 33, 78

Abby, 182
Abdaly, Taimour Abdulwahab al, 189
Abdulmutallab, Umar
  see Underwear Bomber
Abdurakhmenova, Djennet, 185
Abrahms, Max, vii
Abu Aisha, Darine, 188
Abu Amra, Sami, 43
Abu Kamal, Ali Hassan, 41–44, 46,
  58, 112, 177, 191
Abu-Shaduf, Mustafa, 185
Adkisson, Jim David, 183, 192
Afghanistan
  9/11 hijackers and, 65–66, 85–86
  Al Qaeda and, 26, 65–66, 97
  Atta and, 65, 74
  depression and, 30
  foreign occupation and, 159–62
  Hasan and, 115
  substance abuse and, 58
  suicide terrorism and, 1, 9, 37, 134,
    137, 140–41, 153
  Taliban and, 134, 166
Ahmed, Arien, 60, 179
Ahmidan, Jamal, 143, 181
Akhras, Ayat al, 52–53, 58, 178
Al-Aqsa Martyrs Brigade, 22, 46
Al Qaeda
  9/11 and, 31–32, 66, 113

Afghanistan and, 26
Atta and, 66
bin Laden and, 140–41, 151
Iraq and, 166
Norway and, 158
politics and, 37
suicide terrorism and, 19, 26,
  140–41
U.S. military and, 97
Ali, 185
Alonso, Rogelio, 142
Amara, Sabrine, 185
Araj, Bader, 50
Atran, Scott, 5, 58
Atta, Mohamed, 18, 31, 65–88, 95,
  98, 114, 179, 192
  psychological autopsy, 83–85
Attash, Tawfiq bin, 85, 180
Attiya, Hassan, 68
Austin, Texas, 14, 120, 193
Awadh, Mohamed, 43
Awdeh, Abdalbasit, 188

Bader, Michael, 78
Baer, Robert, 24, 45
Bahri, Nasser al, 141
Balawi, Humam Khalil Abu Mulal
  al, 188
Ballen, Ken, vii
Baraykova, Medna, 183
Basayev, Shamil, 147, 181
Baymuradova, Shahida, 185
Berro, Mohammed Mahmoud, 189
Beslan school attack, 147
bin Laden, Osama, 18–20, 32, 54, 74,
  82, 140–41, 151–52
Bishop, Charles, 182, 217

Breivik, Anders Behring, 153–59, 164, 173, 188
Brym, Robert, 5, 35, 50
Budennovsk hospital attack, 147

Chechnya, 32, 134, 147
Cheney, Dick, 163
Chirac, Jacques, 42
Cho, Seung-Hui, 110, 192
Clarke, Arthur C., 171
Colton, Charles Caleb, 7
Columbine shootings
    differences between Klebold and Harris, 123–24, 126
    fame and, 110–11
    homemade explosives and, 164
    risk and, 147
    suicide terrorism and, 19, 113
    see also Harris, Eric; Klebold, Dylan
cowardice, 7, 140–41, 155, 172
Crewdson, John, 73
Croucher, Matthew, 97–101, 106
Cullen, Dave, 124
cults, 17, 19, 70, 127–30, 132, 138, 148

Darweesh, Amar Khaleed, 43
Degauque, Muriel, 53, 56–58, 178
depression
    Abdulmutallab and, 168
    Atta and, 18, 31, 65, 67–69, 71–77, 80–81, 83, 84, 87–88
    coerced suicide and, 134
    Columbine shooters and, 126
    Dungy and, 28
    indirect suicide and, 145
    Kaczynski and, 154
    mental illness and, 31
    Merari on, 46–47, 50–51
    Nassar and, 59
    Pape on, 29–30, 58, 65
    recruiting of suicide terrorists and, 38–39
    as risk factor for suicide, 61, 131
    Sami and, 9
    suicide terrorism and, 13, 29, 36, 46–47, 134, 153, 156, 195
    see also symptoms of depression
Dickens, Charles, 91
donkey bombs, 36

Doukaiev, Lors, 183
Dungy, Tony, 28
Dying to Win (Pape), 29

Empire State Building shooting, 18, 42, 112, 119, 177

Facebook, 156, 170
Fahs, Bilal, 59, 179
fame, 108–11, 136, 173
foreign occupation, 38, 159–62
Fort Hood shooting, 93, 120, 146, 164, 170, 193

Ganim, Rami, 184
Ganiyeva, Larissa (Fatima), 184
Gazuyeva, Luiza, 185
Ghulam, 134, 180
Goris, Issam, 56–57
Guantanamo, 156
guilt, 17–18, 36, 56, 71, 73, 77–80, 82–84, 109, 131
Gull, Ahmad, 182

Hadayet, Hesham Mohamed, 146, 181, 192
Hadeedy, Mohammed Al, 43
Hafez, Mohammed, 6, 109
Hamas, 23, 46, 166
Hamed, 51, 58, 178
Hamid, Tariq, 24
Hanjour, Hani, 86–87, 114, 180, 192
Harris, Eric, 110–11, 113, 123–26, 147, 164, 192
    see also Klebold, Dylan
Hasan, Nidal, 93–94, 98, 113–17, 146, 164, 170, 173, 180, 193
Hassan, Riaz, 5, 29
Hauth, Volker, 69, 78–81
Hawkins, Robert, 110–11, 192
heroism
    actions and, 105–6
    example scenarios, 94–102
    intent and, 93–94
    oversimplification of, 91–93
    trolley problem, 102–4
    ultimate sacrifice and, 90–91
    war and, 104–5
Hitler, Adolf, 19, 29, 139–41
Hoffman, Bruce, 32

hopelessness, 80–83
Huninee, Sa'er, 183
Hussain, Mohammad, 183
Hussein, Saddam, 141

Idris, Wafa, 59, 178
imagination, failure of, 2–4
Internal Revenue Service (IRS),
    14–15, 17, 120, 177
Iraq
    Al Qaeda and, 166, 205
    Atta and, 65
    Degauque and, 56–57
    depression and, 30
    escapist suicide terrorism and, 141
    foreign occupation and, 159–62
    Hasan and, 115
    remote detonation and, 137
    suicide terrorism and, 1–2, 37, 141,
        159–62
    war on terror and, 65
Iraq War, 160
Islam
    Abdulmutallab and, 168
    Abu Kamal and, 44
    Al Qaeda and, 66
    Atta and, 66–67, 70, 72, 76, 80,
        82–83, 85
    Egypt and, 81
    fundamentalist, 66, 73, 80–81, 166
    Hasan and, 113–15
    Israel and, 23
    martyrdom and, 93, 156
    prohibition against suicide, 52, 67,
        75
    sex and, 82
    suicide terrorism and, 23–24, 34,
        37, 53–57, 64
Islamic Jihad, 34, 46
Israel
    Islam and, 23, 54
    Palestinian terrorism and, 20,
        22–23, 101
    studies of terrorism, 33, 46
    suicide terrorism and, 1, 59–60, 95,
        119, 135, 158, 163, 178, 185
    Wafa al-Biss and, 22–23, 25–26

Jaradat, Hanadi, 60, 95, 179, 228
Jarrah, Ziad, 70–72, 82, 86–87, 179,
    192

Jonestown, vii, 19, 70, 127–30, 132,
    138, 148
Justiciar Knights, 155–56

Kaczynski, David, 167–69
Kaczynski, Ted, 154, 167–68
Kaira, 185
Kamikaze, 132–33
Kasi, Mir Aimal, 146, 181, 191
Kawa, 185
Khadjiyeva, Koku, 184
Khalifa, Ahmed, 81
Khan, Mohammad Sidique, 189
Kix, Paul, vii, 8–10
Klebold, Dylan, 110–11, 113,
    123–25, 164
    see also Harris, Eric
Kmeil, Ayat, 189
Kounjaa, Abdennabi, 143, 181
Kurbanova, Ayman (Rajman), 188

Lamari, Allekema, 143, 181
Larkin, Ralph, 110
Lester, David, vii, 29, 57–58
Lincoln, Abraham, 90, 107, 174
London bombings, 45, 142, 164

Maglad, 70, 72–73, 211
Majed, 136–37, 180–81
Maryam, 182
Masri, Iyad al, 185
Masri, Izz ad-Din al, 188
Massoud, Ahmad Shah, 86
McCarthy, Tim, 96, 99, 101
McDermott, Terry, 70, 74, 79, 81, 87
McGehee, Fielding, vii
McGinnis, Ross, 96–101, 104, 106
Merari, Ariel, 33, 46–47, 49–51
Mingqi, Qian, 186
misconceptions about suicide
        terrorism
    consistent sources are automatically
        reliable, 27
    mentally ill or unstable people are
        not used, 35–36
    political function of act is primary
        motive, 37–38
    suicidal people are crazy and
        irrational, 31–32
    suicidal people are easily
        identifiable, 28–30

suicide terrorists are representative
of regular terrorists, 32–35
Mohtasseb, Mahmoud Al, 43
Moscow theater attack, 147
Mueller, Robert, 163
Murad, 59, 179
Musalayeva, Larisa, 184

Nabil, 185
Naji, Ibrahim, 183
Napolitano, Janet, 169–70, 227
Nassar, Shadi, 59, 110, 179
Nasser, Muhammad, 185
Nazima, 135–36, 180
Nazism, 19, 55, 89, 106, 113,
131–32, 139–40, 166
Neale, Joseph, 183, 192
Nimer, 184
Nock, Matthew, 171–72

Ohnuki-Tierney, Emiko, 132
Oppenheimer, J. Robert, 105

Pape, Robert, 5–6, 29–30, 58, 65
Pastor, Larry, 6, 110
Paul, Ron, 159, 161
Pentagon, 2, 86, 119
Peracha, Fareeha, 134
Petry, Leroy, 97–101, 104, 106
Post, Jerrold, 5, 35, 66, 109
Post-Traumatic Stress Disorder
(PTSD), 47, 61

Qudsi, Shifa Adnan al, 188
Quran, 54

Rafik, 47–49, 58, 130, 177–78
Raiyshi, Reem, 59, 179
Rajaratnam, Thenmozhi, 60, 179
rampage shooters, 19, 109–10,
112–13, 117–18, 121–22, 165
rape, 39, 60, 61, 104, 179, 182, 184,
189
Rashid, Abdalfatah, 188
Reilly, Nicky, 53–58, 178
Reinares, Fernando, 142
reliable sources, 27
remote detonation, 137
Robinson, Ken, 3–4
Russian roulette, 19, 131, 144–46

Sabri, 51, 58, 178
Sadeq, Adel, 5
Saeed, Mohamad Abdulaziz Rashid
see Reilly, Nicky
Saleh, 135, 180
Sami, Qari, 9–10, 58, 130, 153, 177
Samiullah, Qari, 184
San'ani, Abu Muhammad Al, 26,
189
school shooters, 17, 19, 109–12,
117–18, 121–22, 158, 165
Secret Service agents, 19, 95–96,
98–101
self-worth, 1, 60, 71, 73, 131
shame, 77–80
Shehhi, Marwan al, 70, 82, 86, 180,
192, 211
Shneidman, Edwin, 17
social isolation
assassination and, 13
Atta and, 18, 68–71, 74–75, 83–85
Breivik and, 153
Columbine shooters and, 123
Kaczynski and, 154, 167
Sodini and, Hasan, 114–16
suicide terrorism and, 131, 170
Sodini, George, 19, 113–17, 193
soldiers jumping on grenades, 19,
94–101, 104, 166
Soufangi, Mayilla, 185
Stack, Joe, 13–17, 58, 130, 177
substance abuse, 13, 58, 144–45,
178, 195, 196
suicidal killers
Columbine and, 123–26
comparison of Sodini and Hasan,
114–17
delusions of grandeur and, 108–9
fame and glory, 109–11
overview, 107–8
statistics on, 121–23
study of, 117–20
terrorism and, 111–13
suicidal people
depression and, 71–77
guilt and shame, 77–80
hopelessness and, 80–83
identifying, 28–31
sanity and, 31–32
terrorism and, 32–36

suicide
  behaviors of, 10
  coerced, 131–32
  coerced suicide terrorism, 133–37
  escapist, 137–39
  Hitler and the Nazis, 139–40
  indirect, 144–47
  Kamikaze, 132–33
suicide terrorism
  bigger picture and, 174–75
  coerced, 133–37
  conventional wisdom on, 4–6
  escapist, 140–44
  explaining, predicting, and
    preventing, 152–53
  facilitators of, 152–53, 158–59
  families of terrorists, 23–25
  fear and, 6–8
  foreign occupation and, 159–60
  identifying preemptively, 166–72
  indirect, 145–47
  intent and, 37–38
  minimum requirements for, 152,
    158
  misconceptions regarding, 27–38
  motives behind, 27–38
  myth of martyrdom and, 172–74
  preparations for death, 154–56
  remote detonation, 137
  Stack and, 13–17
  study of, 11–12
  suicide and, 8–11
  terrorist leaders, 22–23
  terrorists themselves, 25–26
  types of, 130–31, 148–49
  U.S. and, 163–66
  see also misconceptions about
    suicide terrorism
Suleiman, Andalib Takatka, 52–53,
  58, 178
symptoms of depression 71–77
  appetite and/or weight changes,
    74–75
  decreased energy, fatigue, 73–74
  feelings of hopelessness, 73
  loss of interest or pleasure, 73
  persistent sad, anxious, "empty"
    mood, 72
  restlessness, irritability, 76–77
  thoughts of death or suicide, 75–76
  see also depression

Taliban, 9, 97, 134, 136, 166
Thomas, Evan, 78
Thornton, Charles Lee, 189, 192
Titi, Jihad, 185
torture, 54, 104, 129, 133, 155–56,
  184–86
Townsend, Ellen, 5, 27
Turvey, Brent, 148

Unabomber
  see Kaczynski, Ted
Underwear Bomber, 20, 168–69, 181

Vinas, Bryant Neal, 183
Virginia Tech shootings, 110

Wafa al-Biss, 22–23, 25–27, 58–59,
  130, 177
  family and, 23–25
  motives, 27
  statements, 25–26
  terrorist leaders and, 22–23
Walid, 182
War on Terror, 65
Weise, Jeff, 110, 192
Williams, Brian, 9
Winfrey, Oprah, 51–53, 175
workplace shooters, 19, 112, 117–18,
  121–23, 165
World War II, 70, 89, 105, 139

YouTube, 108, 156

Zahar, Mahmoud al, 23
Zawahiri, Ayman al, 32
Zazi, Najibullah, 189
Zuheir, 48–49, 51, 58, 130, 178